AMERICAN BIRDSONG'S
& Daramis Hancock

This book will take you on a journey of the American Birdsong families as far as back 500 A.D. that includes Kings, Queens, and Saints from England, Scotland, Franks, and Saxons through Daramis Hancock ancestry.

"Alfred The Great", "Charles The Great", "Saint Itta", and "Saint Begga" are a few of the documented linage.

Cheryl Birdsong-Dyer

Leawood, Kansas 66209

ISBN: 978-0-615-70694-8

Library of Congress Control Number 2014900442

Copyright 2013 by Cheryl Birdsong-Dyer.
All rights reserved.

No parts of this book may not be mechanically or electronically reproduced without the express permission of the author.

To my Father & Mother
John Patrick Birdsong
(1931 – 1988)
Della Lorene (Rhynerson) Birdsong
(1936- 2009)

To my husband
Sean Riley Dyer

To my children
Justin Michael Birdsong
Julia Marie Hansett
William John Patrick Hansett
Sarah Jade Birdsong
Webster Riley Dyer
Barbara Petronela Dyer
Jordan Philip Hansett
Jayden Ray Hansett
Jackson Riley Hansett

My grandchildren and future grandchildren, my brothers' sisters, nephews, nieces and cousins

ACKNOWLEDGMENTS

Writing is indeed a sullen art, and writing this book would have been much more difficult without the kind family, genealogist, friends, Sister's at St. Johns Catholic church. I owe thanks first to my parents, who provided me with the deep understanding of what family means. I would like to thank my family for the support in encouraging me to seek understanding of the Birdsong surname. To all of them, and the many people who have given me stories over the years, bless you. Please note as this is a working document, send me any edits, updates and addictions to my email below.

Author: Cheryl Birdsong-Dyer

cherylbirdsongdyer@gmail.com

PREFACE

The stories in this book are gleaned from a vast majority of genealogy collections over a 30 year period. While much mystery surrounded my father's surname "Birdsong" (John Birdsong, Jr.), I was determined to find out more about the origin of the name.

My journey began in 1984 while asking my father about his family. This is where my genealogy research project started and it has not stopped with exception of short periods of time although the Birdsong's was frequently on my mind.

In 1994, while conducting research at the genealogy research center located in the Banister Federal Complex in Kansas City, Missouri. As I recall, while going through rolls of film a grey haired women approached me and asked; "Who are you researching"? I responded with the name "Birdsong", she replied; "I have seen that name before". After several weeks of researching at Banister Federal Complex I learned her name was "Mrs. Howard" and she was a professional Genealogist. Additionally, she was related to the "Jobe's" which was one of my distant grandmother's surname. What were the chances of that?

Over the next seven months Mrs. Howard coached me on how to conduct genealogy research. She shared with me that you must first start with your father or mother and than move backwards, also research family Bibles, War records and published books from the time you are researching. Mrs. Howard had plenty to of great ideas on conducting research. She once said; "It's like a history project, and understanding the history during the period of time of the person you are researching."

A researcher should print maps of the locations where the person lived that they are researching and find the locations of cemetery where they are buried and visit because you may find more relatives.

Additionally, get copies of the census, birth, marriage and death certificates. The researcher should interview family members to find out as much as possible from their memories of the past. These approaches have assisted in my research for this book.

For many years, I have been told that Birdsong family name is Native American. I asked Mrs. Howard if she thought Birdsong was a Native American Indian name. Her response was "No" and if I believed my family line had Native American Indian in our family, then I should research all the grandmother's. If there are Birdsong's that is Native American Indian it will be on the women's side of the family. I do not recall Mrs. Howard's first name but she was an angel in my eyes. She must of have been at least 75 years old in late 1998 and spent countless hours with me doing research over the next seven months. I traveled with her to the Mid-Continent in Independence, Missouri to find published books about the Birdsong's.

INTRODUCTION

Origin of the Name Birdsong

There has been long hypnotized that Birdsong is translated to Vogelsang and that perhaps the name was changed to appear English. The theory is that German Soldiers were the acting police for the King of England and not liked by Colonists. This is known as the "Royal Prussian Army" the army of the Kingdom of Prussia. The army was made up of over 3,000 Dutch and German soldiers by 1646.

Although, this makes for a good story there is no direct evidence to prove the Prussian Army came to help settle the colonies by the King. There is much documentation on about the Prussian Army but my research does not show that the British used them in the settlement of the first colonies. However, they did use them in the American Revolutionary War 100 years later.

Furthermore, the first migration of German immigrants was in 1683 to the colony named Germantown in Pennsylvania. Additionally, there was and still are Vogelsangs in Pennsylvania and they did not change their name to Birdsong

Although at this point we have not discovered who John Birdsong, I (1683's) parents are. The researcher has strong suspension about the relationship between John Birdsong, I and Thomas Bird as they are both located in Charles City, Virginia near James Town during the last part of the 17th Century and families married into similar families and owned land near the same locations such as the "Blackwater swamp"

Origin of the Name Bird

The surname BIRD was first attached to an individual who lived by the sign of the bird; also to one who had the characteristics of a bird. The Irish word for bird is names such as O'Neny (sometimes O'Nena), among the chiefs of Moy Ith (County Derry, Ireland) and McEaneny have been anglicised to Bird since colonists attempted to subjugate the Gaelic way of life.

Also the French name L'Oiseau has been anglicised to Bird. Hugh Le Bird (Hughe L'Oise or Lois or Layse) arrived in England with William the Conqueror in 1066 to fight at the Battle of Hastings. His surname is thought to have been derived from his skill at falconry. By the twelfth century the name LE BIRD was well established in England.

Sometime around the 15th century some families changed the spelling to Byrd. In fact there is at least one example of this taking place in the same family, with two brothers each selecting an alternate spelling's The reason for this is unknown. Several Birds are listed in the Heraldic Visitations of Cheshire 1580, which also describe the Crest used by some Birds at that time. "Byrd is a short and simple English name - Norman in origin.

The first man to bear the name apparently was a great hunter with the Falcon, for he was called Hugo the Bird. A few years later when it became customary to use a sir name this man was called Hugo le Bird. The name was spelled with a i until the beginning of the 18th century when it was gradually changed to Byrd. The Byrds came to England with William the Conqueror. As mentioned the Normans invaded England when William, Duke of Normandy, defeated Harold, son of the Earl of Wessex, at the Battle of Hastings in 1066. The earliest English Byrds settled at Brexton or Braxton and at Chester in Cheshire. Chester lies south of Liverpool on the River Dee close to the border of Wales. It is one of the oldest English towns, dating from about A.D. 48. Many of the Byrd descendants came down to London about the beginning of the thirteenth century to learn trades, such as: silversmiths, goldsmiths, coppersmiths, silk weavers, etc. Some became merchants. A few became artists. The above quote offers a brief review of the early Byrds in England. A search of early genealogical records reveals several versions of a lineage chart starting with Hugo le Bird, who lived in the latter part of the 11th century in England.

The researcher wonders are we related to "the famous Byrds of Virginia." It appears that the two brothers, William and Thomas Byrd, came to Virginia from England in the late 1600s. From William descended the Byrds of Westover, including Adm. Richard E. Byrd and the recent Senator Byrds from Virginia. Could it be possible the "Birdsong's" descends from the Byrds of Virginia?

The researcher ponders about Hugh le Bird and if the "Birdsong's" are related to him, he arrived in England with William the Conqueror in 1066 to fight at the Battle of Hastings. Hugh was a skilled Falconer, hence the name Bird. Hugh lived in Canton (11th & 12th Cent) and married Werburger, daughter of Roger Dombue.

Another great artifact the researcher stumbled upon that needs further research is the surname "Birdswood" it was located in the LDS Family Search engine ""England, Cheshire, Land Tax Assessments, 1778-1832," Birdswood, 1799" The tax owed was for a location in Aston-by-Sutton, Cheshire, England. Although, our Birdsong line was already well established in American, once can hypothesis about this name and its origin as well.

Many have suggested that Birdsong is German and translated from Vogelsang, yet when I submit the translation in webbaesd tools. It translates to "Birds Sang" not "Birdsong". Also, Fowl = Vogel is German, Fogal is Old Dutch word that means "Bird, so the common connection between "Vogel" & "Fowl" is Fogal from Dutch. So, logically if they translated "Vogal" into English, they would have translated to "Fowlsong" instead of "Birdsong". I wrestled with this as Birdsong translates into every language.

After much research on the surname of Birdsong, I came across Byrdsong. After further consideration and not finding "Brydsong" genealogy well documented. I wondered if it could have been just "Bird" or translation "Bryd" and I found this:

"The surname 'Byrd' originates from England. It is derived from the middle English word 'bird', meaning nestling, young bird (Old English 'bridd'), applied as a nickname or perhaps occasionally as a metonymic name for a bird catcher. The metathesized form is first found in Northumberland, but the surname is more common in the Midlands and South of England. It may also be derived from the Middle English word 'burde', meaning maiden, girl, applied as a mocking surname. Public and Civil registry archive's confirm that the surname 'Bird' and or it's variant's, date as far back as the thirteenth century were a 'David le Bird', from the county of Oxfordshire, England, is recorded on the Hundred Rolls in 1273.

Further supports my hypothesis that Birdsong originated from old English name from old English. There was the composer from the early 1600's named "William Byrd" whose family was in the southern part of Virginia during the 1620's. Could it be that our distant grandfather added song after the famous composer?

The Birdsong pedigree has many families connected to them and some have been documented as far back as the 1300's, with Colonel of Antwerp, Duke of Clarence Plantagenet (1338-1368) and Ralph Stafford (1299-1372).

Disclaimer: Although, my research has uncovered much in- formation on the origin of the name Birdsong, there is still allot of work to done. To date there is not enough evidence to conclude that the Birdsong's origin was Native American, German and/or French as many have claimed. However, there is solid evidence they lived in St. Charles Parish (Jamestown, VA) in the early 1700's with many other British descents.

GENALOGICAL CHART
American Birdsong

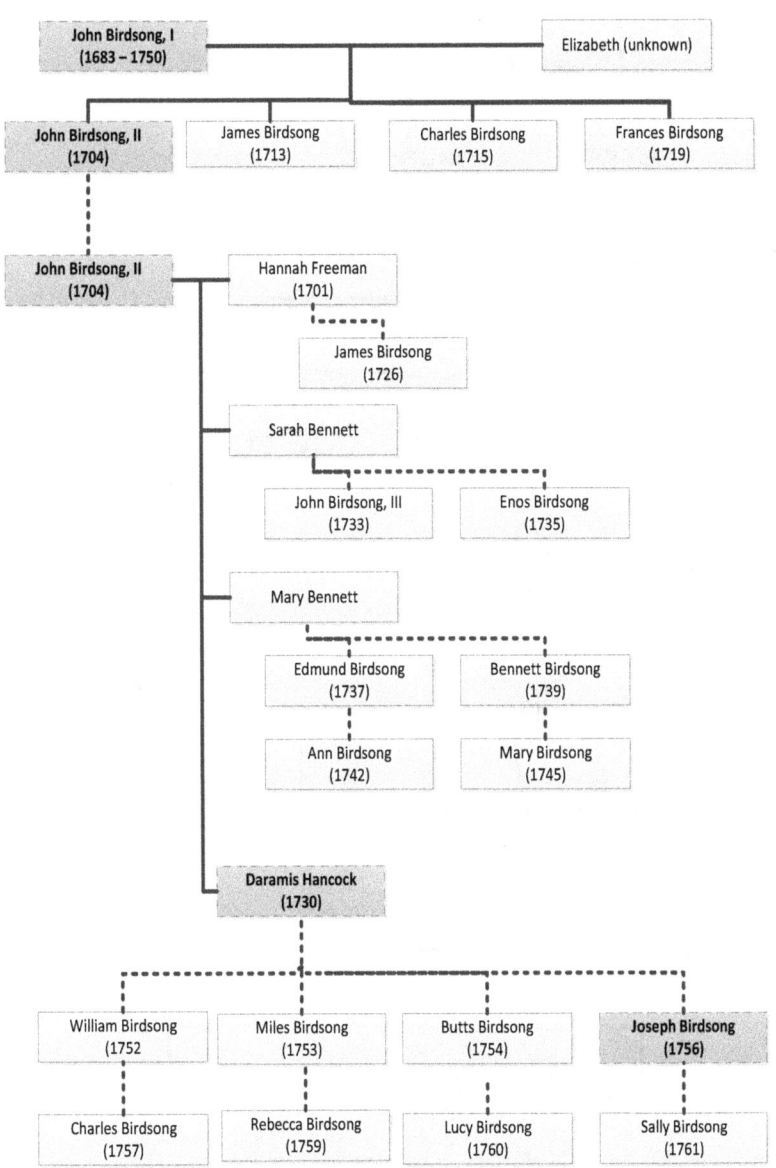

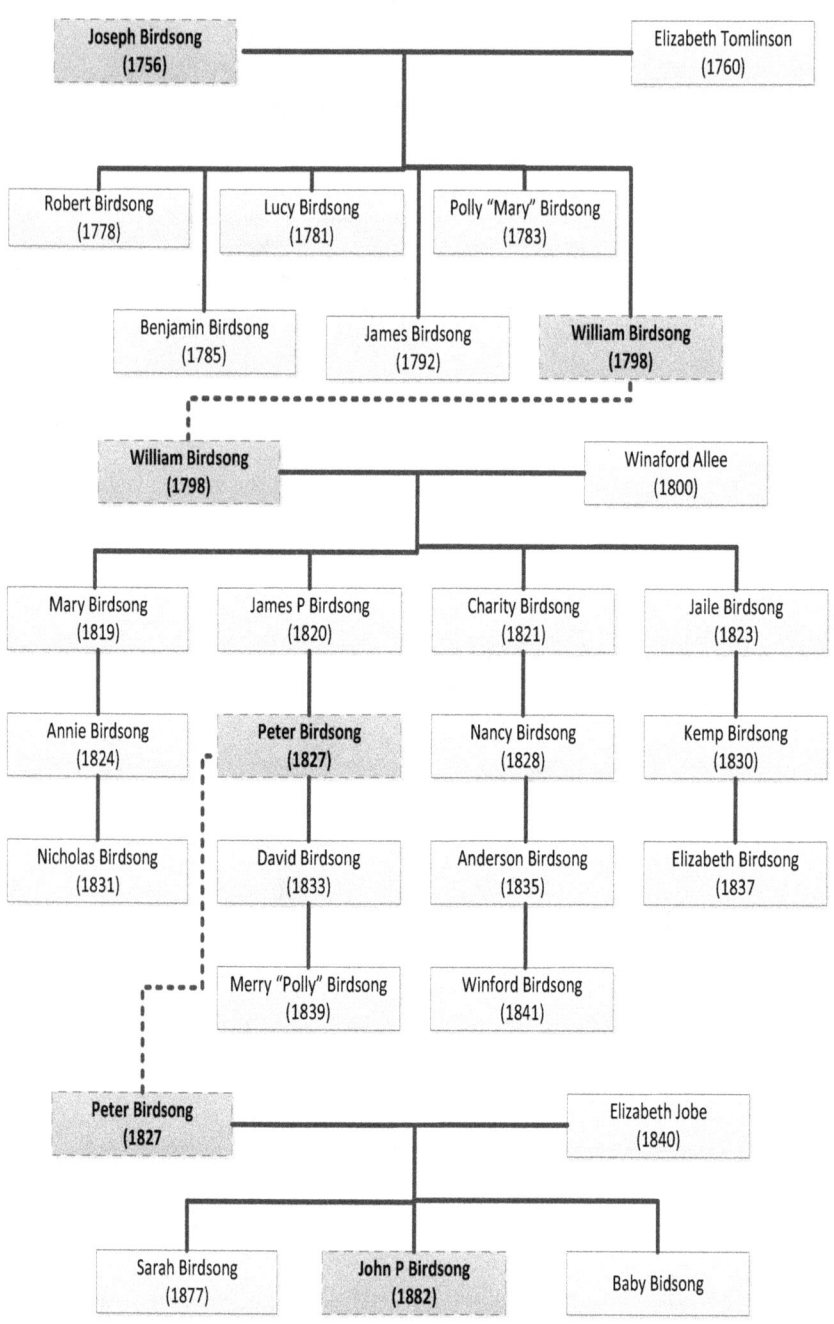

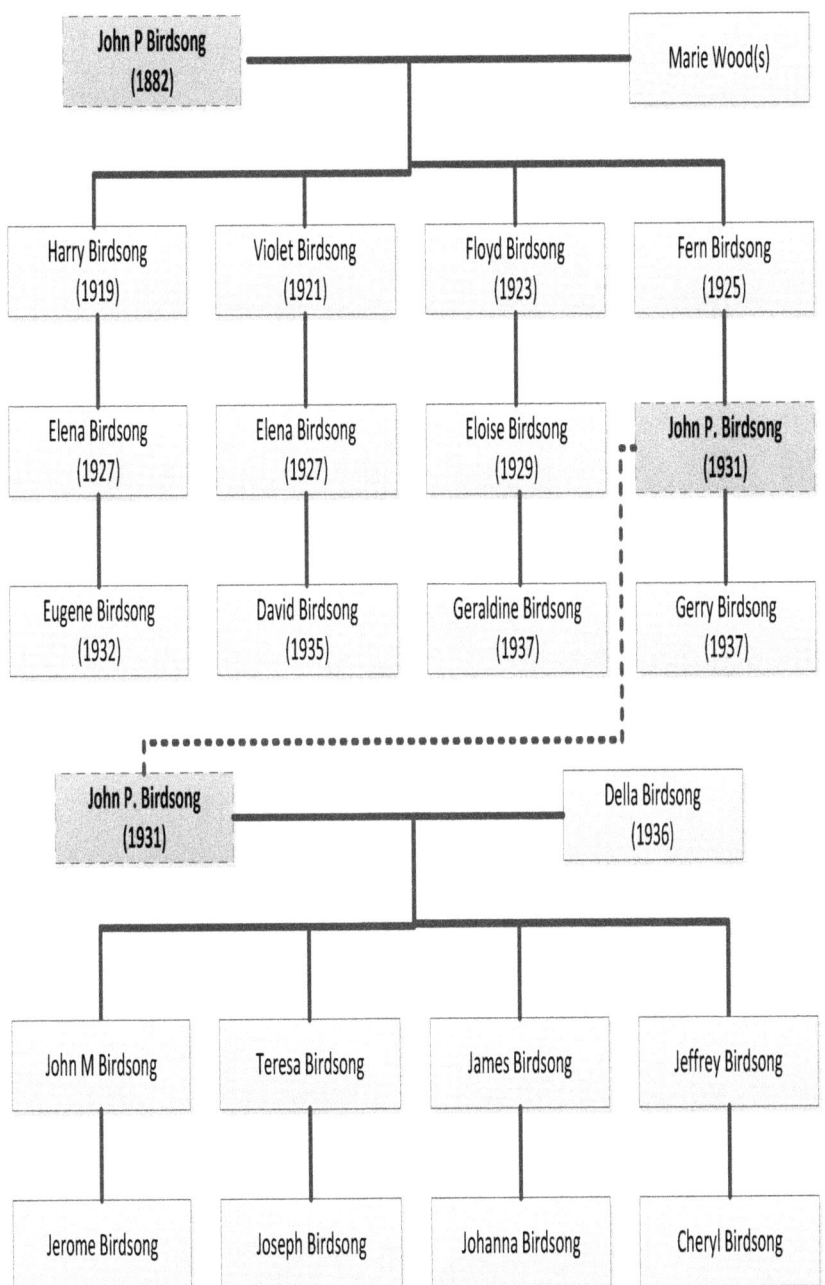

Contents

ACKNOWLEDGMENTS 7
PREFACE 7
INTRODUCTION..9
GENALOGICAL CHART 13
CHAPTER ONE...21
    JOHN I BIRDSONG & ELIZABETH...21
CHAPTER TWO...28
    WIFE OF JOHN DARAMIS HANCOCK, PART I -THE ANCESTRY OF BIRDSONG, II (1704—1785) 32

    PART II - THE ANCESTOR OF ELIZABETH PHILIPS, WIFE OF WILLIAM HANCOCK (1693-1748) 44

    PART III – THE ANCESTRY OF MARY SWAN, WIFE OF WILLIAM PHILIPS (1679-1721) 46

    PART IV – THE ANCESTRY OF MARY HARRIS, WIFE OF MATHEW SWANN (1620-1702)...48

    PART V – THE ANCESTRY OF MARY CLAIBORNE, WIFE OF ROBERT HARRIS (1615-1701)..49

    PART VI – THE ANCESTRY OF LADY ALICE SMYTHE, WIFE OF SIR WILLIAM HARRIS (1556-1616) 53

    PART VII – THE ANCESTRY OF DOROTHY WALDEGRAVE, WIFE OF ARTHUR HARRIS (1526-1597) 57

    PART VIII – THE ANCESTRY OF JOHANNA PERCY, WIFE OF ARTHUR HARRIS (1476-1532)..76

    PART IX – THE ANCESTRY OF MATILDA (EDITH) OF WIFE OF HENRY I BEAUCLERC, KIND OF ENGLAND (1069-1135).......................86

CHAPTER THREE..90
WILLIAM BIRDSONG & ELIZABETH TOMLINSON ....

THE ANCESTERY OF ELIZABETH TOMLINSON, WIFE OF WILLIAM BIRDSONG, SR. (1756-1798) ....

CHAPTER FOUR 97
WILLIAM BIRDSONG & WINAFORD ALLEE ....

WIFE OF WILLIAM BIRDSONG, JR THE ANCESTRY OF WINAFORD ALLEE, (1798-1863) ....

CHAPTER FIVE 115
PETER BIRDSONG & ELIZABETH JOBE ....

THE ANCESTRY OF ELIZABETH JOBE, WIFE OF PETER BIRDSONG, (1827-1918) ....

CHAPTER SIX 128
JOHN BIRDSONG & MARIE WOOD ....

WIFE OF JOHN P BIRDSONG (1882) .... THE ANCESTRY

CHAPTER SEVEN..150
JOHN BIRDSONG & DELLA RHYNERSON ....

THE ANCESTRY OF DELLA RHYNERSON, WIFE OF JOHN BIRDSONG (1931-1988)...

AMERICAN SERVICE..202

BIRDSONG FAMILY CRESTS...204

REFERENCE 205

CHAPTER ONE

FIRST AMERICAN BIRDSONG'S

JOHN I BIRDSONG & ELIZABETH

JOHN BIRDSONG, I born about 1683 probably in England married Elizabeth last name unknown about 1704 in York County, Virginia. His is the first documented ancestor in America.

There is not much known about the first John Birdsong other than he and his wife resided in York County, Virginia and had up to four children. The first documentation of the family of John and Elizabeth Birdsong was found in the register of St Charles Parish. The entry recorded the birth of their daughter, Frances Birdsong on 8th July 1719, is proof that the family was in York County at the time.

Although, John's occupation is unknown, he may have been a farmer based on the location of his and Elizabeth's residence.

Children of the marriage:

1. John Birdsong, II born abt 1704 York County, Virginia; died about 1785 in Sussex, Virginia.

2. James Birdsong, born about 1712 York County, Virginia.

3. Charles Birdsong, born about 1713 York County, Virginia.

4. Frances Birdsong, born 8 July 1719 born about 1712 York County, Virginia.

John Birdsong, I and Elizabeth lived in St. Charles Parish, York County, and Colonial Virginia in late in the 1600's and 1700's. They were members of the St. Charles Parish and documented in the "History and Registers of Charles Parish".

John and Elizabeth registry for Frances Birdsong was the first entry made in the Register of Charles Parish on the Birdsong family. She was born on 8th July 1719, York County, Virginia and baptized on 27th September 1719, York County, Virginia. John was approximately 36 years old when Frances was born.

History of York County, Virginia

During the 17th century, shortly after establishment of the Jamestown Settlement in 1607, English settlers and explored and began settling the areas adjacent to Hampton Roads. By 1634, the English colony of Virginia consisted of eight shires or counties with a total population of approximately 5,000 inhabitants.

Charles River Shire took its name from King Charles I of England. It was located on the Virginia Peninsula on the Charles River (also named for the younger son of King James I. During the English Civil War, Charles River County and the Charles River were changed to York County and York River, respectively. The river, county, and town of Yorktown are believed to have been was named for York, a city in Northern England.

Charles River Shire became York County in 1643. The first courthouse and jail were located near what is now Yorktown although the community, founded as a port for shipping tobacco to Europe, as variously called Port of York, Borough of York, York, Town of York, until and Yorktown was established in 1691. Never incorporated as a town, Yorktown is the county seat of York County.

The Chiskiack Tribe of Native Americans lived on the south side of the York River on the grounds of the present-day Naval Weapons Station Yorktown near Yorktown until the 1630s, when conflicts with the English colonists caused them to move.

It is one of the five original shires of Virginia considered extant in the original form almost 400 years later, making it one of the oldest counties in the United States.

The Birdsong's were early members of the St. Charles Parish it was the last colonial church of Charles Parish, built about 1708 and burned a century later, on the site of two earlier churches of the parish, built about 1636 and 1682. This parish was first known as New Poquoson Parish in 1635 and was renamed Charles Parish in 1692.

Charles Parish has served York County, Virginia, formerly known as New Poquoson Parish. At least 8 other markers are within 4 miles of this marker, as the crow flies. York County / Warwick County; Battle of Big Bethel; Henry Lawson Wyatt; Poquoson; Young's Mill ; First Peninsula Defense Line; Mathews Mill; a different marker also named Young's Mill.

Inscription: About one mile east, on north (left-hand) side of road (see stone marker and old foundations) stood the last colonial church of Charles Parish, built about 1708 and burned a century later, on the site of two earlier churches of the parish, built about 1636 and 1682. This parish was first known as New Poquoson Parish in 1635 and was renamed Charles Parish in 1692.

Site of first and second Charles Churches

The church as founded in about 1692. Site of Charles Church in George Carrington Mason, Colonial Churches of Tidewater Virginia.

The Virginia State Library Board. Includes brief history, list of ministers, parish register births (1648-1789) and deaths (1665-1787). Kinard, June. Charles Parish Records, York County, Virginia, 1648-1789.

Much research goes into genealogist work and yet still much research needs to be done. Throughout this book the researcher will reference artifacts and documents obtained through the years. As most genealogist will state that their work in never done and it is based on collection of evidence that gets you closer to the facts. Although, there is still much work to be done and many undiscovered findings this is the evidence that has been gathered at this point in my research.

Seeking to understand the origin of the Birdsong name my journey looks for the genealogical location of the first Birdsong's and their occupations. The families they marry, the families that live nearby and the families that attend the same church. Also, understanding what was happening during that time in history will bring to life what it must have been like during their journey.

This leads me into my next section the genealogical locations of the first family. New Poquoson's name was change in 1692 to Charles Parish. This was the parish that recorded John and Elizabeth and their family's births and deaths. The New Poquoson's Parish was established in 1635 through 1692, and then it became Charles Parish. The Parish of early Virginia were formed and divided and sometimes ceased to exist.

The following two paragraphs are excerpts from a publication, "Parish Lines, Diocese of Southern Virginia" This assist in identifying the location of the first Birdsong families in the America.

The New Poquoson Paris never combined with other parishes to form larger ones. On December 12, 1692, the House of Burgesses issued the following order;

"Upon petition of the parishioners of New Poquoson in the County of Yorke, it is ordered that from henceforth forever hereafter that the said parish shall be called and named Charles Parish & the said Parish Church shall be called & named Charles Church. And the River formerly called New Poquoson River shall from time to time at all times hereafter be called, named & written Charles River."

John Birdsong, I owned land and the following was documented by Doctor Emile A. Birdsong, the document was in the following "Northumberland County, Virginia Apprenticeships order".

"211. 16 January 1711/1712—Richd Craford is hereby bound an apprentices to serve John Birdsong three years from this time forward in the occupation & trade of a Tayler [tailor], in consideration were of ye sd John Birdsong doth herby oblige himself during the said term to find & allow ye sd Richard sufficient apparel, diet, washing & lodging, to do an honest endeavor to teach him ye trade and that he will not confine the sd Richd to work about any other labour but the trade of Tayor only in tending corn (to wit) no other labour with a hoe but otherwise to performe such necessary services as are suitable to his circumstances." OB 1699-1713, part 2, 761. As you can see the many mis-spellings in this reference you begin to understand that folks may have difficulty reading and writing during the 1600's and 1700's in the literature." Although, it has been documented John Birdsong, I lived in York County, Virginia this document shows he must have lived in Northumberland County, Virginia as well.

The researcher's assessment of this publication is not an indication that "John Birdsong, I" had been a tailor by trade but may have acquired the skills earlier in his career. The publication states that Richard Craford would work as a labor tending "corn" for trade of John training him as a tailor. This indicates John did have land and planted corn.

The research indicates that "John Birdsong, I" had publications if his name "Birdsong" in both 1719 the birth of his and Elizabeth's daughter Francies and 1711 the contract between him and his apprentice.

The researcher still has many unanswered questions around did the Birdsong's arrive in America. Based on the evidence we may conclude that John Birdsong, I was in America by 1711 and had some type of plantation growing corn.

CHAPTER TWO

SECOND GENERATION

JOHN II BIRDSONG & DARAMIS HANCOCK

Includes related families the Hancock, Phillips (Swan, Harris, Clairborne), Holt (Bailey, Hansford), Spencer, Poynter, & Nickolls

JOHN BIRDSONG, II born about 1704 in York County, Virginia and died about 1785 in Sussex, Virginia. It is believed that John was married four times. His first marriage was to Hannah Freeman, second marriage Sarah Bennet, third marriage Mary Bennett and four and last marriage was to Daramis Hancock. Daramis is the daughter of William Hancock and Elizabeth Phillips.

The focus of this book will be his marriage and children with Daramis Hancock.

Children of John and Daramis:

1. **William Birdsong**, born about 1752 in Sussex County, Virginia.
2. Miles Birdsong, born about 1753 in Sussex County, Virginia.
3. Butts Birdsong, born about 1754 in Sussex County, Virginia.
4. Joseph Birdsong, Sr born about 1756 in Sussex County, Virginia.
5. Charles Birdsong, born about 1757 in Sussex County, Virginia.
6. Rebecca Birdsong, born about 1759 in Sussex County, Virginia.
7. Lucy Birdsong, born about 1760 in Sussex County, Virginia.
8. Sally Birdsong, born about 1761 in Sussex County, Virginia.

As mentioned "John, I" married three times before marrying Daramis. His first wife Hannah Freeman is linked up through the Royal family to Richard II of Normandy as was Daramis. It is clear the Birdsong's socialized with the Royal families. This continues to increase my curiosity if in fact the Birdsong's changed their name from "Le Byrd" / "Le Bird" to Birdsong.

John, I purchased land in 1750 this is the same year he married Daramis. The land description states there is 338 acres on the South side of Blackwater swamp. Beginning and extending his own corner tree thence and extending to a pine in snake branch.

John & Daramis was plantation owners and there are records indicating ownership of slaves.

Damaris Will was filed in Sussex in 1801. Her will notes: Rebekah Blow; Lucy Hix; Sally Clary; and six sons William Miles, Butts, Joseph and Charles Hancock Birdsong, William Birdsong, Two sons listed by John Birdsong were James and John and daughter Ann Lane. Many members of the Birdsong family went to Brunswick County.

Will of Damaris (sic) Birdsong

I Damaris Bidsong of Sussex county being weak of body, but of sound mind/and memory…

1st I give and bequeath to my daughter Rebekah Blow on sorrel horse/ known b the Name of blaz to her and her heirs.

2nd I Give and bequeath to my daughter Lucy Hix on Gray horse known by the name of Tallow, Also one feather bed & furniture which I have made since the death of my husband to her and her heirs also one side Saddle to her and her heirs

3rd I Give and bequeath to my daughter Sally Clary my riding chair and harness to her and her heirs

4th My Will and desire is that after all my just debts and legacies are paid tha all my Stock of any kind and quality….with the residue of my Estate of ever sort as bond notes of hand accompts & also my Crop of all kind shall be equally divided among my three daughters…, also money arising from the labour of my negroes which my five sons William, Miles, Butts, Joseph, and Charles Hancock Birdsong have….Also 80 pound my son William Birdsong shall divide among my daughters. Signed with her mark.

1820 Census Sussex County, Virginia shows list Miles as head of household unsure. John & Daramis were both passed by the 1820 census

1820 Census- Sussex County, Virginia

Heads of Household noted: Miles Birdsong

Cherry Birdsong, Rebecca Birdsong, Lucy Birdsong, Nancy Birdsong, William Birdsong

The Ancestry of (1) Daramis Hancock, Wife of John Birdsong, I (1704-1785)

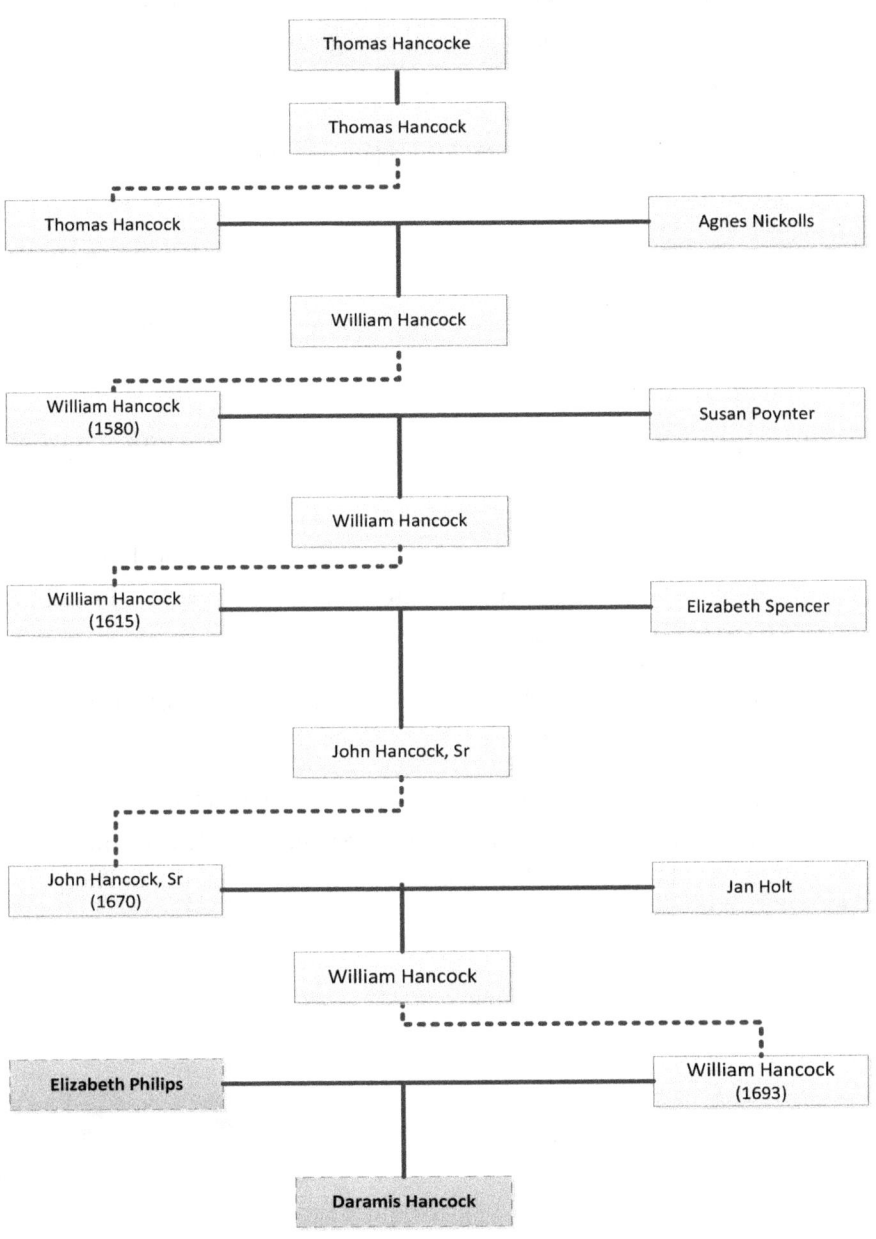

PART I - THE ANCESTRY OF DARAMIS HANCOCK, WIFE OF JOHN BIRDSONG, II (1704—1785)

The story of our English, French & Scottish ancestry is not complete without including the ancestries of at least nine of our "great" grandmothers.

1. Daramis Hancock, wife of John Birdsong, II

2. Elizabeth Philips, wife of William Hancock, mother of Daramis Hancocks.

3. Mary Swan wife of William Philips, mother of Elizabeth Philips.

4. Mary Harris wife of Mathew Swan, mother of Mary Swans.

5. Mary Claiborne wife of Robert Harris, mother of Marry Harris.

6. Alice Smythe, wife of Sir William Harris of Creeksea and "great" grandmother Robert Harris.

7. Dorothy Waldegrave, wife of Arthur Harris who died in 1597 and the mother of Sir William Harris of Creeksea " The Franks" (French) & "King of England" (English).

8. Joanna Percy, wife of Arthur Harris, the great-grandmother of Sir William Harris of Creeksea. "The Franks".

9. Matilda (Edith) Of Scotland, wife of Henry I Beauclerc, King of England. Matilda is one of the grt-grt-grt grandmothers of the Percy's. "The Scottish" & "King of England" (English), & King of Angel-Saxon's.

Daramis Hanock
Royalty lines include:

Alfred the Great, King of Wessex
Matilda (Edith) Of Scotland
Charles the Great, King of the Franks
Saint Itta
Saint Begga
Dorothy Waldegrave
Malcolm III Cammore, King of Scotland
Edward I, II, & III, King of England
Joanna Percy
Sir Henry Percy (Hotspur)

Note the researcher's focus will be Daramis's direct ancestor's line. Starting with the oldest known and documented ancestor.

William Hancock was born in Devonshire, England Abt. 1580. His parents was Thomas Hancock and Agnes Nikolls. He married Susan Poynter. He died March 22, 1622 in Jamestown, James, Virginia

He had the following children:

    1. Simon Hancock in England, born about 1610.

    2. Augustine Hancock in England, born about 1605.

    3. **William Hancock**, Jr. in England born about 1615 married Elizabeth Spencer.

William left his family in England and traveled to America in 1620. He came in search for timber for his shipbuilding business according to an old Hancock Bible record. He lived at Thorpe's House at Berkeley Hundred plantation.

He was a member of The Virginia Company of London which was a group of businessmen who were granted a charter by King Jame I (June 1606) for the purpose of establishing a settlement in the Chesapeake area of Virginia. The first settlement was established at Jamestown in 1607. As an investor in the Virginia Company, William traveled to Jamestown in 1619. According to an old Hancock family Bible, William left England on the ship "Margaret of Bristol" sailing through the Bristol Channel on Sept 16, 1619. Leaving his family behind in England, he was coming to search for lumber for his shipbuilding business.

This group of 39 people set foot in Virginia on Dec. 4, 1619 and proclaimed it a day of Thanksgiving. That location became Berkeley Hundred Plantation, a small village. William Hancock lived at Capt. George Thorpe's house, who wanted to help convert and civilize the Indians. (This was on the north bank of the James River in what is now Charles City County, Virginia) On Good Friday, 22 March 1622 the settlement was attacked by Indians and William was among the 347 who were massacred. Other settlements were attacked also, including Wolstenholme Towne, built in 1620 on the Martin's hundred land grant (now James City County). Those killed in this massacre are supposed to be buried at Carter Plantation.

In 1630, three of William's son Augustine came to Virginia to claim his father's vast estate. Son Simon came in 1635, settling in Princess Anne County, and son William came in 1638. Augustine, Simon and William became wealthy, prominent planters in Virginia.

William Hancock, Jr. was born abt. 1615 in Devonshire, England and died in 1693 in Surry, Virginia, he married **Elizabeth Spencer** and William died about 1693. Elizabeth Spencer is the daughter of Nicholas Spencer, Jr. & Mary Gostwich.

Children: at least one son; **John Hancock, Sr** born about 1670

John Hancock, Sr born about 1670 who married **Jane Holt** about 1699 and John died about 1732. Jane Holt was the daughter of Randle Holt & Elizabeth Hansford.

They had the following children:

William Hancock born between 1693-1694, died April 1768, Sussex County, Viginia.

1. **William Hanock**, born about 1700 Sussex County, Viginia.
2. John Hancock, Jr born about 1702 Sussex County, Viginia.
3. Joseph Hanock born about 1704 Sussex County, Viginia.
4. Elizabeth Hanock born about 1706 Sussex County, Viginia.
5. Mary Hancock born about 1708 Sussex County, Viginia.
6. Duejates Hanock born about 1710 Sussex County, Viginia.
7. Marthat Hanock born about 1712 Sussex County, Viginia.

William Hancock born about 1700 married **Elizabeth Philips**

1. Mary Hancock
2. Benjamin Hancock
3. Sarah Hancock
4. **Daramis Hanock**, born about 1730 Surry Co. Virgina, died about 1797, Surry Co. Vigrinia.

John was not the famous John Hancock but they are likely related back in England or where the Hancock's originally came from. John and Jane had a son named William Hancock. This John Hancock was in Virginia about the same time as the other famous John Hancock's grandfather was in Massachusetts. They are likely related back in England.

Jane's father Randall Holt, Jr. died in 1679; he was likely a yeomen in the Bacon's Rebellion. This rebellion of the settlers was because the Government would not form an Army to protect the settlers from the Indian raids on the settlement.

The early settler's took matters into their own hands and formed their own Army that included farmers and plantation owners.

The Harris family includes Mary Harris, Robert Harris daughter who married Mathew Swann. She is the grandmother of Elizabeth Phillips who married William Hancock, this is Daramis Hancock's grandparents

William Hancock was born about 1693 and died April 1768 in Sussex Co., VA He married Elizabeth Philips, daughter of William and Mary (Swann) Phillips .William and Elizabeth had a daughter named **Damaris Hancock** born about 1730, Sussex County, Virginia; died 1802, Sussex County, Virginia.

Elizabeth Phillips is mentioned in the "Adventurers of Purse and Person, Virginia, 1607-1624/5.

William Hancock left a will 11 Aug. 1764-18 April 1765.

Additional information appears in this book as well and indicates that Hartwell Philips, a grandson of William Philips, Sr., also married a Hancock. "Jane (Jean) Hancock, born 15 Aug. 1741, married, (bond 24) February. 1762, Hartwell Phillips, son of John and Martha (Crafford) Phillips, of Edgecombe Co., North Carolina, who married (2), born in 1772, Feraby Jones and left will about 1807."

THE ANCESTRY OF JANE HOLT, WIFE OF JOHN HANCOCK, (1670—1732)

Mary Bailey & Randall Holt, Sr.

After the death of Mary's first husband she then married her second husband Randall (or Randolph) Holt, **Sr. Randall Holt** was born about 1607 in Prestbury, England, the son of Randall/Randolph and Elizabeth (Pott) Holt, who were wed in the Prestbury church. Randall was probably a nephew of Dr. Pott(s), the Virginia Colony physician who later became governor.

Randall Holt's is the first mention of the Holt family found in the American colonies. The court ordered that upon release from his indenture he was to be given "one suit apparel from head to foot and three barrels of corn."

Randall Holt probably came to the Jamestown Colony in 1621 onboard the ship George as a young teen and indentured servant to Dr. John Potts. Randal was released from his indenture in 1625 and in 1628 he married Mary Bailey, who also may have been from Prestbury. It was a fortunate match. She was the sole heir of John Bailey of Hog Island, one of the richest men in the Virginia Colony.

The Bailey Family Legacy

The Council of Jamestown had appointed Robert Evers as Mary's guardian at her father's death and ordered that 490 Hog Island acres be deeded to her. Randall and Mary settled on this island in the

James River. He added 400 acres to his wife's property in 1636 and another 400 acres in 1639. In 1650, Randall Holt Jr., obtained a grant for 1022 Hog Island acres as "son and lawful heir". He received a major's commission in the British Colonial forces and was a member of the governing House of Burgesses. In 1668, Randall Holt Jr. was appointed Justice for Surry County. In 1679, the year he died, he was granted a patent for 1,450 acres on Hog Island.

Mary Bailey and Randall Holt, Sr. had a son named Randall (or Randolph) Holt, Jr. There is not a known birth date and he died in 1679 – Virginia. John Bailey, was born in 1580. His ancestors were from Lancashire County, England. This is on the west coast of England, between Wales & Scotland, on the Irish Sea coast. It is assumed that this is where he immigrated to @ 1000 A.D. when surnames were granted by the tax collectors

Randall Holt, Jr married **Elizabeth Hansford**, before Oct 1663. Randall Holt, Jr, born about 1629 in Surry County, Virginia (Hogg Island, James City County, Virginia); died before 2 Sep 1679 in Hogg Island, Surry County, Virginia. He was the son of Randall (Randolph) Holt and Mary Bailey. Elizabeth Hansford, born after 1645 in probably York County, Virginia; died before 3 May 1709 in Surry County, Virginia.

She was the daughter of Major John Hansford and Elizabeth. Randall & Elizabeth had Jane Holt. Randal Holt may have died of some of the many plagues of that area, or have been killed by Indians.

Children of Randall Holt and Elizabeth Hansford are:

    1. Captian Thomas Holt, born between1664 - 1679 in Surry County, Virginia; died before 17 Mar 1729/30 in Surry County, Virginia; married Frances Mason before 1696.

    2. John Holt, born about 1664 in Surry County, Virginia; died 1705 in Surry County, Virginia; married Mary Binns before 1685; born about 1666 in probably Surry County, Virginia.

    3. **Jane Holt**, born between 1664 - 1679 in Surry County, Virginia; died before 15 Jan 1733/34 in Surry County, Virginia; married **John Hancock** before 1709; born about 1670 in Surry County, Virginia; died before 17 May 1732 in Surry County, Virginia.

    4. William Holt, born about 1664 in Hogg Island, Surry County, Virginia; died before 18 May 1726 in Lawnes Creek, Surry County, Virginia; married Elizabeth Seward before 1692.

On 6 Aug 1650, Randall Holt re patented Hog Island and the adjacent tract of his father's, amounting to 1022 acres. It is assumed that Randall Jr had reached his majority at this time. In 1679 he patented 1450 acres in Surry County Member of House of Burgesses 1656; appointed Justice for Surry County, 22 Dec 1668. Census of Tithables Surry County: 1668, 1674, 1678. Randall's occupation was a Planter as stated in his Will on 2 Sep 1679, Surry County, Virginia.

Elizabeth made her Will 4 Mar 1708/9; probated 3 May 1709 in Surry County, Virginia. "Leg: to grandson Charles, son of John, Dec'd; to grandson Joseph Holt, son of John; to grandson Benjamin, son of John; granddaughter Mary Seward; bequest to son Thomas and dau-in-law Frances; to Thomas

Edwards; sons William and Thomas Holt; dau Jane Handcock, wife of John Handcock; and Lucy, wife of Joseph Mountfort.Tax Record: Quit Rent, Surry County, Virginia 1450 acres Will proved: 3 May 1709, Surry County, Virginia"

Notes for Randal Holt, Sr;
Census of Tithables Surry Co: 1683, 1688, 1694, 1698, 1702.
In 1687 in Cavalry Militia of Surry Co. Virginia
In 1703 he petitioned the House to be keeper of the ferry across the James River to Archer's Hope Creek.
Military: Calvalry, Surry Co., Virginia

Our immigrant John came to Virginia in 1618, settled on Hog Island in Surry County, Virginia. Surry County was a small island in the James River mostly likely what we know as Jamestown. This is where the early settlers kept their hogs. Only the caretakers and a few people lived on it. John was a very earl immigrant because Jamestown was only 11 years old at the time. John migrated there before the Mayflower by a couple of years. There is no information on his wife.

John Baily's only child **Mary Bailey** was first mart to a Mr. Bagby. He likely died of Malaria or some of the early plagues of the low lying Jamestown area.

John Hansford & Elizabeth Jands

John and Elizabeth had a daughter named **Elizabeth Hansford**. They also had a son Charles Hansford that married Elizabeth Foliott-Mode, Charles was a Captain in the Colonial Militia of York County, Virginia and died in 1702. The Hansford ancestors were from Dorset & Staffordshire England. John came from England in 1651 and settled in York County, Virginia. He patented land in Gloucester County, Virginia in 1653. He patented land in Gloucester County, Virginia in 1653 and was the Justice of the Peace in 1655. He must have brought his wife and children from England with him because he only lived ten years after coming to America. He died in Virginia in 1661

Colonel John Hansford in 1655 served on the Justice's Bench of York County. He married **Elizabeth Jands**, daughter of Elizabeth Jands. He was a member of The Virginia Company Of London which was created by King James I for the purpose of colonizing in America. The first settlement was established at Jamestown in 1607. As an investor in the Virginia Company, William traveled to Jamestown in 1619 aboard the "Margaret" of Bristol. He was a member of a group that founded Berkeley Hundred. On 22 March 1622 the settlement was attacked by Indians and William, along with many others, was massacred.

Shortly after 1630, three of William's sons came to America. Augustine, Simon and William became prominent planters in Virginia and established a family line that today includes many thousands of their descendants. From Virginia, their descendants migrated throughout the southeastern and midwestern states and today are living in all parts of the country. The information found about this Hancock family is the result of the efforts of many reearchers. No genealogy is ever complete. It is the hope that it provides guidance for future researchers to continue to discover.

John Hansford's will, dated 9 May 1654, was proved on 24 June 1661 and was recorded in York County Records No. 3 1657/62, page 122. It showed his wife was Elizabeth, sons were John, William, Thomas, and Charles, and daughters were Elizabeth, Mary, and Margaret; also he possessed over 2,170 acres of land and livestock.

A transcription follows:

John Hansford of Cheesecake, York. To my eldest sons John Hansford and William Hansford 600 acres of land lying upon Claybanke Creek on the north side of York River to be equally divided between them 3 cows apiece etc. To my two sons Thomas and Charles Hansford 500 and odd acres of land lying at the rear of Felgates Creek which I heretofore bought of Mr. Weston's daughter to be equally divided between them. To my son Thomas one young horse colt and to my sons Thomas and Charles 3 cows, 2 heifers etc. To my daughter Elizabeth my old grey mare and 3 cows, etc. To my daughter Mary my younger mare, and to my sd daughter Mary and my daughter Margaret 3 cows etc. Sons under 21, daughters under 15. To daughter Elizabeth 1,000 acres of land lying on the south side of the Matapony River, the rights and bounds whereof do appear at the office in Jamestown. To my godson John Morley, son to my neighbor Thomas Morley, one heifer. To my servant Ennis one heifer with calf. To my wife Elizabeth Hansford my devident of 70 acres of land whereon my dwelling house stands for her life, and after her death to my son Thos. Hansford, and I ordain her sole exix. Francis Willis, Edmund Peeters, Supervisors. To Robert Jones who now instructs my children 500 lbs. of tobacco. Witnesses John Rolands, Ennis Mackintosh (Enoch), Robert Jones.

Additional notes:

Maryland Land Records, Liber 2, fo. 254; Records Provincial Court, Liber B, fo. 224. This John Hansford or Handford (father of Col. Thomas Hansford who was educated {executed in Accomac Co   Va) for his share in Bacon's Rebellion) was perhaps the principal creditor of Weston; though he may have been a connection, for the court record seems to show that Weston, in his will, had named him as executor. He was probably the son of Sir Humphrey Handford of London, one of the Virginia Company, and descended from the armorial family of Handford of Cheshire and Worcestershire. Mr. Tyler says that the Virginia Hansfords had seventy acres of land in York County, which had originally belonged to Weston.

The Ancestry of (2) Elizabeth Philips, Wife of William Hancock (b. c. 1686; d. c. 1768)

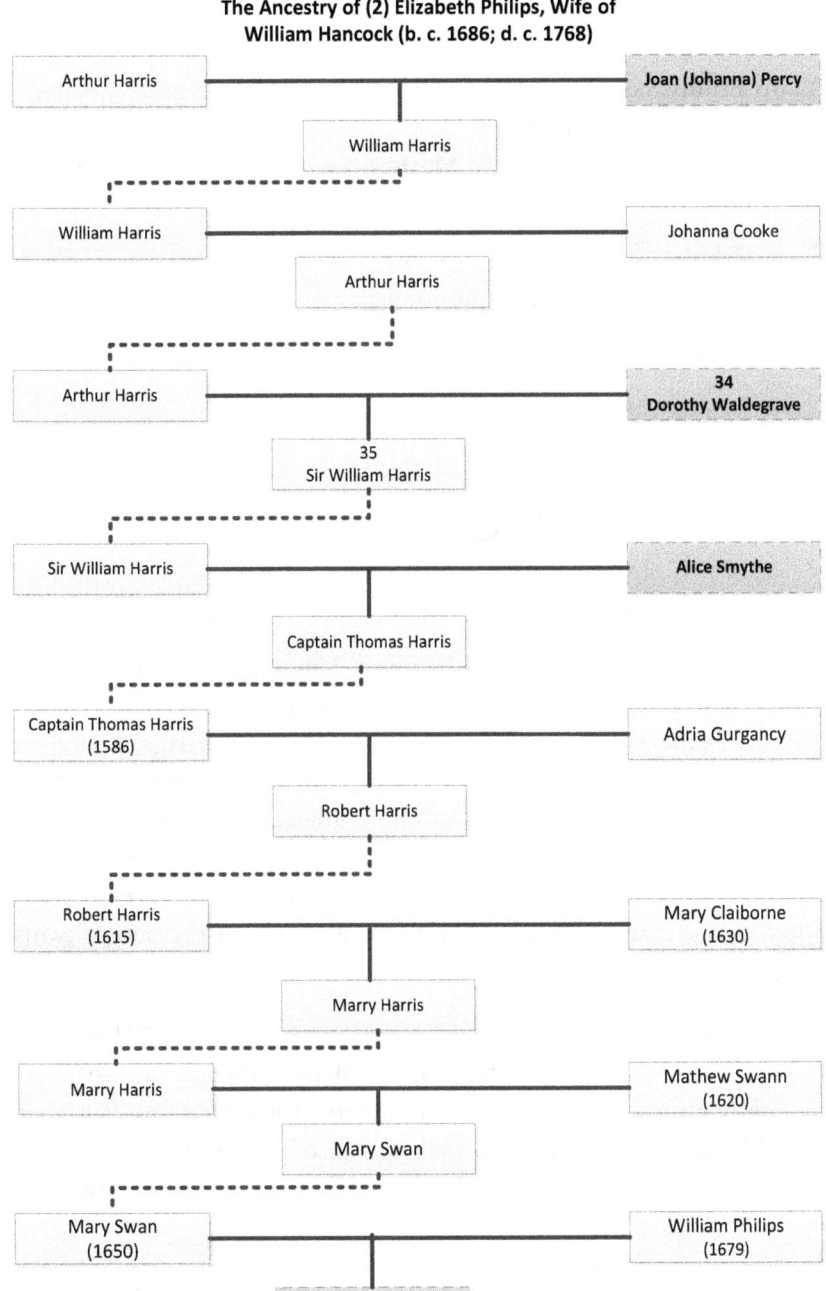

PART II - THE ANCESTOR OF ELIZABETH PHILIPS, WIFE OF WILLIAM HANCOCK (1693-1748)

William Philips born about 1679 and died about 1721 in Surry County, Virginia married to **Mary Swann**. William Philips, first known ancestor, married Mary Swann, daughter of **Mathew Swann**, a prominent early citizen of Surry.

William and Mary Swann had the following children:

1. John Philips unknown birth date.

2. William Philips unknown birth date.

3. Swan Philips unknown birth date.

4. Matthew Philips unknown birth date.

5. Anne Philips unknown birth date.

6. Mary Philips unknown birth date.

7. **Elizabeth Phillips** married **William Hancock**

As mentioned William Philips is the earliest Philips ancestor found in America. This Southside Virginia Families, Volume 2 book spells William Philips last name with one "L". I will do the same on this page, having no reason to spell it otherwise as I have not seen the hand written copies of either William or Mary's wills or the deeds shown on this page. It was also customary to name one of your children after the mothers name as you see here. The average family in those days would have between seven to twenty children over a span of 30 years. Not to mention one or two sets of twins.

Will of William Philips:

The will of William Philips, dated 2-14-1721, probated 4-19-1721 mentioned wife Mary, sons John, William, Swann, and Mathew Philips, the last three being under the age of 16 years, and daughters: Anne; Mary; and Elizabeth Philips. The inventory of William Philips, signed by Mary Philips in April 1721, listed personal property on the Blackwater plantation, the Round Hill plantation and the "Home" plantation.

Will of Mary (Swann) Phillips, 1727
Phillips, Mary. Leg - To daughter, Mary Edwards, wife of John Edwards, my Plantation where I live for her life, then to my daughter, Ann Phillips. To daughter, Ann, one negro, and at her death said negro to my granddaughter,

Ann Edwards. Gives daughter, Ann Phillips, 25 lbs, current money, 8 new pewter dishes, falling table, 6 Russia chairs, tankard, riding horse, etc; if no issue to go to granddaughters, Mary Hancocke and Ann Edwards. Bequest 40 shillings. To sons, William and Swann Phillips; dau. Eliz. Hancocke and Mary Edwards, each six pounds cur money. To John Edwards, my son-in-law, four bbls. corn, to son, Wm. Phillips and Wm. Harrison the same. Rest of est to be equally divided among my five children, Wm. and Swann Phillips, Eliz. Hancocke, Mary Edwards, and Ann Phillips. Friend, Carter Crafford, exer. 28 Mar 1727. April 19, 1927. Wit: Wm. Newsum, Samuel Taylor, John Ruffin. Surry County, Virginia Book 7, page. 697. "Wills and Administration of Surry County, Virginia 1671-1750", p. 129. Note: Mary's executor, Carter Crafford is her brother-in-law who married her sister Sarah Swann. (Carter Crawford).

PART III – THE ANCESTRY OF MARY SWAN, WIFE OF WILLIAM PHILIPS (1679-1721)

Matthew Swann, Jr was born 1661 in Surry County, Virginia. This Matthew married **Mary Harris**, daughter of **Robert Harris** and **Mary Claiborne**. Matthew and Marry (Harris) Swann had three known children: Elizabeth, Mary and Sarah Swann.

The name Swan was English and meant "Knights attendant" and the name Phillips was Welsh.

The Swan's were believed to be of Huguenot ancestry (French), who had fled to Ireland. Since they are French descent, they may have come out of the Isle of Jersey, where the first Swan farm was located between France and Ireland. The Swan family has been tracked back to Mary's father Mathew Swan family also tracked backed to William Swan and Judith Green.

Mathew Swann born about 1620 and died about 1702 son of **William Swann** married his second wife **Mary Harris** in 1675 and had **Mary Swann** who married **William Phillips**.

Mathew married Mary Harris-Spiltimber in 1675 in Virginia. Mary's first husband was Anthony Spiltimber who died then she married Mathew. Mathew was part of the Nathanial Bacon crew for the Bacon's Rebellion, he also rebelled against taxation.

He started the first tax revolt in America. On December 12th 1673 (three years before the Bacon Rebellion) at Lawnes Creek Parish Church, in Surry County, Virginia some of the Parishioners met, to declare that they would not pay their public taxes (British taxation, without representation).

That Church is now known as "The Birthplace of Freedom", due to this meeting. At that time, it was against the law to assemble for stirring up trouble, so they arrested them. William Hancock was also part of this group. Matt was the organizer of the group. They were all fined, but because public opinion was with their cause, the fines were dropped.

Mathew helped Nathanial Bacon form his little Army and one of his sons was supposed to be the first American born person to be hanged for participating in the Bacon Rebellion.

This infuriated the King of England, Charles the second; who had appointed William Berkeley as Governor of Virginia. The King was trying to populate the new colony and his own Governor is killing the settlers. Thus, Governor William Berkeley was removed as Governor of Virginia and recalled to England by the King.

Matthew Swan, the ringleader of this protest against high taxes, has many descendants in Virginia and the South. In 1675 he married Mrs. Mary Spiltimber, widow of Anthony Spiltimber and daughter of Robert Harris. His will was dated December 14, 1702 and probated Jan. 5, 1702. He mentioned daughter, Elizabeth, wife of John Drew, daughter, Sarah; Elizabeth, daughter of John Drew; son-in-law, John Drew; daughter, Mary, wife of William Phillips; and grandson, John Phillips.

Executors were John Drew and Sarah Swann. Witnesses were Arthur Allen, William Chambers, John Allen, and Robert Ruffin.

Children:

1. Elizabeth, married (1) John Drew, d. 1703 (2) John Sugars. (No children.)

2. **Mary,** married **William Phillips** of Surry County, Virginia, who in his will dated Feb. 14, 1720/21, probated April 19, 1721, mentioned wife, Mary; sons, John, William, Swann, and Mathew Phillips (the three last named under 16 years of age); and daughters, Anne, Mary.

PART IV – THE ANCESTRY OF MARY HARRIS, WIFE OF MATHEW SWANN (1620-1702)

Major Robert Harris was born about 1615 in Virginia to **Captain Thomas Harris** and **Adria Gurgancy**. He married **Mary Claiborne** in 1650. Robert died in 1701.

Children of Robert Harris & Mary Claiborne:

1. **Mary Harris** born about 1650 married **Mathew Swann**
2. Colional William Harris born about 1652
3. Mathew Harris born about 1661

Major Robert Harris was born about 1615 either in Jamestown or Henrico County, Virginia. As an adult he lived in York County, Virginia where he received a land grant in 1685 for the transportation of three people into the Virginia Colony. He moved from there to a plantation called "The Forks", which he probably built, in Hanover County, Virginia about 1650 he also married Mary Claiborne-Rice that year. It was her second marriage and evidently his second marriage also, because he was 35 years old. Robert died about 1701 in Virginia. Mary Claiborne died about 1699. They had a daughter named Mary Harris born about 1650 in Virginia who was married to Mathew Swann

Robert and Mary also had a son named Mathew Harris 1661/1727, who had a son William Harris, Sr which had a son named William Harris, Jr born about 1748 who married Elizabeth Wagstaff and their daughter was Susanne Harris who married Nathaniel Jones.

PART V – THE ANCESTRY OF MARY CLAIBORNE, WIFE OF ROBERT HARRIS (1615-1701)

Colonial William Claiborne was born in 1587, in England. He was married to **Elizabeth Butler** from England. He was 34 years old when he emigrated from England to Virginia in 1621.

He came with the Royal Governor Wyatt of Virginia. William may have come from a royal family as most people who traveled with Royal Government were also from a royal family. Also, he was appointed by the King and appointed Governor. He was also Secretary of State of Virginia in 1625. He was a member of the Council 1625-1660. He was made the Treasurer of Virginia for life, in 1642. He was the Deputy Governor in 1653. He was first in Command against the Indians in Virginia 1629 and 1644. He was one of three Commanders appointed to rule Virginia under Cromwell, who had taken over England and he had one grant of 24,000 acres of land in King William Colony of Virginia.

He died in1676 in Virginia at the age of 89 years old. Some believed although he was old enough to die a natural death that it may have been due to the Bacon's Rebellion. William and Elizabeth likely had several children but the only one on record is **Mary Claiborne** (William1) born about 1630. She would have been born about the time that her parents came from England (1621). Mary married her first husband Mr. Rice, because she was Widow Rice when she married **Robert Harris**.

THE ANCESTRY OF ADRIA GURGANCY, WIFE OF CAPT THOMAS HARRIS (1586-1658)

Captain Thomas Harris was born on 10 June 1586 of Crixe Essex, England and died on 30 March 1658 in Henrico County, Virginia, he was married to **Adria Gurgancy**. His parents was **Sir William Harris** and **Alice Smith (Smyth)**. Thomas immigrated to American about 1611 and they had a son named **Major Robert Harris** in 1615. Reportedly a member of the Virginia Company in 1609, he arrived in America 1611 aboard the Prosperous, and settled in Henrico County, Virgina.

He was a member of the House of Burgesses in 1623, 1639 and 1646. A deed for 820 acres in Henrico County, Virginia on Feb. 25, 1638 names the "first wife" of **Captain Thomas Harris** as **Adry Harris** married first **Adria Gurgany** (b. about 1598; d. by Sep. 11, 1626), the daughter of Edward Gurgany, Sr. and Ann. Ann Gurgany is named as the widow of Edward in a deed of 700 acres in Henrico County, Virginia on Jul. 11, 1637, in which 400 of the said acres are said to have been granted to Edward Gurgany in 1617 and bequeathed by his widow to **Captain Thomas Harris**. Edward arrived in America aboard the Phoenix on Apr. 20, 1608, and was a Burgess in 1619.

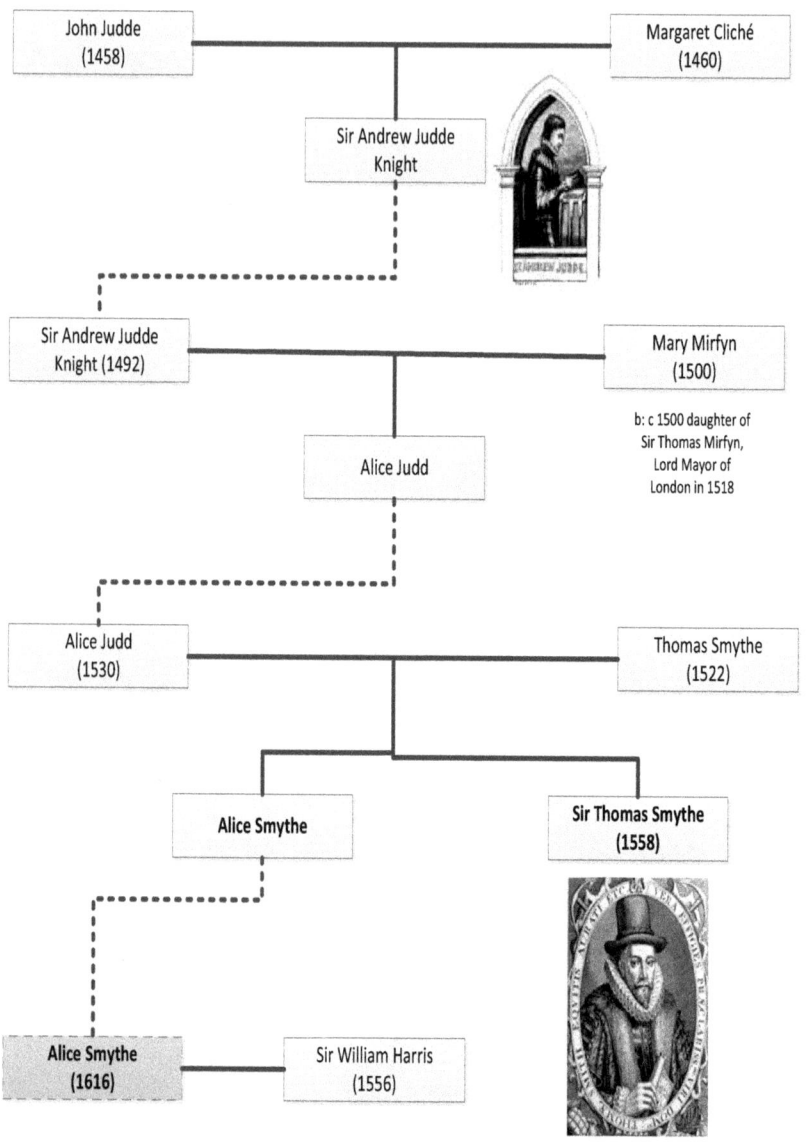

PART VI – THE ANCESTRY OF LADY ALICE SMYTHE, WIFE OF SIR WILLIAM HARRIS (1556-1616)

Sir Andrew Judd; born c 1492 Tonbridge, Kent; died 4th Sep 1558 buried: 14th Sep 1558 St. Helen's Church, Bishopsgate, London.

Andrew was born at Tonbridge (about 40 miles from London) in Kent County, England. He was the son of **Margaret Chichle** of Canterbury and **John Judd** (also spelled Judde). Margaret Chichle of Canterbury born c 1460 daughter of Valentine Chiche and great- niece of Archbishop Henry Chichele. **John Judd** born about 1458.

Andrew, at the age of 17 years, moved to London and worked in the fur trade. He served an eight year apprenticeship and worked as a stapler, skinner and merchant in London and in Calais (Calais, on the continent, was then a part of England). Andrew was quite successful in the London business arena and in public service. He served as; Mayor of the Staple, Master of the Skinners Company, Sheriff of London and Alderman of London. He made his home in the Bishopsgate community of London. Andrew served as Lord Mayor of London in the years 1550-51. After serving as Mayor, Andrew was knighted by King Edward VI, (son of King Henry VIII) Sir Andrew Judd aspired to build a free grammar school for the youth of his hometown, Tonbridge. He secured a charter from King Edward VI for that purpose in 1553. The school which he built in Tonbridge is still in existence serving the young people of England.

Andrew married **Mary Mirfyn** born c 1500 daughter of **Sir Thomas Mirfyn**, Lord Mayor of London in 1518. After Mary's death, Andrew married a second time, and, also, a third time. Andrew is buried at St. Helens Church, Bishopsgate, in London.

Children of Mary Mirfyn and Sir Andrew Judd:

> 1. Martha Judd; born c. 1522; died 1578. Martha married Robert Golding.

> 2. **Alice Judd**; born c 1530; died 1593 Will proven on 12th May 1593

Alice married Thomas Smythe born 1522 son of John and Joan Smythe; died 7th Jun 1591. Thomas was best known as Mr. Customer Smythe of Ostenhanger (now Westenhanger), Kent. His parents were Joan Brounckner, a daughter of Robert Brounckner of Melkshan, and her husband, John

Smythe, Esquire (died 1538), of Corsham, County Wiltshire.

Thomas was appointed by Queen Elizabeth I to be her "Collector of the Queen's Majesties Subsidy for tonnage and poundage, and farmer for the Custome and Subsidy inwards". From this office, he received his nickname, "Customer". Thomas Smythe constructed the central part of Corsham Court, in Wiltshire, in 1582.

This edifice, which exists today, was sold by Thomas' son, Henry Smythe, on June 21, 1602 to the Methuen family.

The children of **Alice Judd** and **Thomas Customer Smythe**:

    1. Andrew Smythe; died as an infant.

    2. Sir John Smythe; died about 1609.

    3. Sir Henry Smythe; birth date unknown.

    4. Sir Richard Smythe; died about 1628.

    5. Robert Smythe; birth date unknown,

    6. Simon Smythe; died about 1596.

    7. Sir Thomas Smythe; born about 1558; died September 4, 1625.

    8. Mary Smythe; birth date unknown. Mary married Robert Davys.

    9. Ursula Smythe; birth date unknown. Ursula married Simon Harding.

    10. Jane Smythe; birth date unknown. Jane married Sir Thomas Fanshawe.

    11. Catherine Smythe birth date unknown. Catherine married Sir Roland Hayward.

    12. Elizabeth Smythe birth date unknown. Elizabeth married Sir Henry Fanshawe.

    13. **Alice Smythe**; died about 1616. Alice married Sir William Harris of Creeksea.

Alice Smythe Harris of Cheeksea Place and the aunt of our immigrant ancestor, John Harris (1588-1638).

Thomas was knighted by King James I in 1603. He was a friend of King James and served as the King's Ambassador to the Tsar of Russia.

Thomas secured from King James the charter to establish the Virginia Colony in North America. He was the Treasurer and operating officer of the corporation, the Virginia Company of London, which actually established and operated the colony in its early years.

Sir Thomas Smythe; born about 1558; died September 4, 1625.

Thomas was the brother of Lady Alice Smythe Harris and the brother in law of Sir William Harris of Creeksea Place. Thomas was born in Ostenhanger (now Westenhanger) in Kent. Thomas was skilled as an English entrepreneur and statesman. He accumulated a considerable fortune from commerce.

1617: Smyth/Southamptono Hundred named for Sir Thomas Smyth its principal investor, Smyth's Hundred was established at Dancing Point in the former Paspahegh territory. The orginal grant was for 80,000 acres on the north side of the James River, constituting most of modern-day Charles City County. This was one of the earliest, largest and best financed of the private plantations. The plantation invested in a brickyard, a mill for toll grinding, iron production, tobacco, corn, and animal husbandry and in the transportation of 300 settlers.

Thomas was an active member of the London Haberdashers and Skinners Companies. He was an organizer in 1600, and, except for the period 1606-07, served as governor of the East India Company until 1621. He served as governor of the Muscovy and French Companies. He was special Ambassador for King James to the Tsar of Russia in 1604-05. Thomas was knighted in 1603 by King James I.

Sir Thomas obtained the Charter of the Virginia Company (of London) in 1609 and was Treasurer until 1618 when charges of embezzlement, later proved to be false, forced his resignation. His labor, perseverance and money were largely responsible for the success of the Virginia Colony.

As governor of the Somers Islands (Bermuda) Company, organized in 1615, Thomas developed the Bermuda Islands with close economic and political ties to Virginia. He was also a major promoter of voyages to find a Northwest Passage to the Orient. Smith Sound (between Ellesmere Island and Greenland) was named in his honor, by its discoverer, William Baffin, in 1616. The Smythes are interred at St. Marys Church at Ashford, England. Some of their tombs are ornated by statues of them

PART VII – THE ANCESTRY OF DOROTHY WALDEGRAVE, WIFE OF ARTHUR HARRIS (1526-1597)

Dorothy Waldgrave ancestry is was part of the Carolingian Dynasty below is a history of the Dynasty.

Carolingian Times & the Catholic Church

The relationship between the Carolingian Empire and the Catholic Church was one of mutual benefit and political expediency: the papacy gave spiritual legitimacy to the the rule of the Frankish kings, while the kings in turn provided the Church with military protection and might. Together, the Carolingian rulers and the Catholic Church strove for the political and religious unification of Western Europe.

Establishment of the Carolingian Dynasty

In 754, Pepin the Short, the son of Charles Martel, and acsester of Dorothy Waldgrave was made king of the Franks by Pope Boniface, establishing what would become the Carolingian dynasty and empire. Pepin helped the papacy establish the Papal States around Rome, and freed Rome from the Byzantine Empire's control. The political merger of the Frankish kingdom and the papacy opened the door for the Carolingian Renaissance. The cultural revival and spiritual unification of Western Europe.

The Ancestry of (7) Dorothy Waldegrave, Wife of Arthur Harris (1526-1597)

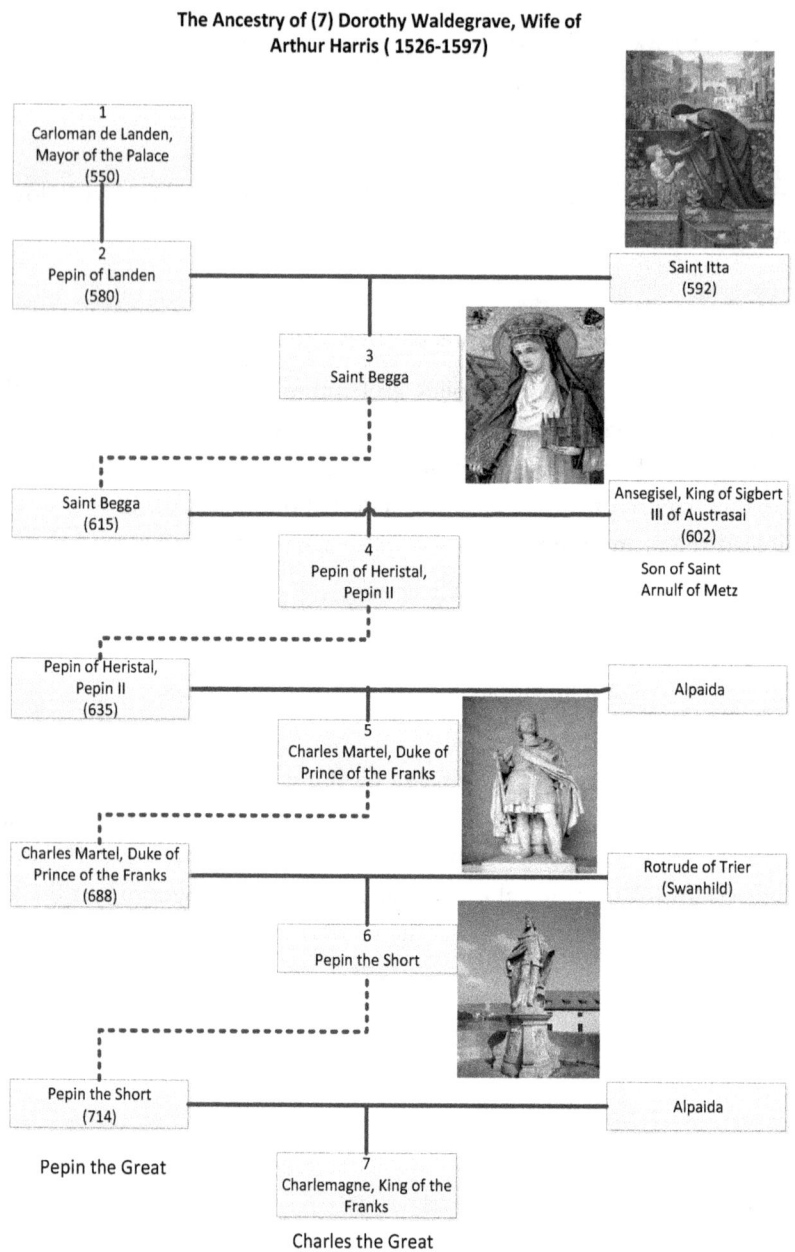

- **1** Carloman de Landen, Mayor of the Palace (550)
- **2** Pepin of Landen (580) — Saint Itta (592)
- **3** Saint Begga
- Saint Begga (615) — Ansegisel, King of Sigbert III of Austrasai (602) — Son of Saint Arnulf of Metz
- **4** Pepin of Heristal, Pepin II
- Pepin of Heristal, Pepin II (635) — Alpaida
- **5** Charles Martel, Duke of Prince of the Franks
- Charles Martel, Duke of Prince of the Franks (688) — Rotrude of Trier (Swanhild)
- **6** Pepin the Short
- Pepin the Short (714) — Alpaida
- Pepin the Great
- **7** Charlemagne, King of the Franks
- Charles the Great

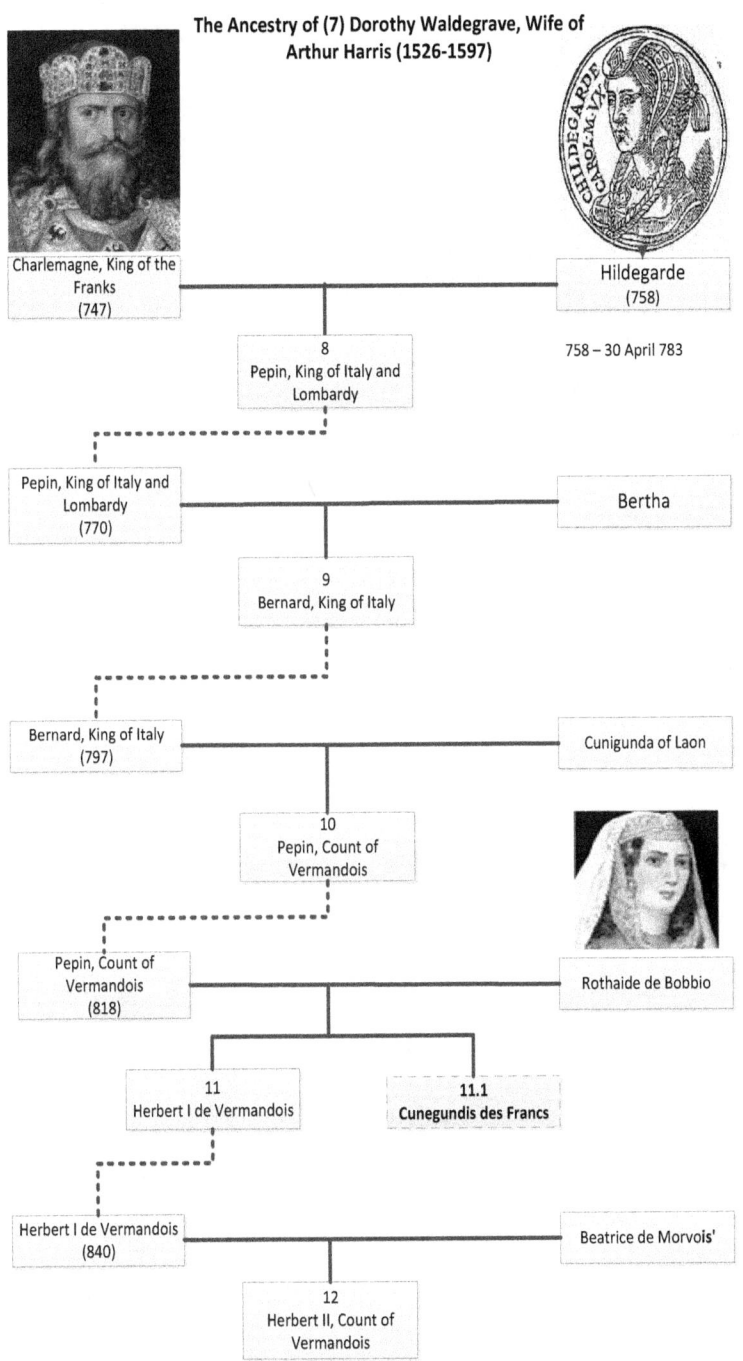

The Ancestry of (7) Dorothy Waldegrave, Wife of Arthur Harris (1526-1597)

Charlemagne, King of the Franks (747)

Hildegarde (758)

758 – 30 April 783

8
Pepin, King of Italy and Lombardy

Pepin, King of Italy and Lombardy (770)

Bertha

9
Bernard, King of Italy

Bernard, King of Italy (797)

Cunigunda of Laon

10
Pepin, Count of Vermandois

Pepin, Count of Vermandois (818)

Rothaide de Bobbio

11
Herbert I de Vermandois

11.1
Cunegundis des Francs

Herbert I de Vermandois (840)

Beatrice de Morvois'

12
Herbert II, Count of Vermandois

The Ancestry of (7) Dorothy Waldegrave, Wife of Arthur Harris (1526-1597)

- **Herbert II, Count of Vermandois (880)** + **Hildebrante (Liegarde)** — daughter of Robert I, Duke of France
  - **13. Albert I, the Pious, Count of Vermandois**

- **Albert I, the Pious, Count of Vermandois (920)** + **Gerberga of Lorraine** — daughter of Giselbert, Duke of Lorraine
  - **14. Herbert III, Count of Vermandois**

- **Herbert III, Count of Vermandois (955)** + **Ermengarde** — daughter of Reinald, Count of Bar.
  - **15. Eudes (Otho), Count de Vermandois**

- **Eudes (Otho), Count de Vermandois (1000)** + **Parvie**
  - **16. Herbert IV, Count de Vermandois**

- **Herbert IV, Count de Vermandois (1032)** + **Adele de Vexin** — daughter of Raoul III, the Great, Count of Valois and Vexin
  - **17. Adelaide de Vermandois, Countess of Vermandois**

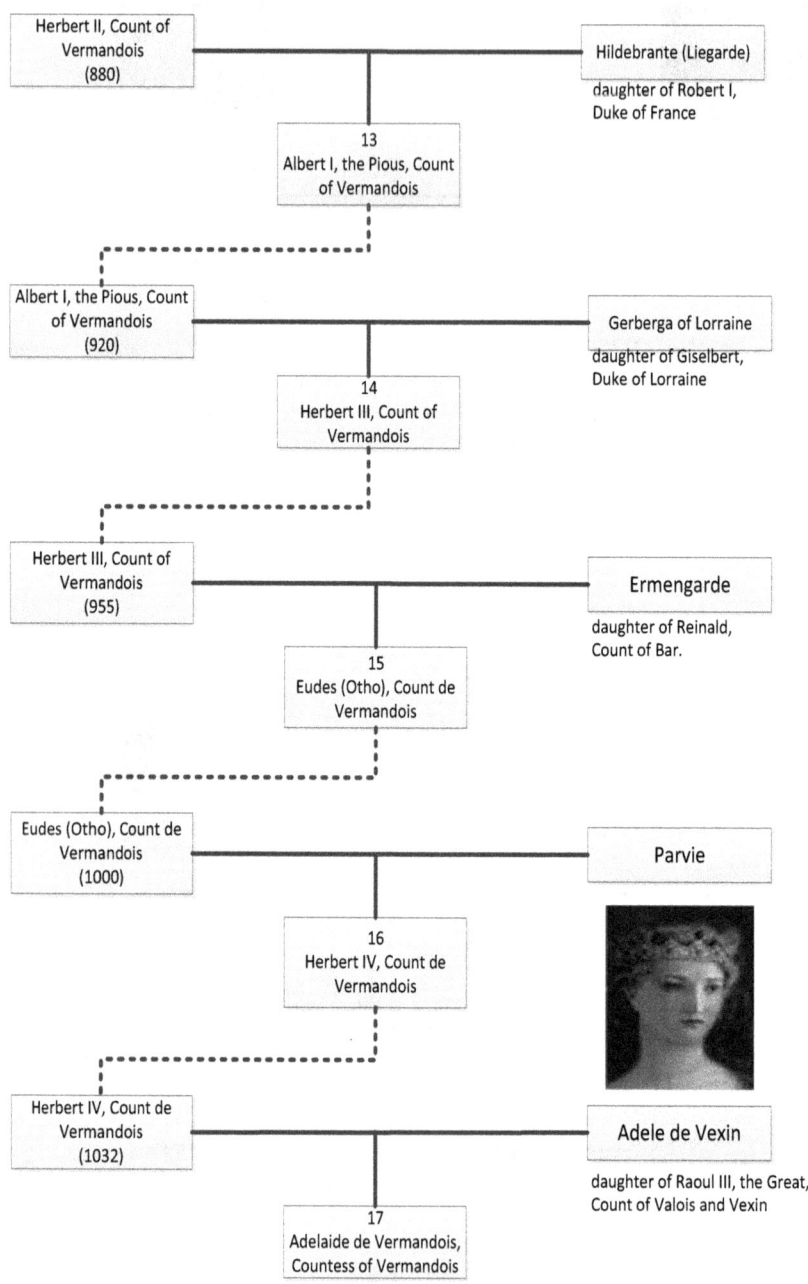

The Ancestry of (7) Dorothy Waldegrave, Wife of Arthur Harris (b. c. 1526; d. c. 1597)

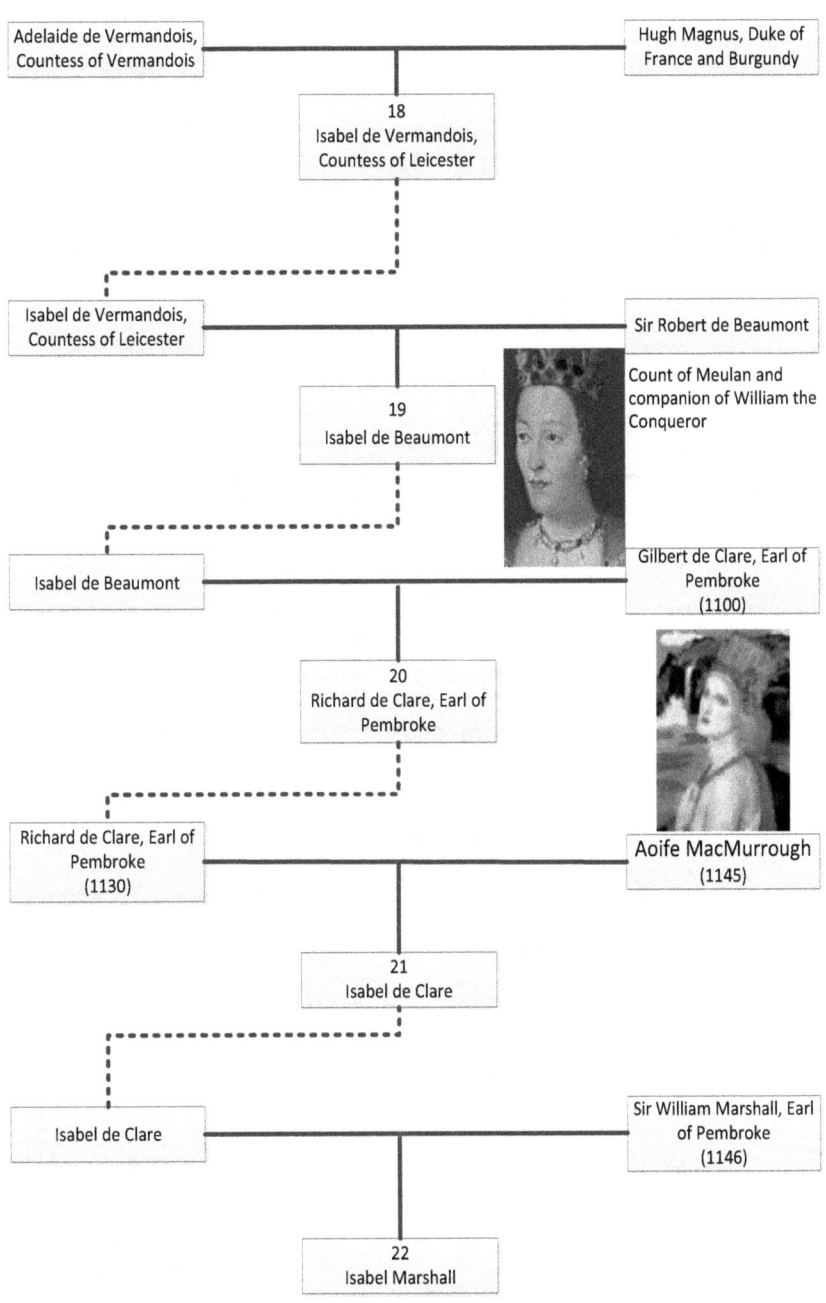

- Adelaide de Vermandois, Countess of Vermandois
- Hugh Magnus, Duke of France and Burgundy
- **18** Isabel de Vermandois, Countess of Leicester
- Isabel de Vermandois, Countess of Leicester
- Sir Robert de Beaumont, Count of Meulan and companion of William the Conqueror
- **19** Isabel de Beaumont
- Isabel de Beaumont
- Gilbert de Clare, Earl of Pembroke (1100)
- **20** Richard de Clare, Earl of Pembroke
- Richard de Clare, Earl of Pembroke (1130)
- Aoife MacMurrough (1145)
- **21** Isabel de Clare
- Isabel de Clare
- Sir William Marshall, Earl of Pembroke (1146)
- **22** Isabel Marshall

The Ancestry of (7) Dorothy Waldegrave, Wife of Arthur Harris (b. c. 1526; d. c. 1597)

- Isabel Marshall
- Sir Gilbert de Clare, Earl of Clare (1180)
  - **23** Sir Richard de Clare, Earl of Clare
- Sir Richard de Clare, Earl of Clare (1222)
- Maude de Lacy, Countess of Lincoln (1237)
  - **24** Sir Gilbert de Clare
- Sir Gilbert de Clare (1245)
- Joan Plantagenet (1272)
  - daughter W Edward I, King of England
  - **25** Elizabeth de Clare

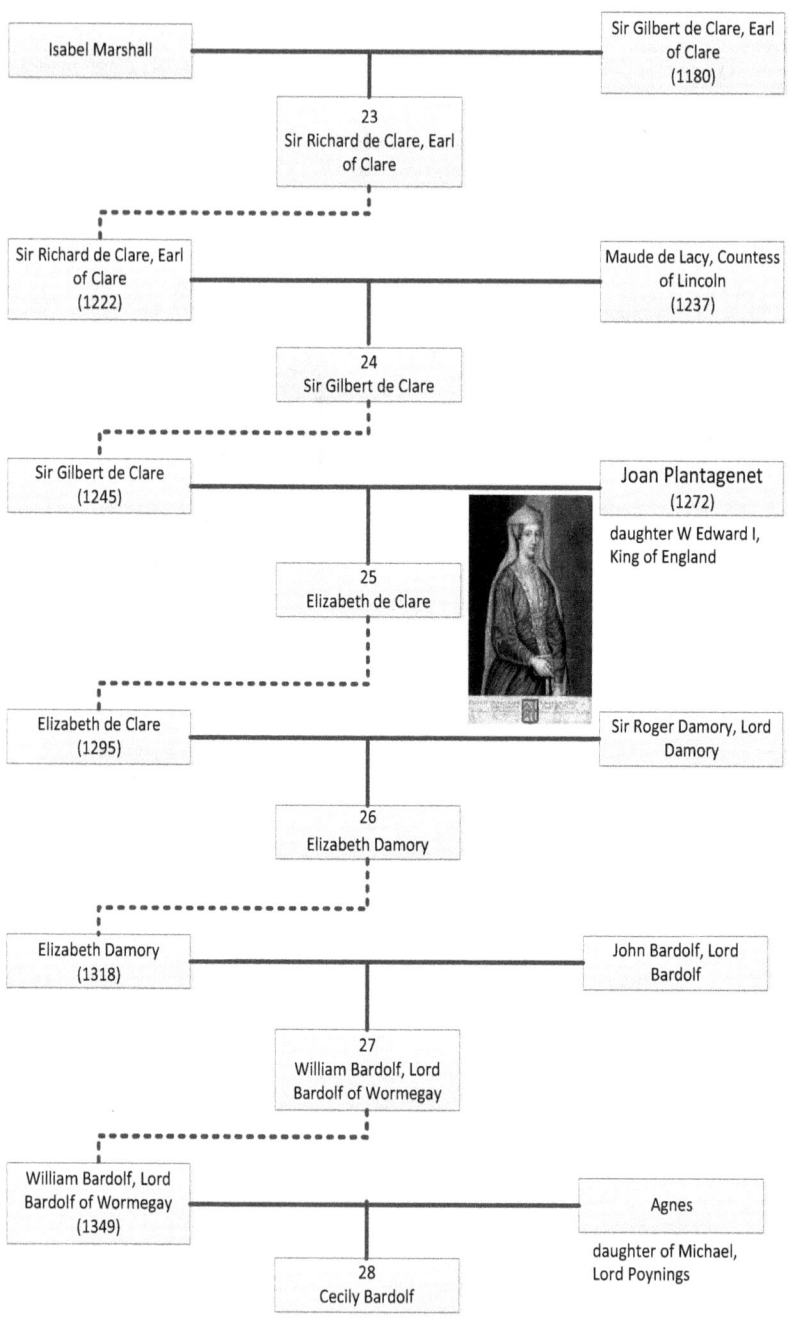

- Elizabeth de Clare (1295)
- Sir Roger Damory, Lord Damory
  - **26** Elizabeth Damory
- Elizabeth Damory (1318)
- John Bardolf, Lord Bardolf
  - **27** William Bardolf, Lord Bardolf of Wormegay
- William Bardolf, Lord Bardolf of Wormegay (1349)
- Agnes
  - daughter of Michael, Lord Poynings
  - **28** Cecily Bardolf

The Ancestry of (7) Dorothy Waldegrave, Wife of Arthur Harris (b. c. 1526; d. c. 1597)

Ancestry of Dorothy Waldegrave, Wife of Arthur Harris (1526-1597)

1. Carloman de Landen, Mayor of the Palace, born c. 550 in Landen, Liege, Belgium and died c. 645 in Landen Liege, Belgium.

2. Pepin of Landen, mayor of the palace of Austrasia born c. 580- 27 February 640, also known as "The Elder or The Old", was the Mayor of the Palace of Austrasia under the Merovingina king Dagobert I from 623 to 629. He married Saint Itta (592–652)

> **2.1** Through the marriage of his daughter Begga to Ansegisel, a, the clans of the Pippinids and the Arnulfings were united, giving rise to a family which would eventually rule the Franks as the Carolingians.

3. Saint Begga, the daughter of Pepin of Landen, 615– 17 December 693. She married Ansegisel, King of Sigbert III of Austrasai, born c. 602 or 610. Son of Saint Arnulf of Metz

4. Pepin of Heristal, sometimes called "Pepin II" Frankish Strongman, born c. 635–16 December 714, was a statesman and military leader.

5. Charles Martel, Duke of Prince of the Franks, was born 688- 22 October 741. He was a Fankish statsman and military leader who de facto ruled Franica and Duck and Prince of the Franks and Mayor of the Palace from 718 until his death. He married **Rotrude of Trier** (Swanhild).

6. Pepin the Short or "Pepin the Great", King of the Franks was born c. 714-24 September 768. He was King from 752 to his death.

7. Charlemagne, King of the Franks, and Emperor of the West - expanded the Carolingian Empire also known as **"Charles the Great"** was born on 2 April 747 and died on 28 January, 813/4. He married (probably, his third) **Hildegarde**, (758 – 30 April 783) was the Germanic daughter of count **Gerold of Vinzgouw** and **Emma of Alamannia**, daughter of **Hnabi, Duke of Alamannia**. She was the second wife of Charlemagne,[1] who married her about 771.

8. Pepin, King of Italy and Lombardy, was born April 770/773 – 8 July 810 at Milan. He was baptized at Rome by Pope Adrian I.

9. Bernard, King of Italy, was born in 797 and died on 17 April 818 at Milan. He married Cunigunde de Gellone born about 797 in Gellone, Savoy, France.

10. Pepin, count of Vermandois, Lord of Senlis, Peronne and St. Quentin, was born in 818 in Vernandois, Normandy and died in 848 in Milan, Italy. (Ref: Moriarty, p. 5; Turton, p. 112.) He married Rothaide de Bobbi (Chrothais) born abt c 820 in Treves, Gard, Languedoc-Roussillion, France and died c. 850 in Austrasia, France. She was the daughter of Walla de Corbie (c. 754 – 836)

11. Herbert I de Vermandois, Count of Vermandois, Siegneur of Senlis, Peronne and St. Quentin, was born ca. 840 and died ca. 902. He married Beatrice de Morvois'

> **11.1** Herbert I, seigneur de Peronne & de S. Quentin+ born 840, died 902 (Dorothy Waldegrave family ancestry) Cunegundis des Francs + born 855 (Johanna Percy family ancestry)

12. Herbert II, Count of Vermandois and Troyes, was born 880-890 and died 943 at St. Quentin. He married Hildebrante (Liegarde), daughter of Robert I, Duke of France.

13. Albert I, the Pious, Count of Vermandois, was born in 920 and died in 987/8. He married Gerberga of Lorraine, daughter of Giselbert, Duke of Lorraine.

14. Herbert III, Count of Vermandois, was born 955 and died 1000. He married Ermengarde, daughter of Reinald, Count of Bar.

15. Eudes (Otho), Count de Vermandois, was born 1000 and died on 25 May 1045. He married Parvie.

16. Herbert IV, Count de Vermandois, was born 1032 and died 1080. He married Adele de Vexin, daughter of Raoul III, the Great, Count of Valois and Vexin.

17. Adelaide de Vermandois, Countess of Vermandois and Valois, died 1120. She married Hugh Magnus, Duke of France and Burgundy, Crusader. He died in 1101.

18. Isabel de Vermandois, Countess of Leicester, died in February 1131. She married Sir Robert de Beaumont, Count of Meulan and companion of William the Conqueror. Re was born 1046 and died on 5 June 1118. They were married in 1096.

19. Isabel de Beaumont married Gilbert de Clare, Earl of Pembroke. He was born ca. 1100 and died on 6 January 1147/8.

20. Richard de Clare "Strongbow", Earl of Pembroke, Striguil, Justiciar of Ireland, was born ca. 1130 and died ca. 20 April 1176. He married ca. 26 August 1171 to Aoife MacMurrough, daughter of Dermot MacMurrough, King of Leinster, at Waterford, Ireland. He was living in 1186.

21. Isabel de Clare, Countess of Pembroke and Striguil born in 1172; died in 1220. She married Sir William Marshall, Earl of Pembroke and Regent of the Kingdom in August, 1189 in London. He was born ca. 1146 and died on 14 May 1219. They are buried at Temple Church.

22. Isabel Marshall died on 17 January 1239/40 at Berkhamstead. She married Sir Gilbert de Clare, Earl of Clare, of Hertford and Gloucester on 9 October 1217. He was born ca. 1180 and died on 25 October 1230 at Penros, Brittany.

23. Sir Richard de Clare, Earl of Clare, of Hertford and Gloucester, was born on 4 August 1222 and died on 15 July 1262. He married (his second) Maude de Lacy, Countess of Lincoln, ca. 25 January 1237/8. She died before 10 March 1288/9.

24. Sir Gilbert de Clare, Earl of Hertford and Gloucester, was born 2 September 1245: at Christ Church, Hampshire and died on 7 December 1295 at Monmouth Castle. He married (his second) Joan Plantagenet (Joan of Acre) on April-May 1290. Joan, the daughter W Edward I, King of England, was born ca. 1272 at Acre, Holy Land, and died on 2 April 1307 at Clare, County Suffolk (England).

25. Elizabeth de Clare was born at Tewkesbury on 16 September 1295 and died on 4 November 1360. She is buried at St. Marys, Ware. She married Sir Roger Damory, Lord Damory (her third) of Bletchingdon, Oxon. He died at Tutbury Castle m 13/14 March 1321/2.

26. Elizabeth Damory was born before 23 -May 1318 and died after 1360. She marries John Bardolf, Lord Bardolf, before 25 December 1327. He was born at Wormegay County Norfolk on 13 January 1313/14 and died on July-August 1363 at Assisi, Italy

27. William Bardolf, Lord Bardolf of Wormegay, County Norfolk was born 21 October 1349 and died on 29 January 1385/6. He is buried at Friar Carmelites, Lynn County Norfolk. He **married Agnes, daughter of**

Michael, Lord Poynings. She died on 12 June 1403. She is buried at Trinity Priory, Aldgate, London.

28. Cecily Bardolf died on 29 September 1432. She married Sir Brian Stapleton of Ingham and Bedale. He was born before 1380 and died in August 1438. They are buried at Ingham Priory.

29. Sir Miles Stapleton of Ingham and Bedale was born 1408 and died 30 Sept ber-1 Oct 1466. He is buried at Ingham Priory. He married (his second Katherine de la Pole of Grafton Regis. She was born 1415 and died 13/1 Oct 1488. She is buried at Rewley Abbey.

30. Elizabeth Stapleton was born ca. 1440 and died on 18 February 1504/5. She married Sir William Calthorpe, the Sheriff of Norfolk, of Burnham Thorpe, Count Norfolk before 7 March 1463/4. He was born on 30 January 1409/10 and died on 1 November 1494. He is buried at White Friars, Norwich.

31. Anne Calthorpe died ca. 1494. She married Sir Robert Drury of Hawstead, Count Suffolk. He died on 2 March 1535/6 at St. Edmunds. He is buried at St. Mary

32. Anne Drury married **Sir George Waldegrave of Smallbridge**, County Suffolk. He was born in 1483 and died in 1528.

33. Sir William Waldegrave of Waltham-Stow, County Essex and Smallbridge, Count Suffolk, died on 2 May 1554. He married Juliane, daughter of Sir John Rainey ford.

34. Dorothy Waldegrave married **Arthur Harris**, Esquire, of Woodham Mortimer and Crixse, County Essex. He died on 30 June 1597.

35. Sir William Harris died on 20 November 1616 at Crixse, County Essex. He married **Alice Smythe,** daughter of Sir Thomas Smythe of Weston Hangar, County Kent.

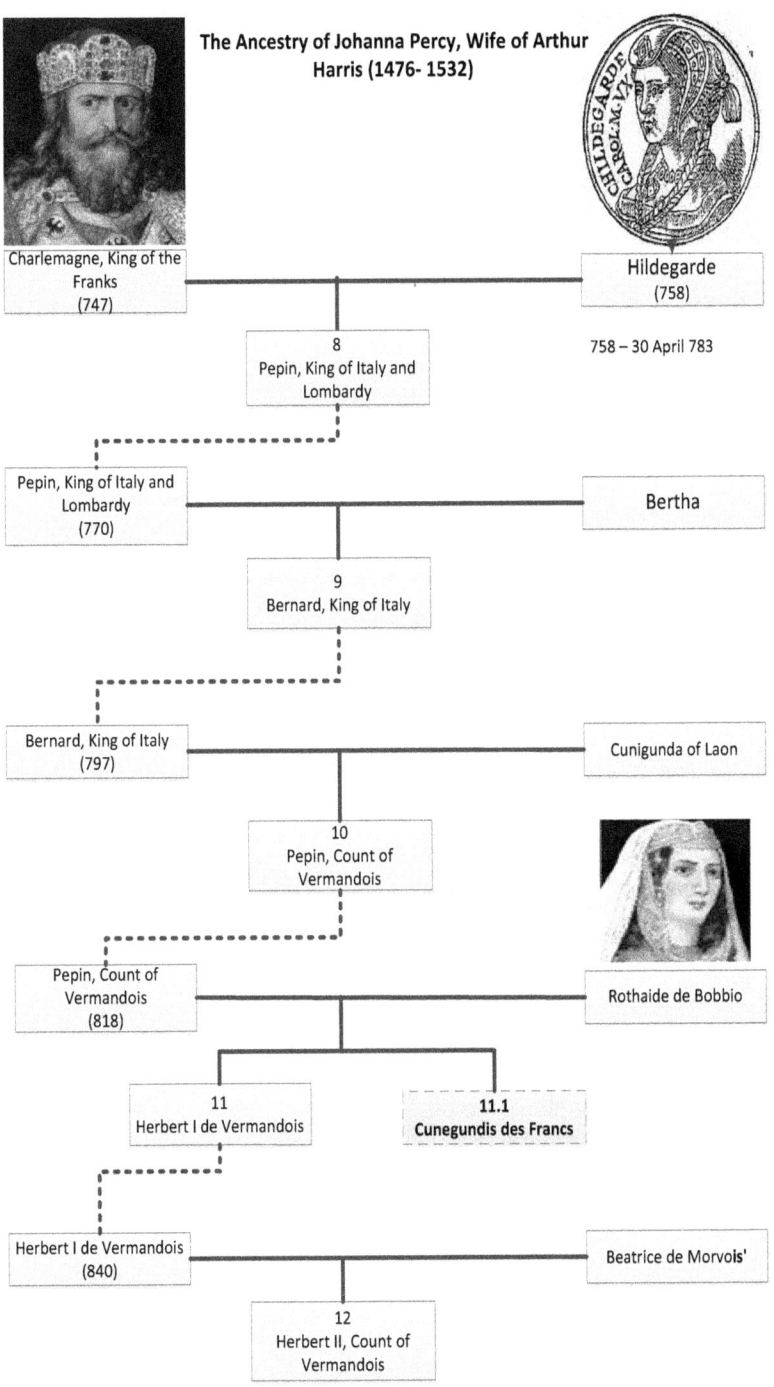

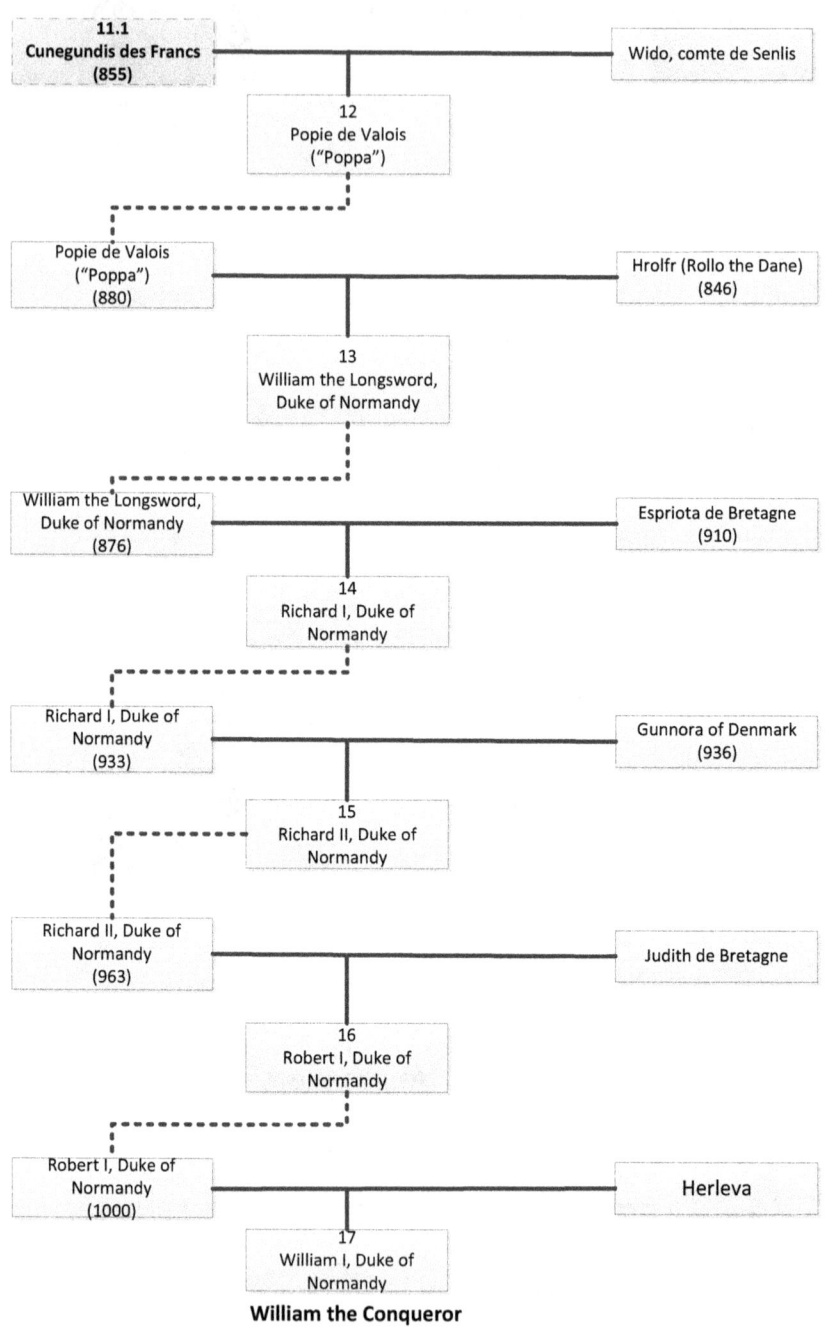

The Ancestry of Johanna Percy, Wife of Arthur Harris (1476- 1532)

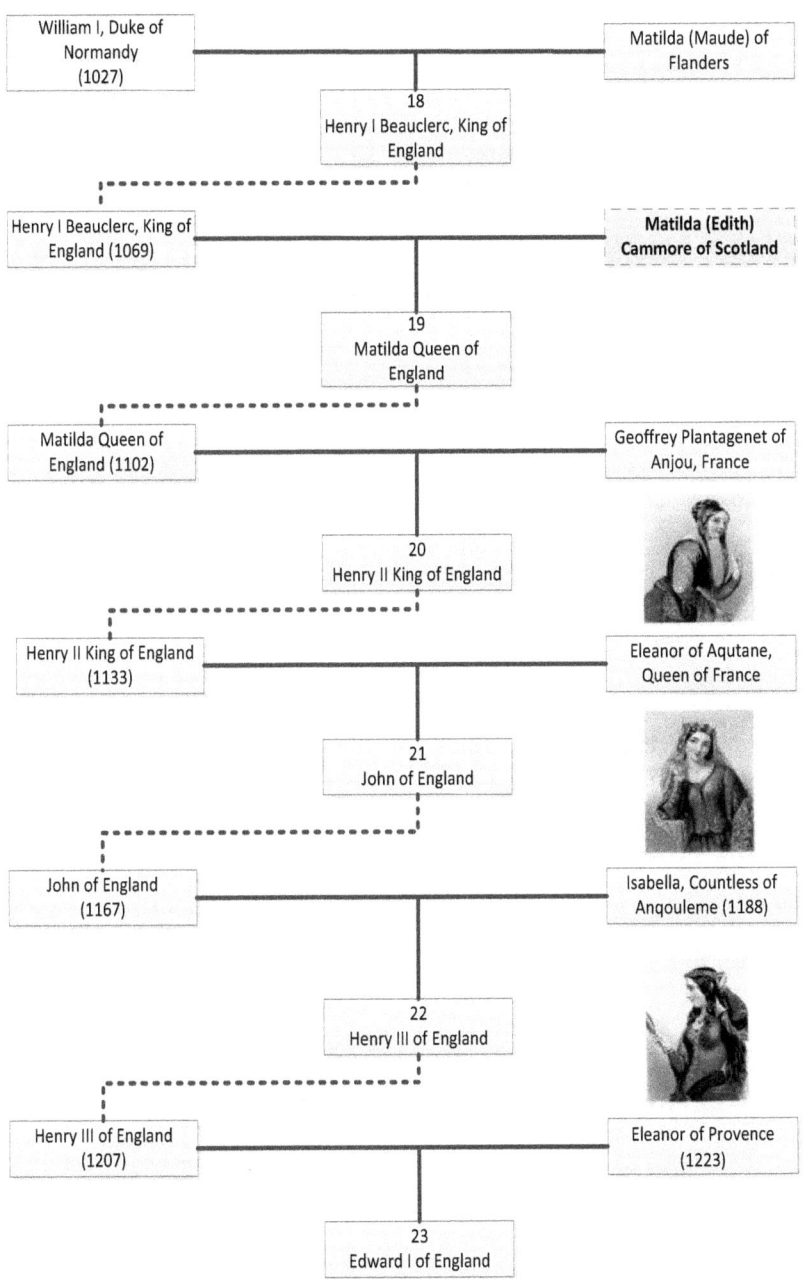

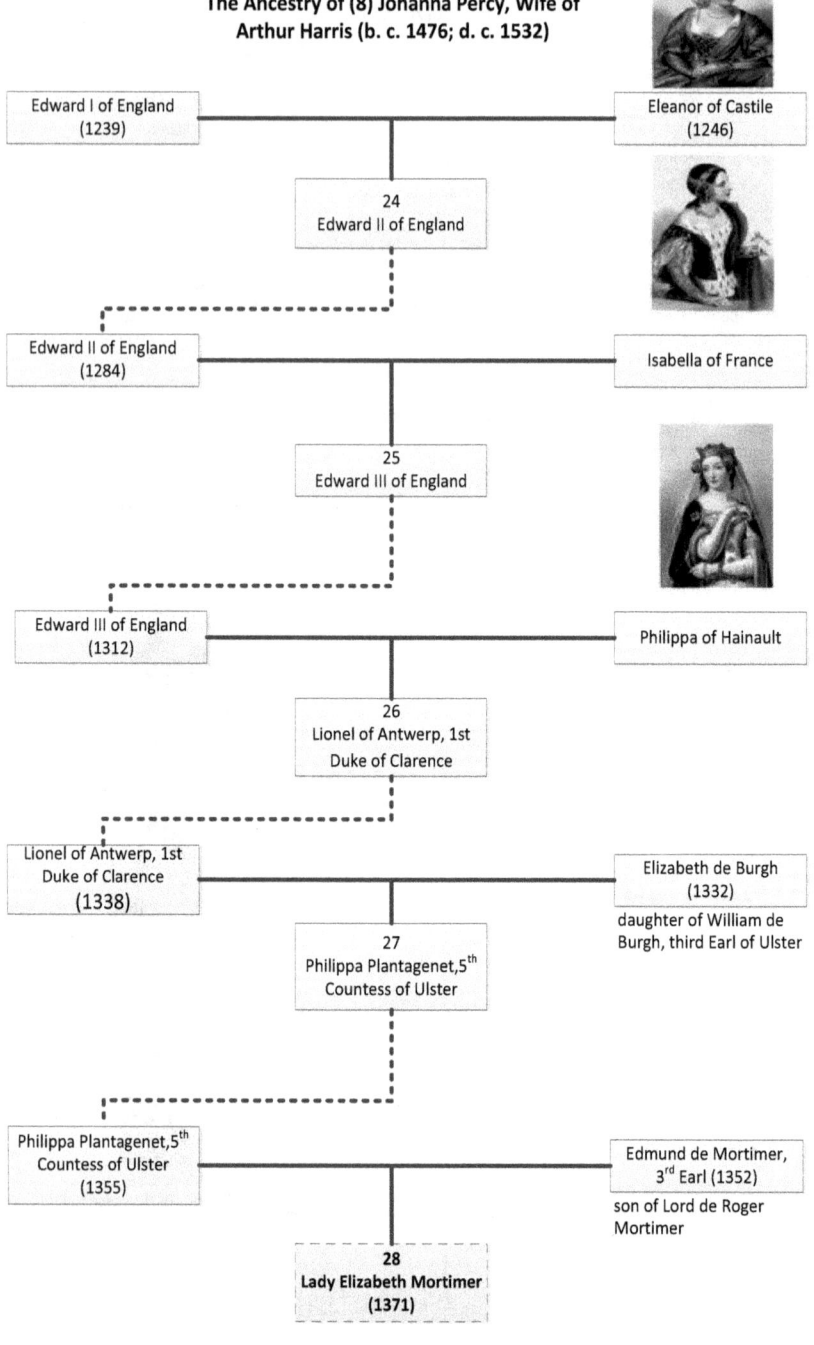

The Ancestry of (8) Johanna Percy, Wife of Arthur Harris (b. c. 1476; d. c. 1532)

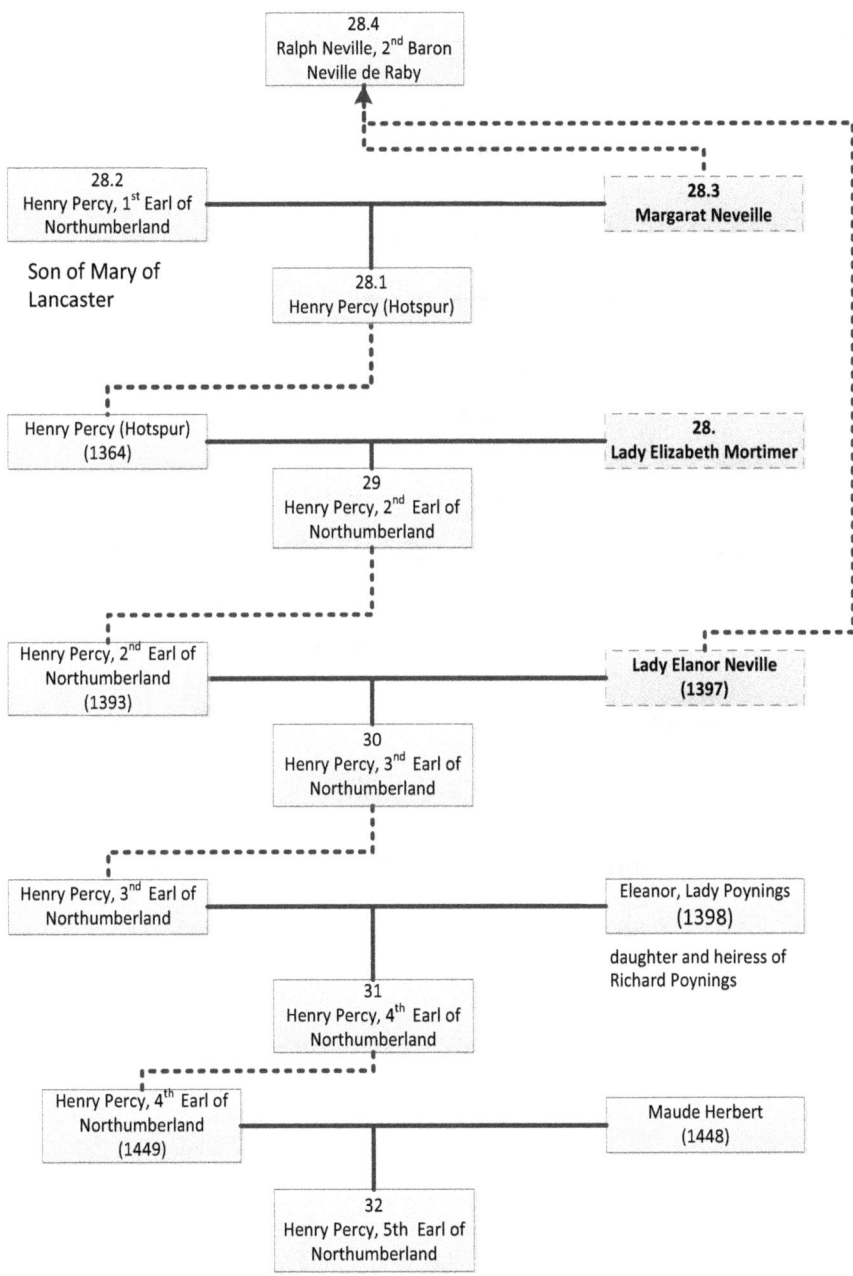

The Ancestry of (8) Johanna Percy, Wife of Arthur Harris (b. c. 1476; d. c. 1532)

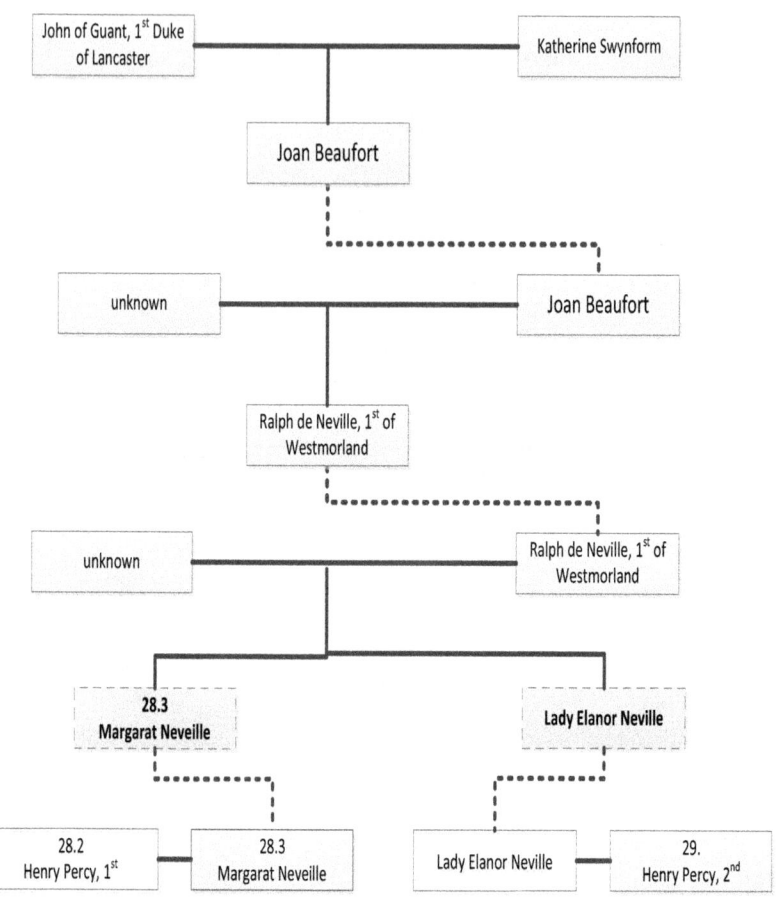

The Ancestry of (8) Johanna Percy, Wife of Arthur Harris (b. c. 1476; d. c. 1532)

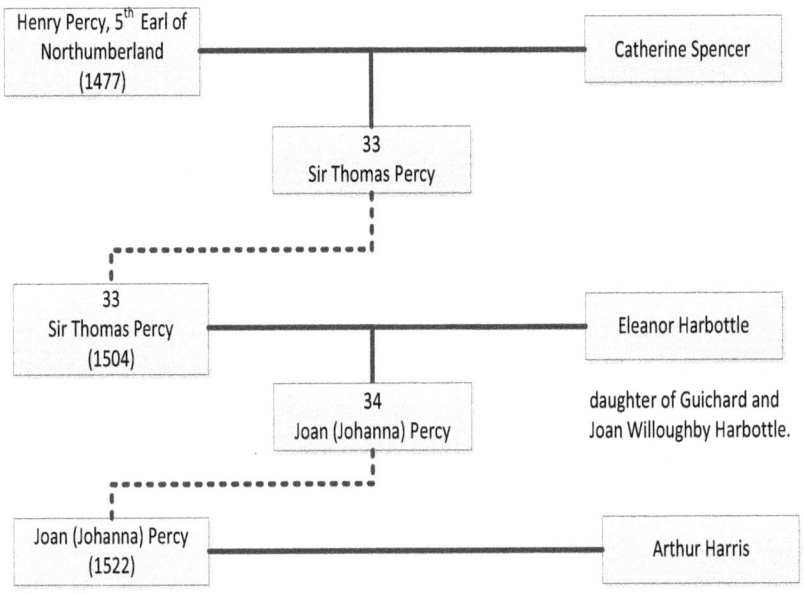

PART VIII – THE ANCESTRY OF JOHANNA PERCY, WIFE OF ARTHUR HARRIS (1476-1532)

1. **Carloman de Landen, Mayor of the Palace**, born 550 in Landen, Liege, Belgium and died 645 in Landen Liege, Belgium. He married Gertrudis of the Bavarians, born 525 Bavaria, Germany d. 596 in Bavaria, Germany. She was the daughter of Agivald of the Bavarians & Lucile d'Alsace.

2. **Pepin of Landen,** born 580- 27 February 640, also known as "The Elder or The Old", was the Mayor of the Palace of Austrasia under the Merovingina king Dagobert I from 623 to 629. Through the marriage of his daughter Begga to Ansegisel, a son of Arnulf of Metz, the clans of the Pippinis and the Arnulfings were united, giving rise to a family which would eventually rule the Franks as the Carolingians.

3. **Ansegisel, King of Sigbert III of Austrasai**, born 602 or 610 and his wife was Saint Begga, the daughter of Pepin of Landen.

4. Pepin of Heristal, sometimes called "Pepin II" Frankish Strongman, born 635 16 December, was a statesman and military leader.

5. **Charles Martel, Duke of Prince of the Franks**, was born 688- 22 October. He was a Fankish statsman and military leader who de facto ruled Franica and Duck and Prince of the Franks and Mayor of the Palace from 718 until his death. He married Rotrude of Trier (Swanhild).

6. **Pepin the Short or "Pepin the Great"**, King of the Franks was born 714- 24 September. He was King from 752 to his death.

7. **Charlemagne, King of the Franks**, and Emperor of the West expanded the Carolingian Empire also known as "Charles the Great" was born on 2 April 747 and died on 28 January, 813/4. He married (probably, his third) Hildegarde, daughter of Count Geroud of Swabia. She died on 30 April 783.

8. **Pepin, King of Italy and Lombardy**, was born on 12 April 781 and died on 8 July 810 at Milan. He was baptized at Rome by Pope Adrian I.

9. **Bernard, King of Italy**, was born in 797 and died on 17 April 818 at Milan. He married Cunigunde de Gellone born about 797 in Gellone, Savoy, France.

10. **Pepin, Count of Senlis, Peronne and St. Quentin**, was born in 818 in Vernandois, Normandy and died in 848 in Milan, Italy. He married Rothaide de Bobbi (Chrothais) born abt c 820 in Treves, Gard, Languedoc-Roussillion,

France and died c. 850 in Austrasia, France. She was the daughter of Walla de Corbie (c. 754 – 836). His second wife was N.N. de Vermandois.

Children of Pepin II, seigneur de Peronne & de S. Quentin and N. N. de Vermandois : Pippin, comte + born c 845, died a 28 Jan 893 Bernhard, comte près de Laon born c 845, died a 878 *Herbert I, seigneur de Peronne & de S. Quentin+ born c 850, died 902 (Dorothy Waldegrave family ancestry) Cunegundis des Francs + born 855

11. Cunegundis des Francs born abt 855 married Wido, comte de Senlis before 875.

12. Popie de Valois ("Poppa") born abt 880 she married Hrolfr (Rollo the Dane). Rollo Rognvaldsson "the Dane" Duke of Normandy born about 0846 Maer, Nord-Trondelag, Norway died about 0931 Notre Dame, Rouen, Nornandie, Neustria buried Notre Dame, Rouen, Nornandie, Neustria

13. William the Longsword, Duke of Normandy, born 0876 Normandie, Neustria died 0942 France. Spouse (2nd): *Espriota de Bretagne born abt 0910 married Abt 932 Of, Normandy, France. 2nd Duke of Normandy from 927 to 943, was also Duke of Aquitaine and died in 942, slain by Arnulf of Flanders with whom he had in good faith gone to confer.

14. Richard I, Duke of Normandy, "The fearless" ("Sans Peur") born 933 in Fâecamp, Normandie, died 0996 Fâecamp, Normandie. He married three times; he married the mother of Richard II, Duke of Normandy in 962. Her name was Gunnora of Denmark Duchess of Normandy daughter of the King of Denmark. She was born abt 936 and died abt 1031 in France.

15. Richard II, "The Good" Duke of Normandy, born about 0963 Normandie died 28 August 1027 Fâecamp, Normandie buried Fâecamp, Normandie; he married Judith de Bretagne (Judith Brittany) (of Rennes) born 0982 Bretagne, France died 16 June 1017 Normandie, France married about 1000 Normandie, France

16. Robert I, "The Magnificent" Duke of Normandy and Count of Heimois, born 22 June 1000 Normandie died 22 July 1035 Nicea, Bithynia, Turkey buried Nicaea, Bithynia, Turkey. He had one son by Herleva (c. 1003-c. 1050) William I, Duke of Normandy.

According to one legend, still recounted by tour guides at Falaise, it all started when Robert, the young Duke of Normandy saw Herleva from the roof of his castle tower. The walkway on the roof still looks down on the dyeing trenches cut into stone in the courtyard below, which can be seen to this day from the tower ramparts above. The traditional way of dyeing leather or garments was for individuals to trample barefoot on the garments which were awash in the dyeing liquid in these trenches. Herleva, legend goes, seeing the Duke on his ramparts above, raised her skirts perhaps a bit more than necessary in order to attract the Duke's eye.

The latter was immediately smitten and ordered her brought in (as was customary for any woman that caught the Duke's eye) through the back door. Herleva refused, saying she would only enter the Duke's castle on horseback through the front gate, and not as an ordinary commoner. The Duke, filled with lust, could only agree. In a few days, Herleva, dressed in the finest her father could provide, and sitting on a white horse, rode proudly through the front gate, her head held high. This gave Herleva a semi-official status as the Duke's mistress. She later gave birth to his son, William, in 1027 or 1028.

17. William I, "William the Conqueror", Duke of Normandy; born c. 1027/28 at Falaise, Normandy; died September 9, 1087 at Rouen, Normandy (now France). William was Duke of Normandy and the **Conqueror of England** in 1066 A. D. He was crowned as the first Norman King of England on Christmas Day in 1066. William's wife was Matilda (Maude) of Flanders. William was King of England (1066 to 1087).

18. Henry I Beauclerc, King of England; born 1069; died December 1, 1135. Henry was King of England (1100-1135). He married Matilda (Edith) Cammore of Scotland born 1079 Dunfermline, Fifeshire, Scotland and died 1 May 1118 buried in Westminster Abbey, London, Middlesex, England. She was the daughter of the King of Scotland.

19. Empress Matilda, known as "Matilda Queen of England"; born 7 February 1102 in Westminster, London, Middlesex, England; died September 10, 1167 in Notre Dame, Rouen, Seine Maritime, France.

She was named by her father as heir to the throne of England. She actually served as the reigning monarch for only a short period of time. Matilda was not shy because she was a woman. However, her marriage to Geoffrey Plantagenet of Anjou, France did not help her cause. Geoffrey was from a family who were enemies of Matilda's own people. Matilda defended her claim to the throne by raising an army, which was not an unusual way too politic in her day. Matilda's cousin, Stephen of Blois, served as King of

England in place of Matilda. Matilda's son, Henry Plantagenet, became the King after Stephen.

20. Henry II King of England (Plantagenet); born 5 March 1133 at LeMans; died July 6, 1189 in Chinon. He was King of England (1154-1189). He married to Eleanor of Aqutane, Queen of France born on 25 July 1137 in Aquitaine and died 1 April 1204 in Fontevraud Abby. Her parents were William X, Duke of Aquitaine, and Aenor de Chatellerault. Eleanor of Aquitaine was one of the wealthiest and most powerful women in Western Europe during the High Middle Ages. As well as being Duchess of Aquitaine in her own right, she was queen consort of France and of England.

Henry II, also known as Henry Curtmantle, Henry FitzEmpress or Henry Plantagenet, ruled as Count of Anjou, Count of Maine, Duke of Normandy, Duke of Aquitaine, Count of Nantes, King of England and Lord

21. John of England (Plantagenet); also known as John Lackland born 24 December 1167 in Beaumont Palace; died 19 October 1216 in Newark-on-Trent. He was King of England (1199-1216). He signed the Magna Carta in 1215. He was married to Isabella, Countless of Anqouleme born abt c. 1188 and died on 31 May 1246.

22. Henry III of England (Plantagenet); born 1 October 1207 in Winchester; died 16 November 1272 in Westminster. He was King of England (1216-1272). He was married to Eleanor of Provence born abt. 1223 in Aix-en-Provence and died 26 June 1291 in Amesbury.

23. Edward I of England (Plantagenet); born 18 June 1239 in Palace of Westminster; died 7 July 1307 in Burgh by Sands. He was King of England (1272-1307). Edward was also known as Edward Longshanks and the Hammer of the Scots. Edward married Eleanor of Castile. She was born in 1246 and died in 1290. She was the daughter of King Ferdinand III of Castile.

King Edward I of England, who had Sr. William Wallace a 13th century Scottish leader hanged, drawn, and quartered for high treason and crimes again English civilians. The movie Braveheart is based on this event in history.

24. Edward II of England (Plantagenet); born 25 April 1284 in Caemarfon Castle; died 21 September 1327 in Berkeley Castle. He was King of England (1307-1327). He married Isabella of France.

25. Edward III of England (Plantagenet); born 13 November 1312 Windsor; died 21 June 1377 in Sheen. He was King of England (1327-1377). Edward married Philippa of Hainault. He is noted for his military success and for restoring royal authority after the disastrous reign of his father, Edward II.

26. Lionel of Antwerp, 1st Duke of Clarence (Plantagenet); born 29 November 1338, Antwerp; died 17 October 1368 in Alba. Had he not preceded his father in death, Lionel may well have succeeded to the throne of England. Lionel married **Elizabeth de Burgh**, daughter of William de Burgh, third Earl of Ulster. Elizabeth de Burgh born 6 July 1332 in Carrickfergus Castle and died 10 December 1363 in Dubin.

27. Philippa Plantagenet, 5th Countess of Ulster; born 16 August 1355 in Etham Palace and died 5 January 1382 in Cork. She married Edmund de Mortimer, 3rd Earl of March in 1368. He was born 1 February 1352 and died 27th December. He was the son of Lord de Roger Mortimer.

28. Lady Elizabeth Mortimer, born 12 February 1371 in Usk and died 20th April 1417 in Trotton with Chithurst. She was the granddaughter of Lionel of Antwerp, 1st Duke of Clarence, and great-granddaughter of King Edward III, was in the line of succession to the English crown. Her first husband was Sir Henry Percy, known to history as 'Hotspur'

Henry Percy (Hotspur) born the 20 May 1364 and died Spofforth, Harrogate and died 21st July 1403 he was the oldest son of Henry Percy, 1st Earl of Northumberland and Margarat Neveille, daughter of Ralph Neville, 2nd Baron Neville and Maud Neville. Henry's grandmother Mary of Lancaster was Henry III of England's great granddaughter. He was so named by the Scots because of the zeal with which he patrolled the Scottish border. The Percy family had enormous prestige and influence in England. They were closely related to several other families with close ties to the royal family.

After a time, Henry failed to keep his commitments. The Percy's agreed to help others depose Henry IV, They, again, raised an army. Henry, however, learned of the effort and engaged them with his own forces.

Sir Henry Percy (Hotspur) was killed in the battle on July 21, 1403. His father escaped and continued the fight. The elder Percy was captured in due time. As a lesson to others, Henry IV had the elder Percy killed. His head was hung on the London Bridge. His body was cut into chunks and delivered in parcels to the other Earls in England.

29. Henry Percy, 2nd Earl of Northumberland; born 3rd February 1393 in Alnwick Castle and died 22nd May 1455 in St Albans. He was killed in the battle of Towton. He married

Lady Elanor Neville (born c. 1397 – 1472) she was the second daughter of Ralph Neville, 2nd Baron Neville (died 1425) and Joan Beaufort, daughter of John of Guant, 1st Duke of Lancaster and Katherine Swynform.

He was an English nobleman and military commander in the lead up to the Wars of the Roses. His Father and grandfather were killed in different rebellions against Henry IV in 1403 and 1405 respectively, and the young Henry spent his minority in exile in Scotland. Only after the death of Henry IV in 1413 was he reconciled with the Crown, and in 1416 he was created Earl of Northumberland.

Many Percy family lives were lost as results of War of Roses, which lasted for 85 years. For example, Henry Bolinbroke, the son of John of Gaunt, insisted that the Percy's assist him in his efforts to depose King Richard II and become King himself. They did assist him. They raised an army and removed Richard from the throne. Bolinbroke became Henry IV. He rewarded the Percy's for their help.

30. Henry Percy, 3rd Earl of Northumberland; He married Eleanor, Lady Poynings on or before 25 June 1435. She was born in 1398 and died in 1472. The daughter and heiress of Richard Poynings, and granddaughter of Robert Poynings, 4th Lord Poynings.

In consequence of his marriage to Eleanor, Lady Poynings, Henry Percy was summoned to Parliament from 14 December 1446 to 26 May 1455, by writs directed Henrico de Percy, chivaler, domino de Ponynges. His wife was a legatee in the 1455 will of her mother, Eleanor, Countess of Arundel.

In 1448, Percy was captured following his father's defeat at the Battle of Sark. During the Wars of the Roses, Percy followed his father in siding with the Lancastrians against the Yorkists. On December 30, 1460, Percy is known to have fought on the Lancastrian side at the Battle of Wakefield. He commanded the Lancastrian van at the Battle of Towton on March 29, 1461, in which he was slain fighting. He was buried at St Denys's Church, York

31. Henry Percy, 4th Earl of Northumberland, born 1449; died April 28, 1489. He had married Maude Herbert, b 1448 and died 27 July 1485/1495

after 1473 but before 1476. She was the daughter of Sir William Herbert, the first Earl of Pembroke and Anne Devereaux. Henry and Maude had eight children.

Henry was confined in the Tower of London from the time of his father's death until October 27, 1469. At that time, he was given his freedom by King Edward 111 and restored to the Earldom. In April 1489, Percy held temporary residence in his estates of Yorkshire. Henry VII had recently allied himself to Anne of Brittany against Charles VIII of France. Taxes rose to finance the military action. Sir John Egremont of Yorkshire led a riot in protest at the high taxation, known as the Yorkshire rebellion. Percy was targeted by the rioters as he approached the city and lynched on 28 April. He was buried at Beverley Minster. Yorkshire was formerly a stronghold of support of Richard III. Percy may have been killed in vengeance for Richard..

32. Henry Algernon Percy, 5th Earl of Northumberland & Lord Poynings; born 13 January 1477 and died 19 May 1527. He married Catherine Spencer, birth unknown, she died in1542, and she was the daughter of Sir Robert Spenser and Eleanor Beaufort.

How important Northumberland's position was can be seen from The Northumberland Household Book, which was edited from the manuscript in possession of the Duke of Northumberland by Thomas Percy in 1770.

33. Sir Thomas Percy; born about 1504 in Alnwick, Northumberland, England and died 2 June 1537. He married **Eleanor Harbottle**, daughter of Sir Guichard and Joan Willoughby Harbottle. He was father of Thomas Percy, 7th Earl of Northumberland and Henry Percy, 8th Earl of Northumberland. A daughter, Joan, married an Arthur Harris of Prittlewell, Essex and had issue.

He was a participant in the 1537 Bigod's Rebellion in the aftermath of the Pilgrimage of Grace, a Roman Catholic uprising against Henry VIII of England. He was convicted of treason and hanged, drawn and quartered at Tyburn.

Eleanor Harbottle born about 1504 and died May 18, 1566. As mentioned Eleanor was the daughter of Sir Guischard Harabottle of Horton, Northumberland (January 6, 1485-September 9, 1513) and Joan or Jane Willoughby and the sister and coheiress of George Harbottle of Beamish, Durham. Their father died at Floddon Field. Eleanor married Sir Thomas

Percy of Prudhoe (c.1504-x. June 2, 1537) and was the mother of two sons who eventually became earls of Northumberland, Thomas (June 10, 1528-August 22, 1572) and Henry (1532-June 21, 1585). Their other children were Joan (c.1521-August 22, 1572), Guiscard (c.1526-d.yng), Richard, Mary (buried February 7, 1597/8), Catherine, and Jane. Eleanor's second husband, to whom she was married after November 10, 1540, was Sir Richard Holland of Denton, Lancashire (March 25, 1493-1548), by whom she had another Mary (d. before 1570) and Richard (d.1548+). Holland's will was dated March 27, 1548.

34. Joan (Joanna) Percy, born about 1522 in Prittlewell, Essex Co. England and died 22nd August 1572 in Southminister, Essex Co. England. Joan married **Arthur Harris**, born about 1466 in Prittewell, Southminster Parish, Essex, England and died 1544 he was the son of William Harris and Anne Jernegan. Joan and Arthur were the great-grandparents of Sir William Harris of Creeksea (d. November 14, 1616).

These are views of Ainwick Castle, Northumbria, which was a fortress along the old border with Scotland. This property came into the possession of the Percy family in 1309. The Percy's were Normans. Our ancestor, Sir Henry (Hotspur) Percy (1364-1403) lived here

The Ancestry of Matilda (Edith) Of Scotland, Wife of Henry I Beauclerc, King of England (1069-1135)

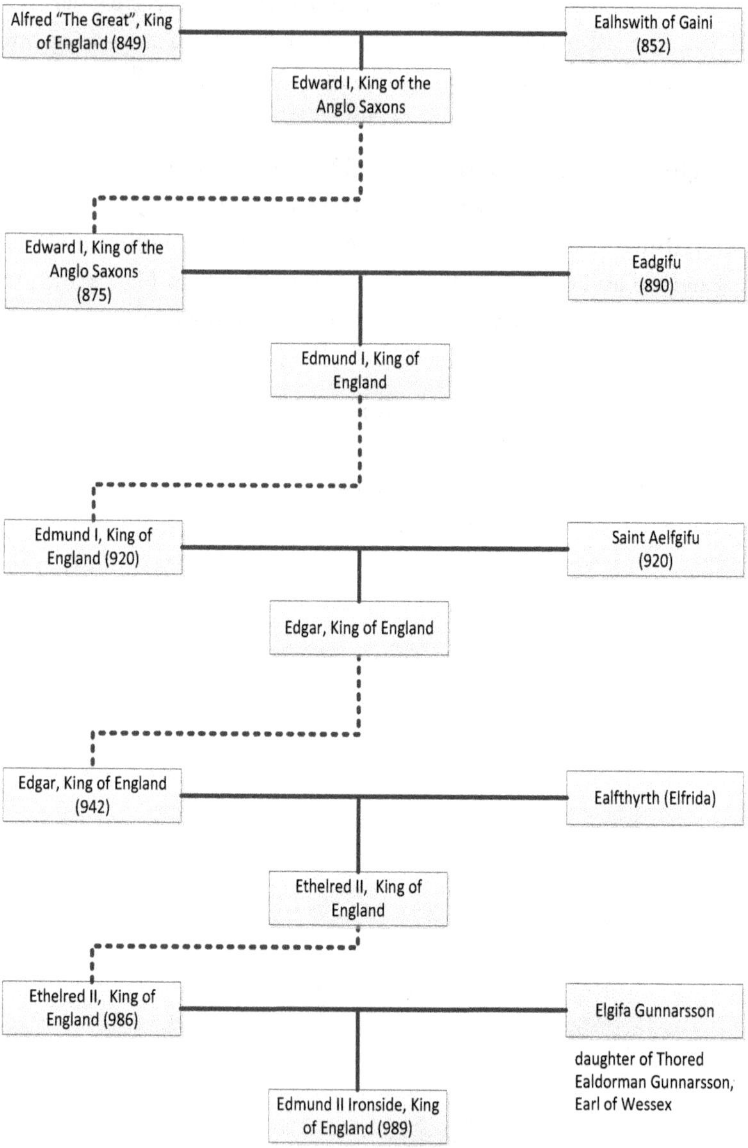

- Alfred "The Great", King of England (849) + Ealhswith of Gaini (852)
  - Edward I, King of the Anglo Saxons

- Edward I, King of the Anglo Saxons (875) + Eadgifu (890)
  - Edmund I, King of England

- Edmund I, King of England (920) + Saint Aelfgifu (920)
  - Edgar, King of England

- Edgar, King of England (942) + Ealfthyrth (Elfrida)
  - Ethelred II, King of England

- Ethelred II, King of England (986) + Elgifa Gunnarsson, daughter of Thored Ealdorman Gunnarsson, Earl of Wessex
  - Edmund II Ironside, King of England (989)

The Ancestry of Matilda (Edith) Of Scotland, Wife of Henry I Beauclerc, King of England (1069-1135)

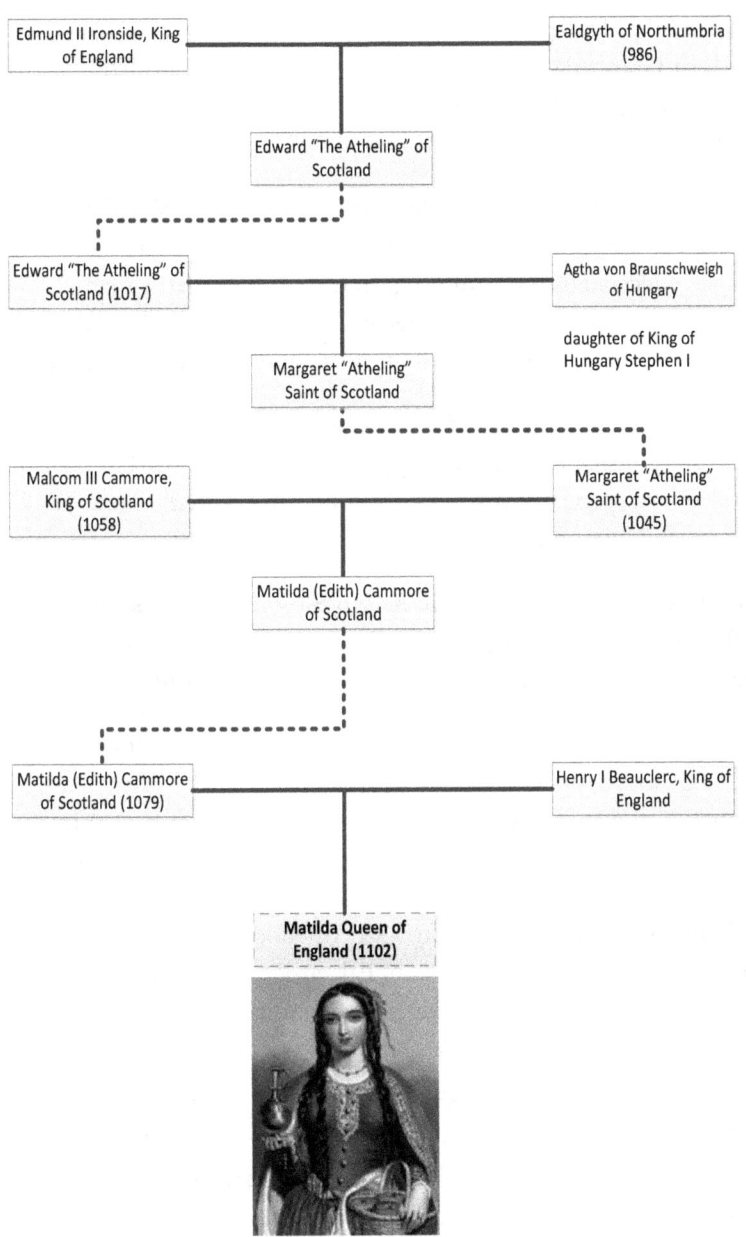

Matilda Queen of England (1102)

PART IX – THE ANCESTRY OF MATILDA (EDITH) OF WIFE OF HENRY I BEAUCLERC, KIND OF ENGLAND (1069-1135)

1. **Alfred "The Great", King of England**, born about 849 in Wantage, Berkshire, England and died 26 October 899, Winchester, Hampshire, England, buried in Hyde Abbey, Winchester. He married 868 to **Ealhswith of Gaini** (daughter of **Aethelred "Mucil" Ealdormand of the Gaini**) in England. She was born about 852 in Mercia, England and died 5th December 905, St Mary's Abbey, Winchester, Dorest.

   Alfred was the fifth son of **Aethelwulf, king of the West Saxons**. At their father's behest and by mutual agreement, Alfred's elder brothers succeeded to the kingship in turn, rather than endanger the kingdom by passing it to under-age children at a time when the country was threatened by worsening Viking raids from Denmark.

   It is for his valiant defence of his kingdom against a stronger enemy, for securing peace with the Vikings and for his farsighted reforms in the reconstruction of Wessex and beyond, that Alfred - alone of all the English kings and queens - is known as 'the Great'.

2. Edward I "The Elder", King of the Anglo Saxons, born about 875 and died 17 July 924. He married **Eadgifu** (daughter of Sigehelm Ealdormand of Kent) she was born about 890 in Kent, England and died about 961.

THE REIGN OF KING EDWARD THE ELDER (899-924): "Following the death of King Alfred, on 26 October 899, the distinctively Alfredian polity established in the early 880s, comprising Wessex, its south-eastern extensions, and 'English' Mercia, and symbolised by the royal style 'king of the Anglo-Saxons', passed intact to Edward the Elder, securely based at Winchester. Acting in close co-operation with Athelred and Athelflad, rulers of the Mercians (under Edward's authority), Edward extended his rule over the southern Danelaw; and in 920 he gained the submission of the Scots, the Northumbrians, and the 'Welsh' of Strathclyde.

3. Edmund I "The Magnificent", King of England, born in about 921, Wessex, England and died 26 May 946, in a fight at Pocklechurch by Leofa, an exiled thief. His burial is in Glastonbury Abbey, Somerset, England. He married **Saint Aelfgifu** born about 920, Wessex, England.

King Edmund I of England or Edmund the Deed-Doer was born in Wessex in 921 as a son of Edward I the Elder of England, King from 899 till 924, and half-brother of Athelstan of England, king from 924 till 939.

Athelstan died on October 27, 939 and Edmund succeeded him as King. Shortly after his preclamation as king he had to face several military threats. King Olaf I of Dublin conquered Northumbria and invaded the Midlands. When Olaf died in 942 Edmund reconquered the Midlands. In 943 he became the god-father of King Olaf of York. In 944,

Edmund was successful in reconquering Northumbria. In the same year his ally Olaf of York lost his throne and left for Dublin in Ireland. Olaf became the king of Dublin as Olaf Cuaran and continued to be allied to his god-father. In 945 Edmund conquered Strathclyde but conceded his rights on the territory to King Malcolm I of Scotland. In exchange they signed a treaty of mutual military support. Edmund thus established a policy of safe borders and peaceful relationships with Scotland. During his reign, the revival of monasteries in England began.

Edmund was murdered in 946 by Leofa, an exiled thief. He had been having a party in Pucklechurch, when he spotted Leofa in the crowed. After the outlaw refused to leave, the king and his advisors fought Leofa. Edmund and Leofa were both killed. He was succeeded as king by his brother Edred, king from 946 until 955.

4. Edgar "The Peaceful", King of England, born about 942 and died 8 July 975 buried in Winchester Cathedral, Glastonbury, England. He married **Ealfthyrth "the Fair" (Elfrida)** (daughter of Ordgar Ealdormand, Earl of Devon) in 965. She was born about 945 and died about 1000, Wherwell King Edgar (about 942-July 8, 975) was the younger son of King Edmund I of England. He won the nickname, "the Peaceable", but in fact was a stronger king than his brother, Edwy, from whom he took the kingdoms of Northumbria and Mercia in 958. He officially succeeded Edwy as king of England in 959. It was his decision to appoint Dunstan (eventually canonised as St. Dunstan) as Archbishop of Canterbury, but it is alleged that Dunstan at first refused to crown Edgar because he disapproved of his way of life.

5. Ethelred II "The Unready", King of England, born about 968 and died 23 Aprifl 1016. He married 985 to Elgifa Gunnarsson (daughter of Thored Ealdorman Gunnarsson, Earl of Wessex) in Wessex, England.

Ethelred succeeded to the throne aged 10 following the death of his father

King Edgar and subsequent murder of his half-brother Edward the Martyr. His nickname "The Unready" does not mean that he was ill-prepared, but derives from the Anglo-Saxon unræd meaning without counsel. This is also a pun on his name, the Anglo-Saxon form of his name, Æþelred, which means "Well advised".

6. Edmund II Ironside, King of England, Edmund was born in England 989. Edmund died 11/30/1016 at 27 years of age. He married in 1015 **to Ealdgyth of Northumbria** born about 986. He was nicknamed Ironside for his military prowess. He was elected king of England by the population of London on his father's death in 1016 He was murdered at instigation of brother in law Edric of England.

7. Edward "The Atheling", "The Exile" of Scotland, born about 1017 in Wessex, England, and died about 1057 in London England married Agtha von Braunschweigh of Hungary (daughter of King of Hungary Stephen I)after 1034, Newcastle-Upon-Tyne

8. Malcom III Cammore, King of Scotland; born 1058; He married Margaret "Atheling" Saint of Scotland, born in about 1045 and died on 16 Nov 1093.

"Atheling, Margaret (St.) the Exile, Born: 1045, Hungary Died: 16 Nov 1093, Edinburgh Castle, Scotland. Interred:

Dunfermline Abbey, Fife, Scotland, Canonised 1250 and her feast day is 16th November. In 1057 she arrived at the English court of Edward the Confessor. Ten years later she was in exile after William defeated Harold at the Battle of Hastings. She fled to Scotland where she was married against her wishes to King Malcolm to whom she bore six sons and two daughters. Her unlearned and boorish husband grew daily more graceful and Christian under the queen's graceful influence. Her remains were removed to Escorial Spain and her head Douai, France."

9. Matilda (Edith) Cammore Of Scotland born 1079 Dunfermline, Fifeshire, Scotland and died 1 May 1118 buried in Westminster Abbey, London, Middlesex, England. She married **Henry I Beauclerc**; born 1069; died December 1, 1135. Henry was King of England (1100-1135).

Matilda (Edith) of Scotland, Princess of Scotland was born in 1079 or 1080 and, as she was destined to become a nun, she went to Romsey where her Aunt Christina was the Abbess. However, in 1100 Henry I, the new king of England, demanded her hand in marriage; and on 11 November 1100 at Westminster she became his queen. Upon her marriage she adopted the name Matilda in honour of the king's mother. They had two, possibly three children. One was **Matilda Adelaid** wife of **Geoffrey Plantagenet**. Queen Matilda built a leper hospital at St. Giles-in-the-Fields, London, and founded the Augustinian Priory at Aldgate. She was aged only about thirty-eight when she died

CHAPTER THREE

THIRD GENERATION

WILLIAM BIRDSONG & ELIZABETH TOMLINSON
Includes related families the Tomlinson

William Birdsong, SR, born about 1752 in Sussex County, Virginia. He married **Elizabeth Tomlinson** about 1776 in Sussex, Virginia. Elizabeth Tomlinson was born 15 March 1760 in Albernarte Parish, Sussex, Virginia and died 13 January 1799. Elizabeth was the daughter of Thomas Tomlinson and Mary Cotton. William married a second time to Cherry Hargrove after Elizabeth's death.

The focus of this book will be the children William had with Elizabeth Tomlinson.

Children of William and Elizabeth Tomlinson:

1. Robert Birdsong, born about 1778 in Sussex County, Virginia.

2. Lucy Birdsong, born about 1781 in Sussex County, Virginia.

3. Mary Birdsong, born about 1783 in Sussex County, Virginia.

4. Benjamin Birdsong, born about 1785 in Sussex County, Virginia.

5. James Birdsong, born May 29th 1792 in Sussex County, Virginia.

6. **William Birdsong, Jr** born about 1795 in Sussex County, Virginia.

Although, there is not much documented it appears they live in Sussex County, Virginia

William was likely a planter or farmer however there is not evidence at this point in my research that supports this theory.

James and William Jr. are listed in service records in War of 1812. The War of 1812 lasted from 1812 to 1815. William was enlisted on May 27th 1814 at Norfolk, Virginia.

He was in Captain William Parson's Company of the Virginia Militia. They were fighting the Indians during this war, but in Norfolk, William Birdsong Jr at 19 years old was fighting the British. He was discharged on November 30th 1814 after only six month of service.

His brother James enlisted on September 1st 1814 and only served six weeks. The researcher wonders if he may have been injured during the war.

Both William and James received land grants for their tour of duty. These two brothers were still in their home state of Virginia in 1814 when discharged but evidently went to Barren County, Kentucky shortly after being discharged. This makes you wonder if they traveled there to meet up with their father William Birdsong, Sr.

The census of 1810 was likely burned in Washington during the War of 1812 we do not have that information to help establish if William and his brother James was raised by their Father and step-mother or if relatives raised them.

Sussex County is next to Surry County Virginia. It is between the James River and the North Carolina border. This area is just thick with our old Birdsong's. William was the son of John and Damaris Hancock Birdsong.

THE ANCESTERY OF ELIZABETH TOMLINSON, WIFE OF WILLIAM BIRDSONG, SR. (1756-1798)

Thomas Tomlinson, born by 1690, Virginia; died 5 Feb 1750/1, Albemarle Parish, Surry County, Virginia. Thomas married Elizabeth Cooke, about 1712. Elizabeth Cooke born by 1697, Virginia; died 27 Jan 1750/1, Albemarle Parish, daughter of William Cooke, Jr. and Rebecca Jones.

Children of Thomas and Elizabeth Cooke

> 1. William Tomlinson, born about 1715, Sussex County, Virginia, died Between Feb 1758 and Mar 28 1758, Brunswick County, Virginia.

> 2. **John Tomlinson Sr,** born about 1695 in Charles County, Virginia died about 1760 in Sussex County, Virginia.

Thomas Tomlinson, "being sick and weak," wrote his will 31 Jan 1750/1. He left to his son William, Negro boy Lewis; to his son Thomas, Negro girl Jenny; to his son Benjamin, the plantation where Thomas lived, Negro man Daniel, woman Juda, boy Joiner and girl Tabb; and 10 shillings Virginia currency each to his daughters Sarah Carter, Elizabeth Moss and Amy Carter. He named his son Benjamin Tomlinson as executor; the witnesses were Joseph Carter, Joseph Carter, Jr., and Henry Gee.

The Will was presented in Surry Court 19 May 1750 (O.S.), "and the executor therein being within the age of 21 years," on the motion of John Tomlinson, certificate was granted him to obtain letters of administration for the estate of the deceased with the will annexed during the minority of the executor. John Tomlinson posted bond, with Richard Carter and Wyke Hunnicutt his securities.

Thomas appears in Surry court records in 1715 and in 1716 patented land on Main Blackwater Swamp in Surry. In 1726 he patented land in Brunswick County, Virginia.

John Tomlinson, Sr. was born about 1695 in Charles City, Virginia and died 1761 in Sussex, Virginia. He married **Mary Chappell** on 1739 in Abemarle, Surry, Virginia, daughter of Thomas Chappell and Elizabeth Jones. John Tomlinson married Mary Chappell about 1739, Abemarle, Surry, Virginia.

Children of John Tomlinson and Mary Chappell are:

1. **Thomas Tomlinson**, born about 1723, Surry, Virginia, Albemarle, Sussex, Virginia.

2. John Tomlinson, born about 1720, Prince George, Virginia; died 06 Aug 1781, Greensville, Virginia.

3. Nathaniel Tomlinson, died 03 Dec 1801 in Lancaster, South Carolina.

4. Rebecca Tomlinson, born about 1720 in Surry, Virginia, died 26 Sep 1764 in Sussex, Virginia.

5. Henry Tomlinson, born about 1723 in Surry, Virginia, died 1748 in Amelia, Virginia.

6. William Tomlinson, born about 1725 in Surry, Virginia, died 19 Dec 1759 in Sussex, Virginia.

7. James Tomlinson, born in, Surry, Virginia, died about 1779, Brunswick, Virginia.

8. Sarah Tomlinson, born in Surry, Virginia, died about 1812 in Chatham, North Carolina.

9. Benjamin Tomlinson, born in Surry, Virginia, died 15 Jun 1759 in Sussex, Virginia.

10. Mary Tomlinson, born in Surry, Virginia, died 26 Sep 1764 in Lancaster, South Carolina.

11. Elizabeth Tomlinson, born in Albemarle County, Surry, Virginia, died about 1759 in Sussex, Virginia.

12. Burell Tomlinson, born in Albemarle County, Surry, Virginia, died Jan 1765 in Albemarle, Surry, Virginia.

13. Anne Tomlinson, born in Albemarle County, Surry, Virginia, died about 1858.

Thomas Tomlinson (son of John Tomlinson and Mary Chappell) was born 1723 in Surry, Virginia, and died 07 Mar 1793 in Albemarle, Sussex, Virginia. He married **Mary Cotton** on 1749 in Surry, Virginia,

Children of Thomas Tomlinson and Mary Cotton are:

1. Lucy Tomlinson, born 27 Sep 1764 in Sussex, Virginia, died 08 May 1848

in Todd, Kentucky.

2. William Tomlinson, born 17 Aug 1749 in Albemarle County, Surry, Virginia, died 07 Mar 1808 in Sussex, Virginia.

3. Ann Tomlinson, born about 1757 in Sussex, Virginia, died 04 Mar 1830 in Sussex, Virginia.

4. Mary Tomlinson, born about 1757 in Sussex, Virginia, died 1810 in Sussex, Virginia.

5. Robert Tomlinson, born 09 Jul 1757 in Albemarle County, Surry, Virginia, died 09 Jul 1757 in Albemarle, Surry, Virginia.

6. **Elizabeth Tomlinson**, born 15 Mar 1760 in Albemarle County, Surry, Virginia, died 13 Jan 1799, Sussex, Virginia, married **William Birdsong, Sr.**

7. Burwell Tomlinson, born about 1767 in Sussex, Virginia, died 03 Dec 1795 in Sussex, Virginia.

8. Benjamin Tomlinson, born about 1770 in Sussex, Virginia, died 07 Sep 1797 in Sussex, Virginia.

CHAPTER FOUR

FOURTH GENERATION

WILLIAM BIRDSONG & WINAFORD ALLEE
Includes related families the Allee, Bybee

William Birdsong, Jr. *(JOHN ^{I}, JOHN ^{II}, WILLIAM SR, ^{III})* born 14th January 1798 in Sussex County, Virginia; died 11 September 1863 in Moniteau County, Missouri. William was married to **Winafrod Allee** on May 3rd 1816 in Barren County, Kentucy by Rev. Ralph Petty. Winaford Allee was the daughter of Rev David Allee (1762-1835) and Charity Bybee. Winaford born 15 January 1801 in Barren County, Kentucky; died 25 May 1886 in Moniteau County, Missiouri.

Children of William Birdsong and Winaford Allee:

    1. Mary Birdsong born14 April 1819 in Barren County, Kentucky.

    2. Rev. James Birdsong born 30 January 1820 Barren County, Kentucky.

    3. Charity Birdsong born 14 October 1821 Moniteau County, Missouri, died 28 December 1888 St Louis, Missouri.

    4. Jaile Birdsong born 7 April 1823 in Moniteau County, Missouri.

    5. Annie Birdsong, born 22 September 1824 in Moniteau County, Missouri.

    6. **Peter Birdsong**, born 18 May 1827 in Moniteau County, Missouri.

    7. Nancy Birdsong, born about 1829 in Moniteau County, Missouri.

    8. Kemp Birdsong, born about 1830 in Moniteau County, Missouri

    9. Nicholas Birdsong, born 27 October 1831 in Moniteau County, Missouri.

    10. David Birdsong, born 27 November 1833 in Moniteau County, Missouri.

    11. Anderson Birdsong, born 13 January 1835 in Moniteau County, Missouri.

    12. Elizabeth Birdsong, born 18 November 1837 in Moniteau County, Missouri.

    13. Merry Birdsong, born 23 August 1839 in Moniteau County, Missouri.

    14. Wilford Birdsong, born 15 January 1941 in Moniteau County, Missouri.

William and Winaford married in Barren County, Kentucky and moved west settling in Moniteau County, Missouri. William served in the War of 1812 and was likely a farmer in Moniteau County, Missouri.

William enlisted at age 19 years old in Sussex County, Virginia in the War of 1812. He served from May 27th 1814 to November 30th 1814 in the Virginia Militia at Norfolk Virginia and received a land grant for his war service. His brother James Birdsong also served in the War of 1812.

William and James traveled together and appear stayed close throughout their military service in 1812. They also got married about the same time when William and Winaford married; William's brother James Birdsong married Margaret (Peggy) Hill. They were all in the Glovers Creek Baptist Church.

William and Winaford were born before the Louisiana Purchase of the Missouri Territory. Sometime in 1820, they and their families all came on the same wagon train to Moniteau County, Missouri. They settled near Clarksburg, Missouri. William Jr. and Winaford Allee Birdsong's daughter was Charity Birdsong born October 14th 1821 in brand new Missouri which became a State that year.

Mary Birdsong and Rev. James Birdsong born in Barren County, Kentucky. William and Winny probably came to Moniteau County, Missouri the following spring after James birth. The trip took up to three months by covered wagon pulled by oxen.

Winaford was a member of Glovers Creek Baptist Church in Barren County, Kentucky. They already had their first two children, when they pioneered to Missouri on the same wagon train that David & Charity Allee, Winafords parents came at time this is sometime in 1820 to Missouri at the time was the western frontier. They settled 1 ½ miles northeast of Clarksburg, Missouri in Moniteau County, Missouri near Winafords relatives. They later moved about five miles northeast of California, Missouri.

On September 11th 1863 William Birdsong, Jr died in Moniteau County, Missouri of smallpox during the Civil War at the age of 68. Smallpox was deadly in those days that his own children had to dig his grave and bury him in Old Salem Cemetery in Moniteau County, Missouri.

After William's death, Winaford received a pension that was honored for Williams War service of 1812. She lived with her daughter Charity Cooper who was widowed about a year before William's death. Charity's husband Luke Cooper had died of a fever (likely Typhoid), in the service of the Civil War. Winaford helped Charity raise her three children.

Winaford lived for more than twenty years after Williams death, she died on May 25th 1886 at the age of 86, at her son Peter's home. This fact was recorded by Peter, when he had her Government pension stopped. Her daughter Charity, died just two years later at the age of 67 in St. Louis, Missouri according to her obituary.

Notes on William and Winafords Children:

Mary Birdsong, there is no record of her marrying or having children.

James Birdsong, Records show that James Birdsong married Mary Beatty on December 1st 1844 in Morgan County, Missouri and also that James married Mary Scroggins on March 9th 1845 in Morgan County, Missouri.

The 1850 census showed him and his wife Mary in Morgan County, Missouri. Apparently, his first wife that he had married died and he remarried. The children of Rev James Birdsong and Mary Birdsong are:

1. Louisa Birdsong born about 1841

2. Sarah (Sally) Ann Birdsong born September 7th 1842 and married Tom E. Allee.

3. Winaford Birdsong born about 1849

4. Rev. W.S. (Bud) Birdsong

Charity Birdsong married Luke Cooper on February 10th 1845 when Moniteau County, Missouri just about three days old. Luck was born there on June 19th 1825 the son of George & Rebecca Cooper, Luke died at Waynesville, Missouri in the Civil War, just about 50 miles from home.

Charity died on December 28th 1888 at a hospital in St. Louis, Missouri. She is buried at Old Salem Church in Moniteau County, Missouri.

Luke and Charity had a son named James Franklin (Frank) Cooper born on September 5th 1853 in Moniteau County, Missouri and he was only nine years old when his father died in the Civil War. Charity Birdsong and Luck Cooper had the following children;

    1. Jane Ann Cooper born Sept 29th 1847

    2. James Franklin (Frank); born Sept 5th 1853/died April 22nd 1925. He married Anna Safronia born Aug 6th 1856/died Oct 25th 1939

    3. John Patrick Cooper; born May 15th 1857/died after 1925. He married Nancy Ladorra Apperson

Jaile Birdsong born April 7th 1823 and married Levi Bybee

Annie Birdsong born September 22nd 1824 and married Thomas Jerden Scott on January 1st 1843 in Cole County, Missouri. Annie and Thomas had the following children;

    1. William Scott born about 1844

    2. Noah Scott born about 1845. He married Josephine Bowlin

Peter Birdsong born May 18th 1827 and married Elizabeth Redmon and had one child;

    1. James Birdsong (1850).

Peter Birdsong second marriage to **Elizabeth Jobe** on Sept 9th 1877 and their children are;

    1. Sarah Melissa Birdsong born July 1st 1877 married to Charles Walter Orr before 1902 and died February 8th 1959.

    2. **John Birdsong** born on 24 Aug 1882 in Moniteau County, Missouri, died 29 Aug 1966 in Kansas City, Missouri. John married Marie Lula Wood

    3. Baby Birdsong

Kemp Birdsong born about 1830 and married Kiziah Jane Howard they had no children then he married his second wife Nancy Allee and their children are;

    1. James W Birdsong born about 1854

    2. Sarah Alice (Jane) Birdsong; born about 1857

    3. George Washington Birdsong born about 1860. He married Catherine Apperson

    4. Newton Leonard Birdsong; born about 1865 married Mary Dipa Sartin Jasper (Jap) Montgomery Birdsong; born about 1868 he married Dora Adams

Nicholas Birdsong born Oct 27th 1831. He married Frances Huff on April 2nd 1856 and had one child;

    1. Elizabeth Jane Birdsong; birth unknown

David Birdsong; born Nov 27th 1833

    1. Gerhardn Birdsong; birth unknown

    2. Isabel Birdsong; birth unknown

Elizabeth Jane Birdsong born Nov 18th 1837 and married Elias Scott on April 15th 1852.

Wilford Birdsong born Jan 15th 1841 this is the last child of William and Winny Birdsong. This son was born after the 1840 census and evidently died before the 1850 census.

The Ancestry of Winaford Allee, Wife of William Birdsong, Jr (1798-1863)

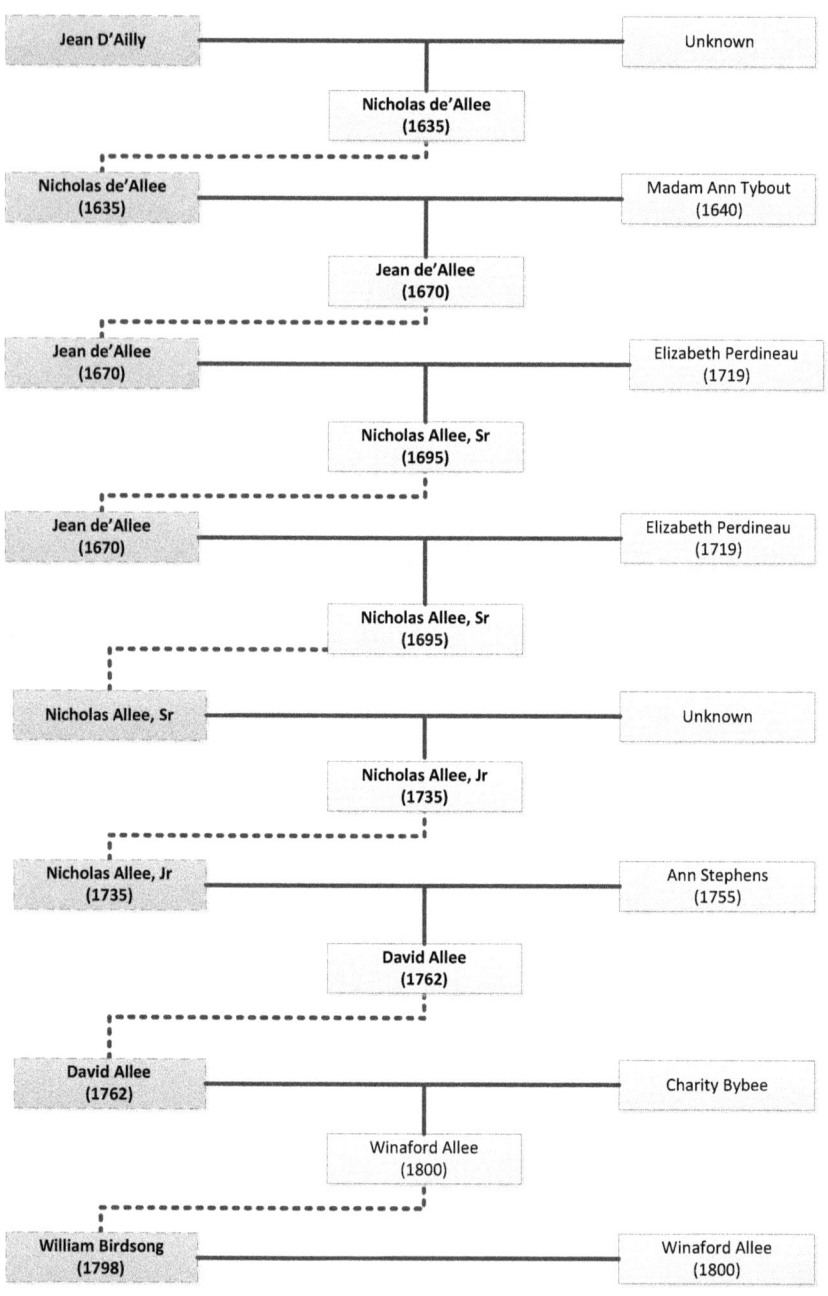

THE ANCESTRY OF WINAFORD ALLEE, WIFE OF WILLIAM BIRDSONG, JR (1798-1863)

The name d'Ailly was usually the name of the Catholic branch of the family while those of the Huguenot branch usually used dally.

The name Dally and d'ailly is from the Latin de Alliaco and was traced to 1090 A.D. in northern France, to the area called Alliacum by the Romans, when they occupied the area around what is now Amiens. Source: letter from David S. Dalley of Plainfield, New Jersy dated 16 Feb 1926 to my great-grandfather, Rev. Joseph W. Dally in Ridgewood, New Jersy.

The reading of records is greatly complicated by the fact that these people were French living with Dutch and German people in a country which spoke English. So, one finds our family name recorded as Daille, Dalje, Allje, Alje, Alley, Allie, Allyee, Alyie, Alyea, and Allee, the last two being the most common, at least since 1700.

It is assumed that **Jean d'Allee / D'Ailly Sr.** born about 1594 at Chattellerault, France; died about 1670 he was the father or blood relative of Nicholas and Jean d'Allee. We are also assuming that **Nicholas** and **Jean d'Allee** were bothers or cousins in France and fled together in 1682.

Jean d'Allee / D'Ailly Sr. was educated at Poitiers and Saumur; and in 1626 became the Huguenot minister at the great church at Charenton. He was the president of the last national synod held in France in 1659, which met at Loudun. Of his works, the best known is the treatise, "Du vrai emploi des Peres", which was translated into English by Thomas Smith under the title, "A Treatise concerning the right use of the Fathers 1651". (H.M Baird: The Huguenots and the Revocation of the Edict of Nantes", 1895, Vol. 1, p. 412).

Nicholas de'alle, (Jean [1]) born about 1635 in Flanders, Artois, France and he died about 1700 in Hackensack, New Jersy. He married **Madame Ann Tybout** between 1655 -1665. She was born about 1640 in France and died in 1705 in New Jersey.

Nicholas D'Ailly was a French Huguenot apparently born in Artois, in the Normandy Province of France, in 1640. At some point prior to 1663 he fled from France to Mannheim, Germany and joined a group of Huguenots there. From Mannheim, they traveled to Holland and it is believed he emigrated along with his wife, **Madame Tybout** and fifteen year old son Jan, about

1663. Certain records say that they were aboard the Dutch ship Da Trouw (The Faith) although no ships passenger list or other document has been found which would support this.

Notes on Nicholas D'Ailly: Education: Poitiers and Saumur.

Occupation: 1626, Huguenot minister at the great church at Charenton.

Children of Nicholas D'Ailly and Ann Tybout are:

> 1. Alley D Allee, born about 1658, France.
>
> 2. John D Allee, born about 1665, Artois, France, died 16 Mar 1717/18, Kent County, Delware.
>
> 3. **Jean D Allee**, born about 1672, Dunois, died about 1719, New York, New York married to **Elizabeth Perdineau** in about 1695.
>
> 4. Rachel De Allee, born about 1670, France.

Notes on Nicholas De'Allee's son John D. Allee

The earliest settlements of Delaware were made along the navigable rivers and bays. One of the early grants of land in lower New Castle County was issued in 1765 by James, Duke of York to Peter Bayard for a tract called Bampties Hook, now Bombay Hook. The quit rent then was six bushels of wheat annually. The land originally owned by the Indian, Mehockesett and called Neuwsings or Navasink was surveyed in May 1680 to John Dawson. Three years later, in 1683, William Penn created Kent County out of the lower part of New Castle County and from the upper part of the county below which he called Sussex. Meanwhile other land transfers were made at Bombay Hook and the names of Francis Richardson, Francis Murray and E. Peterson appears as landholders there.

About the same time, there came to Hackensack, New Jersey, the Huguenot, **John Allee**, born in Artois, France, about 1665. He was a son of the Reverend **Pierre de Allie** who fled France to escape religious persecution. In 1706, John Allee of Hackensack, New Jersey, bought the 600 acre tract of land in Kent County called "Woodstock Bower" from John Albertson and John Manford, both of New York. An adjacent tract of 360 acres was acquired by John Allee of "Duck Creek" in 1711. He seems to have acquired additional land and exerted his efforts in developing it for his family. The exact date of his death is not known, but his will probated March 16, 1718, named his sons, Peter, Abraham, Johanus, Jacob, and daughters, Hannah,

Mary, Elizabeth, Rachell, Jane Vanwinkle (wife of Simon) and Susannah Vangasco (wife of John). The three sons, Peter, Abraham and Johanus were the executors.

Jean D Allee (Nicholas [2] Jean [1]), born about 1672, Dunois, died about 1719, New York, New York married to **Elizabeth Perdineau** in about 1695.

Children of Jean D Allee and Elizabeth Perdineau;

> 1. Jean Allee born about 1692 "from an Island, near France" died about 1752 spouse Susanna Dassier.
>
> 2. **Nicholas John Allee** born 7 July 1695.
>
> 3. Peter Allee born about 1700 France died about 1779.
>
> 4. William Allee born about 1702 France. He married Marion Coutant.
>
> 5. Benjamin Allee born about 1710/12 France.

Nicholas John Allee (Jean[3], Nicholas [2], Jean [1]) born 7 July 1695 in France.

Children of Nicholas John Allee:

> 1. **Nicholas Allee**, born 1 May 1735 Montgomery/Henrico County, Virginia.
>
> 2. Thomas Allee, born about 1724.
>
> 3. James Allee, born about 1728.

Notes for Nicholas John Allee

Halifax Virginia voting records before 1764

Pittsylvania land entries, 1750s area with Jeremiah Stover

Nicholas Allee (Nicholas [4], Jean[3], Nicholas [2], Jean [1]) was born 01 May 1735 in Montgomery/Henrico County, Virginia, and died 20 Jul 1808 in Montgomery County, Virginia. He married (1) **Ann Stephens** on about 1755 in Halifax County, Virginia. He married (2) Mary Dennis on 04 Jun 1794 in Montgomery County, Virgina.

Children of Nicholas Allee and Ann Stephens

> 1. Keziah Allee, born about 1760, Virginia.
>
> 2. **David Allee**, born 25 April 1762, Richmond, Halifax/Pittsylvania

County, Virginia, died 03 Jan 1835, California, Cooper County, Missouri. He married **Charity Bybee**.

3. John Allee, born 08 Jul 1764, Washington, Virginia, died about 1842, Putnam County, Indiana.

4. William Allee, born about 1780, Pittsylvania/Franklin County, Virginia, died about 1826, Barren County, Kentucky.

5. Sarah Allee, born about 1768.

6. Jemima Allee, born about 1770, Virginia.

Nicholas Allee served in the militia in Virginia during the French and Indian War. He was severely wounded by the Indians in a skirmish believed to have been fought near Ft. Duquense. Receiving 25 pounds as compensation from the colony of Virginia, he moved to South Carolina, where he stayed a few years, then returned to Virginia. In 1767 he was a resident of Pittsylvania County, later removing to Montgomery County in the lower Shenandoah Valley, where he died in 1808.

Ann Stephens was born 1738 in Halifax County, Virginia, and died before 1797 in Virginia. It is thought that Ann Stephens was a Powhatan Indian. Nicholas married Ann Stephens in 1755. Legend says she was a Powhatan Indian. The Powhatans were known to be a suspicious and dangerous tribe unless convinced that the European settlers had friendly intentions. Some English officials have credited them with saving early settlements by teaching them how to cultivate tobacco. This allowed a measure of commercial success, especially in Virginia.

On January 1756 Nicholas Allee was on the private payroll of Captain Robert Steward's Company, Troop of Light Horse, Cumberland Fort, Virginia, commanded by General George Washington.

Early in 1757 he furnished provisions for the Prince Edward Company Militia. In June of that same year he was wounded while fighting at the Battle of Fort Duquesne at Pittsburg, Pennsylvania. This battle was also known as Braddock's Defeat.

On Thursday, September 28, 1758 he presented a petition to the Virginia House of Burgesses stating that he ought to be paid for a disabling wound he received last year in June. He explained that he was ordered out as a guide to a part of the Brunswick Militia which was sent as protection for the inhabitants.

Then in a skirmish with some Indians he was shot twice through the body and his right arm was broken. This incident had entirely disabled him from making a livelihood for himself and his family. The petition was received to be read and considered at that time. The next day it was recommended that he receive 25 pounds. But before receiving it, he, with his family and others, went to South Carolina where they remained for six years. (1758 - 1764)

In 1764 Nicholas returned to the House of Burgesses and again presented his claim for provisions for troops in battle. The first request had been denied.

His name appears on the tax list of Pittsylvania County, Virginia in 1767. It was then clear that he was a tax-paying resident, a member of the community. On May 31, 1770 Nicholas appeared once more before the House of Burgesses to request payment for provisions which he had provided in 1757. He was questioned about the delay in making the claim. He was able to convince the membership that he had indeed been absent six years. The house approved 3 pounds, 9, 9 1/2 for 372 pounds of pork and 2 barries of corn which he had furnished the militia.

On August 27, 1772 he and Ann sold land to Robert Stockton of Pittsylvania County, Virginia. Land Records show that as of May 31, 1774 he owned 546 acres on the Little Branch of New River. On April 5, 1774 a survey was made in Fincastle County on the South side of Little River, a branch of New River for Thomas Allee. This is by the Montgomery County line where we later find Nicholas. On April 5, 1787, Jane Alley (former relative of Captain John Jennings) was entitled to pay of her husband, Thomas, who died of wounds received at Buford's Retreat.

Again Nicholas furnished material or service in the war effort for Botetourt County, Virginia from 1780 - 1784. He paid taxes for the years 1782, 1784 - 1787. Although he paid taxes here, he may have lived in Franklin County as early as 1786 since he signed marriage bonds for his children in 1786 and 1787. They were Jermima, Keziah, David, Jonathan, Buford and William. The first daughter, Sarah, was married, though the county of her marriage was not identified.

Some time before 1794 his wife, Ann, died and he married Mary Dennis. They were married on June 4, 1794 or April 13, 1795 in Montgomery County, Virginia, where they made their home. She was the daughter of Joseph Dennis. All the children of Nicholas and Ann were married except William at the time. Nicholas and Mary had seven more children.

On May 20, 1808 Nicholas Allee made his will. It was probated July 20, 1808. The Last Will and Testament of Nicholas Allee, 20 May, 1808, Montgomery County, Virginia.

In the name of God Amen this twentieth day of May in the year one thousand, eight hundred and eight.

I, Nicholas Allee of Montgomery County, and State of Virginia, being advanced in years and weak in body, but of sound mind, memory, and understanding do see cause to make this my last will and testament; that is to say, I commend my soul to Almighty God and my body to the grave, to be buried in a Christian like manner at the discretion of my wife and Exrs [sic]. And as touching such worldly Estate as it pleased God to bless me with in this life, I dispose of the same in the following manner and form.

It is my will and I do ordain that all my lawful debts, funeral expenses and Doctor charges, if any there be, shall be paid and lawfully discharged.

I will and bequeath unto Mary, Daughter of Joseph Denis, deceased who is married to me and lives with me now as my wife and home keeper - Seven Cows and calves, one Beef cow, my mare that goes by the name of the young Roan, and her choice three of the rest of my horses, all my sheep and Hoogs [sic]. All my Household furniture, Beds and bedding, her saddle, and every other article thereunto belonging without exception. All the grain, Hay, and fodder that is on my plantation, Growed and Growing, the croppers' part excepted at the time of my decease.

I also will unto the said Mary, all the land that I now possess in this county, during her natural life, if she remains unmarried if she chusses [sic] to Live on it and if she will not chuse [sic] to live on it or should marry then the land to be sold by my Exrs [sic] for the most that can be got for it and the price thereof to be equally divided between my seven children by the said Mary, namely, Anne, Nicholas, Merry, Betty, Joseph, Isaac, and Hannah, she drawing a childs; part and I will unto the said Mary all or any Legacy or Legacies that has or shall fall to her from her fathers Estate.

I bequeath unto Thomas Denis that now lives with me one cow & calf. The ballance [sic] of my property is to be sold and the price thereof, with my cash, to pay the following? Legacy to my six children by my former wife, to wit: Sarah Stephens, Jemimah Hays, Keziah Robins, David, John, & William Allee,

Twenty pounds each, and to Rhoda Cox, my Grand daughter, five pounds. If my negro Poll will find a man that will give fifty five pounds for her, she may chuse [sic] her own master; if not, if any of my children will take her at the same they may the oldest having preference, and if they will not she shall be sold to the highest bider [sic].

And it is my will that if my children by my wife Mary, should be like to suffer, or not be well brought up, they shall be bound out by my Exrs [sic], in such places and with such men as will be likely to bring them up in the fear of God & make them able to gain an honest living when of lawful age.

And if my wife Mary should die before the youngest of my children by her shall be of lawful age, the two thirds of her dowry to go to my children by her, and the one third is to be at her own disposal; and whereas my son David Allee hath worked for me after he was of lawful age and my son William hath left property on my plantation for which they had no satisfaction in lieu thereof, I will unto the sd [sic] David & William the Waggon [sic] they bought of me, exclusive of the forementioned legacies. And it is my will that the balance of my property, if any there be after the above legacy is paid the one half thereof go towards the Education of my children by the sd [sic] Mary, and the other half to be divided equally between my six aforementioned oldest children.

My wearing apparel and my large Bible, I will to my son David. And I do nominate my friend, Peter Saunders, and John Long, to be Exrs [sic] of this my last will and Testament as Witness whereof I set my hand and seal the day and date above written the words she drawing a childs part was underlind [sic] before it. Signed [sic] and acknowledged in presence of us Edward Gray, John Long, and At Montgomery July Court 1808

This last will and Testament of Nicholas Allee, deceased, was presented in Court and proven by the oath of Edward Gray, Junr. and John Long, the witnesses, thereto subscribed, and ordered to be recorded, and on the motion of Peter Saunders, Junr. and John Long, the Executors, therein named, who make oath and entered into bond with security according to law. Certificate is granted them for obtaining a probate thereof in due form.

Rev David Allee (Nicholas [5], Nicholas [4], Jean[3], Nicholas [2], Jean [1]) Born in Pittsylvania, Virginia, April 25, 1762. He dies in January 1835, David married Charity Bybee (of Welsh descent) Dec 4, 1784 and lived on land given to him by his father. **Winnaford Allee** was the daughter of Rev David Allee and Charity Bybee. David was said to be of French, Spanish & English descent. The family story shared for many years is that David's ancestors landed in Maryland in route from England, on Easter Sunday in the mid 1600's. David was reported to also be descendant of an Indian maiden from the Pamunkey Tribe (Powhatan Indian of Pocahontas tribe).

David was only 13 years old when he first volunteered for six months service in the American Revolutionary War. David clearly felt strongly about the education of the youth. He built and taught the first school in his neighborhood, in a log house on his property in 1825. He died in January 1835 after a long and painful affliction (said to be cancer).

"David Allee, of French and English descent, was born on April 25, 1762 in Pittsylvania co., VA. His parents were Nicolas and Ann Allee. David was only 13 years old when he entered the Revolutionary War, volunteered for 6 months. Signed up 3 more times, making his service on VA front 2 years."

In 1795, David moved to Barren County, Kentucky, 1806 was ordained a minister at Glover's Creek Baptist Church and started new profession at the age of 44. In 1820 settled in Moniteau County, Missouri (Northeast of Clarksburg) he brought along 10 of 11 children. All married but one of them. Nicholas married Tempey Hill, Betsy married Thomas Scott, Buford married Suzanna Evans, Anne married Kemp Scott, Winifred married William Birdsong, Polly married Capt Stephen Cole, Jerusha married James Hill, William married Anna Hill, and Charity married Carrick Howard. David never married. John remained in Kentucky. All built identically sized houses and types. William and Nicholas returned to Kentucky and brought mother-in-law, Mildred Hines "Granny" Hill and her family including 6 sons"

Rev Allee rode Saline, Morgan, Moniteau, Cooper, Cole, Callaway, Boone and Howard Counties preaching. First formed Mt Pleasant Baptist Church 1823 Died Jan 1835 buried Allee Cemetery northwest of California or Mt Pleasant Cemetery, Clarksburg, Missouri.

David Allee, of Cooper County, Missouri, May 6, 1833 served in Henry, Spring of 1777, under Captain Peter Herston, Lieutenant William Ferguson.

Joined seven other companies under Colonels Shelby and Christie, and on the French Broad the companies divided and went in different directions in pursuit of the Cherokees. They marched to the towns of Choto, Chilhowie, and Tuckaluckee.

On the return they remained at Long Island on the Holston until Christie's treaty with the Cherokees was concluded. This service was six months. July, 1778, went out from Botetourt under Captain Thomas Cummings, and Colonal Charles Lynch. Had a fight with tories at the head of Little River in Botetourt, where they took Job Hale and William Terry, two tory captains. At Sinking Creek, in Montgomery, they disarmed a good many tories, and at Tom's Creek in Wythe, they disarmed others. Here they were discharged.

Then volunteered under Captain Joshua Martin, of Colonel Abraham Penn's regiment, marched to the Dan River, and as the British were not in Virginia as reported, they were discharged, just after the battle of Guilford.

Volunteered six months in the rangers under Captain Arbuckle, who scouted the country from Daniel Rand's bottom on New River to Point Pleasant. Served another six months under Captain Arbuckle and Colonal Floyd, being stationed at Point Pleasant to watch the frontiers.

First Salem Church

Near California, Walker Township, Moniteau County, Missouri

David Allee married to Miss Charity Bibee in 1784, who was of Welsh extraction and made him a useful and devoted wife. He was converted when a young man, immigrated to Kentucky in 1795, and soon afterwards commenced preaching the gospel to dying men. He immigrated to Missouri in 1820, (some historics give the date as 1819) settling in what is now the southeast part of Cooper County, and united with the Pisgah Church. Two years after he aided in the organization of Mount Pleasant Church, of which he and his family became members and so remained until his death. He was active in the organization of Concord Association in 1823 and ever sought to promote its prosperity. When the question of forming the "Central Society" (now General Association) was agitated, he advised its formation. David was granted 200 acres for his service during the American Revolutionary War.

CHAPTER FIVE

FIFTH GENERATION

PETER BIRDSONG & ELIZABETH JOBE

Peter Birdsong (John [I], John [II], William, Sr., [III], William, Jr. [IV]) born 18th May 1827 in Moniteau County, Missouri; died 13th May 1918 in Eldon, Missouri. Peter first married Eliza Redmon and had four children based on the 1850 & 1880 Census. James Birdsong, born 1848, Isaphine born 1864, Alice Ann born 1866, Edmond born 1870.

Peter married his second wife **Elizabeth Jobe** on the 9th September 1877. Elizabeth Jobe was born abt 1840 Moniteau County, Missouri; died 14th January 1912 in Californian, Missouri. Elizabeth Jobe daughter of Abraham Jobe and Clarinda Chandler.

Children of Peter and Elizabeth Jobe:

    1. Sarah Birdsong, born 1 July 1877 Moniteau County, Missouri; died 8 February 1959 Moniteau, Missouri.

    2. **John P. Birdsong**, born 24 August 1882 Moniteau County, Missouri; died 28 August 1966 Kansas City, Missouri.

    3. Baby Birdsong, born about 1883 Moniteau County, Missouri; died at birth.

The 1850 Census – Moniteau County, Missouri show the following for Peter Birdsong, it appears he had family members living with him. He is only 25 years old at the time and Elizabeth Redmond is living with him and she is only 19 years old. They had one child of their marriage James Birdsong and he was born in 1850. He is not listed in the 1850 Census he must had been born after the census was conducted.

Peter Birdsong , Age 25

Estimated Birth Year: 1825

Other People in Household:

Eliza Birdsong 19 years old – Female (This must have been Elizabeth Redmond)

James Birdsong 2 ½ years old – Male - MO

William Birdsong 17 years old – Male - TN

Edwin Birdsong 13 years old – Male - TN

Susan Birdsong 12 years old – Female - TN

Arthur Birdsong 9 years old – Male - TN

James Birdsong 8 years old – Male - TN

Martha Birdsong 6 years old – Female - TN

Samuel Birdsong 4 years old - Male – TN

The 1880 Census – In Linn Township, Moniteau County, Moniteau, Missouri show the following for Peter Birdsong;

Peter Birdsong, 54 years old, occupation as a farmer born in County, Missouri, Father born in Virginia and Mother born in Kentucky. Census shows he was once widowed

Elizabeth Birdsong, 42 years old, wife of Peter, occupation as keeping house, it shows she is ill (cannot read the illness) and that she was born in Missouri, unknown birth place of Father , Mother born in Kentucky. Census shows she was once widowed. It also indicates she cannot read or write.

Isaphine Birdsong, 16 years old, is the daughter of head of household, attended school within the census year. Born in Missouri, both Father and Mother born in Missouri. This is likely the daughter that Peter had with Elizabeth Redmond.

Alice Ann Birdsong, 14 years old, is the daughter, is ill "chilling", attended school within the census year. Born in Missouri, both Father and Mother born in Missouri.

Edmund S Birdsong, 10 years old, Son of head of household, attended school within the census year. Born in Missouri, both Father and Mother born in Missouri. Sarah M Birdsong, 3 years old, Daughter of head of household, Born in MO, both Father and Mother born in Missouri. Sarah is the first born child of John & Elizabeth (Jobe) Birdsong.

The 1900 Census – Moniteau County, Moniteau, Missouri show the following for Peter Birdsong;

Peter Birdsong, Age 73

Estimated Birth Year: 1827

Other People in Household:

Elizabeth Birdsong, 62 years old, Female – Spouse

Sarah Birdsong, 23 years old, Female – Daughter

John Birdsong, 17 years old, Male – Son

Years married: 22

The 1910 Census – Moniteau County, Moniteau, Missouri show the following for Peter Birdsong;

Peter Birdsong, Age 82

Estimated Birth Year: 1827

Other People in Household:

Elizabeth Birdsong, 72 years old, Female – Spouse, number of children (5), number of children still living (2).

Years married: 32

Peter and Elizabeth attended Salem Baptist Church Members and joined in July of 1849.

Peter and Elizabeth are buried in May 1918 near California, Walker Township, Moniteau County, Missouri.

Obituary of Elizabeth

From the Jan 18, 1912 California Democrat newspaper

"Death of Mrs. Birdsong

Mrs. Elizabeth Birdsong wife of Peter Birdsong died at the family residence in this city January 14th The funeral services were held at the house Tuesday, R.L. Hood of the Baptist Church officiating and the interment was at the Jobe cemetery north of town. Mrs. Birdsong was born in this county in 1840, being about 72 years of age, a daughter of Abraham Jobe. She was twice married Birdsong – there were 4 children born of the union, 2 died in infancy and 2 survived, John Birdsong and Mrs. Walter Orr, she is also survived by her husband Peter Birdsong. Mrs. Birdsong was a good woman highly esteemed by her friends and acquaintances, a good wife and dutiful mother, she and her aged husband were living very happily together and her death was a great blow to him."

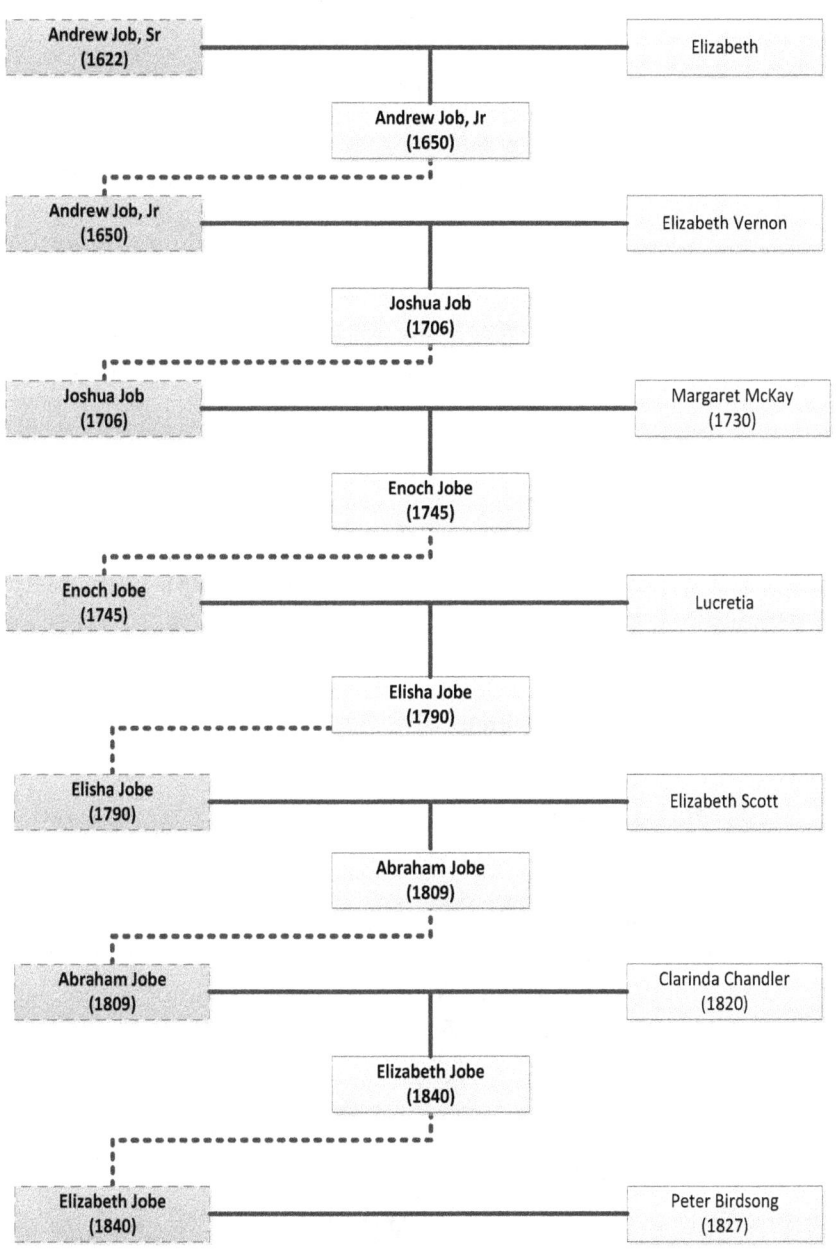

THE ANCESTRY OF ELIZABETH JOBE, WIFE OF PETER BIRDSONG, (1827-1918)

The name Jobe has origins in both English and French. The Jobe family name is linked to the ancient Anglo-Saxon culture of Britain. Their name comes from the baptismal name Job. The surname Jobe referred to the son of Job which belongs to the category of patronymic surnames.

Variant spelling of Job nickname from Old French job, joppe 'sorry wretch', 'fool' (perhaps a transferred application of the name of the Biblical character) from Middle English jubbe, jobbe 'vessel containing four gallons', hence perhaps a metonymic occupational name for a cooper. It could also have been a nickname for a heavy drinker or for a tubby person metonymic occupational name for a maker or seller (or nickname for a wearer) of the long woolen garment known in Middle English and Old French as a jube or jupe. This word ultimately derives from Arabic.

Andrew Job, Sr (Jobe) was born in 1620 in Kent County, England (Fishguard, Wales), and died 29 November 1699 in New Hampshire. He married Elizabeth (unknown) Job.

Andrew Job, Sr was in Scotland in the 1640's and his brother David sailed from Liverpool to American (Portsmouth)

Children of Andrew Job and Elizabeth:

> 1. **Andrew Job, Jr** born in 1650 in board ship coming from Kent, England; died 5 April 1722 in Chester City, Pennsylvania.
>
> 2. Thomas Job, born about 1654.
>
> 3. John Job

Andrew Job, Jr (Andrew, Sr.[1]) was born 1650 in board ship coming from Kent, England, and died 5 April 1722 in Chester City, Pennsylvania. He married **Elizabeth Vernon** on 10 August 1692 in Chester City Pennsylvania, daughter of Thomas & Elizabeth Vernon.

Children of Andrew Job and Elizabeth:

> 1. **Joshua Job,** born about 1706 in Nottingham, Maryland; died 1772 in Woodstock, Shenandoah City, Virginia.
>
> 2. Benjam Job, born about 1693 in Chester City, Pennsylvania.
>
> 3. Jacob Job, born 26 May 1694 in Chester City, Pennsylvania.

4. Thomas Job, born 22 September 1695 in Chester City, Pennsylvania. He married Elizabeth Maxwell 28 August 1725.

5. Mary Job, born 23 January 1697 in Chester City, Pennsylvania. She married John White 31 October 1717.

6. Enoch Job, born 6 November 1700 in Chester City, Pennsylvania.

7. Abraham Job, born 22 June 1702 in Chester City, Pennsylvania.

8. Caleb Job, born 26 May 1704 in Nottingham, Maryland.

9. Hannah Job, born about 1709 in Nottingham, Maryland.

10. Patience Job, born 2 July 1710 in Nottingham, Maryland. She married Robert McCoy.

Andrew Job was well educated and his name is prominent in the early records of the Colony. He was High Sheriff under Penn from 1687 to 1700. He removed to Cecil Co., Md., in 1704, commissioned to survey and locate roads, adjust township lines, settle differences etc.

Joshua Job (Andrew, Jr.^{2}, Andrew, Sr.^{1}), born about 1707 in Nottingham, Maryland; died by 1782 in Woodstock, Shenandoah City, Virginia. He married **Margaret McKay** 11 November 1730, the daughter of Robert McKay and Ann Brown. She was born about 1710, Freehold Township, Monmouth County, New Jersy and died about 1770, Frederick County, Virginia.

Children of Joshua Job and Margaret:

1. **Enoch Jobe**, born about 1745 in Shenandoah County, Virginia; died 19 April 1843 in Cole County, Missouri.

2. Samuel Job

Joshua Job was living on the South River Shenandoah by 26 January 1735/36 when his name appeared on the Peter Wolf/Morgan Morgan list of 49 settlements on the Hite, McKay, Duff and Green 100,000-acre grant land. He was living on the 216-acre tract on Joshua's Bottom willed to him by his wife Margaret's father Robert McKay Sr. Joshua's Bottom was located on the north side of the South River Shenandoah within the "7000 acre South River Tract," down river 40 poles from "Robert McCoys Ford" east of Robert McKay Sr.'s place. Robert McKay Sr. bequeathed the other half of Joshua's Bottom to George Hollingsworth. George and Hannah McKay

Hollingsworth's son Abraham sold his father's inherited 216-acre tract to Edwin Young for 200 pounds on 29 August 1778.

Adam Cunningham's 27 November 1770 deposition stated that Joshua Job had settled on Joshua's Bottom when he arrived at the South River in 1740 and that he was still living there at the time of the 1770 deposition.

Joshua (born 1707) was deceased by 30 May 1782 when his eldest son Enoch Job was appointed administrator of Joshua's estate by the Shenandoah County Court. The inventory of his estate was returned to court on 27 June 1782 and 24 April 1783.

Enoch Jobe (Joshua³, Andrew, Jr.², Andrew, Sr.¹,), born about 1745 in Shenandoah County, Virginia; died 19 April 1843 in Cole County, Missouri. He married **Jennica Odell** on 22 April 1790 Shenandoah County, Virginia, daughter of James Odell.

Children of Enoch Jobe and Jennica:

    1. Abraham Jobe, Sr., born about 1793 in Tennessee or Virginia; died 17 March 1848 in Moniteau County, Missouri.

    2. **Enoch Jobe**

Enoch Jobe was a resident of Shenandoah City, Virginia enlisted February 18, 1776 in Capt. William Croghan's Co., Col. Mualenburg's Regiment of the Virginia Line, served two years as a private and was engaged in the battles of White Plains, Trenton, Brandywine, Germantown and White Marsh. Information taken from a letter from the Department of Interior, Bureau of Pensions, Washington D.C. dated January 7, 1920.

- February 22, 1828 – Military pension allowed
- Veteran of Revolutionary War
- Changed spelling from Job to Jobe
- First Jobe to migrate to Missouri

Enoch Jobe (Enoch Jobe ⁴, Joshua³, Andrew, Jr.², Andrew, Sr.¹,) married **Lucretia (unknown)**

Children of Enoch Jobe and Lucretia:

    1. **Elisha Jobe**, born 1790 in Tennessee; died 1855 in Missouri

Elisha Jobe (Enoch Jobe [5], Enoch Jobe [4], Joshua[3], Andrew, Jr.[2], Andrew, Sr.[1]), born 1790 in Tennessee; died 1855 in Missouri. He married **Elizabeth (unknown).**

Children of Elisha Jobe and Elizabeth:

> 1. Logan Jobe, born 24 February 1805 in Tennessee; died 14 December 1846 in Moniteau County, Missouri.
>
> 2. Bartholomew Jobe, born 6 June 1809 in Tennessee; died 2 March 1878 in Moniteau County, Missouri.
>
> 3. **Abraham S. Jobe**, born 27 April 1810 in Tennessee; died 27 February 1881 in Moniteau County, Missouri.
>
> 4. Elisha Jobe, born in 1810 in Tennessee.
>
> 5. Lucretia Jobe, born 28 February 1811 in Tennessee; died 21 March 1878 in Camden County, Missouri.
>
> 6. Ellen Jobe, born in 1812 in Tennessee.
>
> 7. Polly Jobe, born in Tennessee.
>
> 8. Reuben H Jobe, born 23 December 1816 in Tennessee; died 1859.

Thomas Scott, born in Barren County, Kentucky in 1810, settled near what is now California, Missouri in 1817, married a daughter of Elisha Jobe and from 1830 to his death in 1887 was a preacher or worker in the Missionary Baptist Church.

Abraham S. Jobe, born 27 April 1810 in Tennessee; died 27 February 1881 in Moniteau County, Missouri. He married **Clarinda Chandler** on 26 September 1837 in Cole County, Missiouri. Clarinda was born about 1762 and died in 1835. Both Abraham and Clarinda are buried in the Jobe Cemetery, Near California, Walker Township, Moniteau County, Missouri

Children of Abraham Jobe and Clarinda:

> 1. Logan Jobe born between 1838 - 1839, Walker Township, Cole County, now Moiteau County Missouri, died August 27, 1877 in Moniteau County Missouri.
>
> 2. **Elizabeth Jobe** born in 1840, Cole County Missouri, now Moiteau County Missouri, died January 14, 1912, Moniteau County, Missouri.

3. William Frankline Jobe born February 02, 1845, Near California, Moniteau County Missouri, died April 12, 1923, Moniteau County, Missouri.

4. Reubin Jobe born between 1846 - 1847, California, Moniteau County, Missouri.

5. Mary Eliza Jobe, born about 1848, Moniteau County, Missouri.

6. Nancy Jobe born about 1852, California, Moniteau County, Missouri, died after 1923, probably in Eldon, Miller County, Missouri.

7. Elisha Thomas Jobe, Sr. born between 1854 - 1857, California, Moniteau County, Missouri, died July 10, 1910, Eldon, Miller County, Missouri.

8. M.W. "Fan" Jobe, born between 1857 - 1858, California, Moniteau County, Missouri.

9. Francies "Fannie" Jobe, born about 1862, Moniteau County, Missouri.

Census on Abraham S. Jobe and Clarinda "Charity or Clarissa" Chandler

1840 Cole Co Missouri

Jobe, Abraham Jr. 1 (M) 1810-1820

1 (F) 1810-1820

1 (F) 1820-1825

1 (M) 1825-1830

1 (F) 1825-1830

1 (M) 1830-1835

1 (M) 1835-1840

Census on Abraham S. Jobe and Clarinda "Charity or Clarissa" Chandler

1850 Moniteau Co MO, Dist # 58, 1 Oct 1850, Line 38 F # 547

Job, Abraham 37 M Farmer 600 TN

Clarinda 30 F MO

Logan 11 M MO

Elizabeth 10 F MO

Reuben 3 M MO

Elisha 1 M MO

Census on Abraham S. Jobe and Clarinda "Charity or Clarissa" Chandler

1860 Moniteau Co MO, Twp 45 Range 15, 2 Aug 1860, P O California, line 13 F # 1110

Jobe, Abram 50 M Farmer TN

Clarissa 45 F MO

Logan 22 M MO

Elizabeth 20 F MO

Wm 16 M MO

Reubin 14 M MO

M. E. 12 M MO

Nancy A. 8 F MO

M. W. 6 MO

Census on Abraham S. Jobe and Clarinda "Charity or Clarissa" Chandler

1870 -Moniteau Co, Mo Census - Walker Township

JOB, A. S. 63 TN -Abraham S. Jobe

C (f) 54 MO -Clarinda Chandler

MAUS?, E (f) 28 MO "Domestic"

W (m) 26 MO "Laborer"

R (m) 21 MO

1880 -Moniteau Co, Missouri Census page 15, #140

Abraham JOBE 73 TN TN TN

Clerenda 69 MO TN TN -nee Chandler

Reuben 28 MO TN Mo

Nancy A. 25 MO TN MO

Thomas 22 MO TN MO

Fannie 18 MO TN MO

William BIRDSONG 3 MO TN MO -grandson

CHAPTER SIX

SIXTH GENERATION

JOHN BIRDSONG & MARIE WOOD
Includes related families the Wood & Dobson

JOHN P BIRDSONG (JOHN [I], JOHN [II], WILLIAM, SR., [III], WILLIAM, JR. [IV], PETER [V])

John Birdsong born 24 August 1882 in Moniteau, Missouri, son of Peter Wood Birdsong and Elizabeth Jobe; died 1 September 1966 in Kansas City, Missouri. John married **Marie Wood** born 6 March 1901 in Eldon, Missouri, daughter of Marion Wood & Lillian Dobson; died 31 January 1941 in Kansas City, Kansas.

Children of the marriage:

1. Harry Birdsong, born about 1919 in Moniteau County, Missouri; died Dec 1982 in Sacramento, Califorina.

2. Violet Birdsong, born about 1921 in Moniteau County, Missouri; died 2009 in Kansas City, Kansas.

3. Floyd Birdsong, born about 1923 in Kansas City, Kansas; died 5 July 2000 in Wyandotte, Ottawa, Oklahoma.

4. Fern Lula Birdsong, born about 1925 in Kansas City, Kansas

5. Elena Birdsong, born about 1927 in Kansas City, Kansas

6. Eloise Birdsong, born about 1929 in Kansas City, Kansas; died 27 August 1976 in Arkansas.

7. **John Patrick Birdsong**, born 25 February 1931 in Kansas City, Kansas, died 15 December 1988 Kansas City, Kansas.

8. Eugene Birdsong, born 15 October 1932 in Kanas City, Kansas; died 3 June 2000 Gridley, California.

9. David Birdsong, born about 1935 in Kansas City, Kansas; died in 2000.

10. Geraldine Birdsong, born about 1937 in Kansas City, Kansas; died in 2007, Kansas City, Kansas.

11. Gerry Birdsong, born about 1937 in Kansas City, Kansas; died about 1937 in Kansas City, Kansas.

John & Marie married in Moniteau County, Missouri and until abt 1921 and then moved to Kansas City, Missouri. John was 20 years Marie's senior. John & Marie lived in and around Eldon, Missouri and moved to the Kansas City, Missouri after the birth of their first two children. They then moved to Kansas City, Kansas across the river in a neighborhood called Armourdale. The lived in a small home with as they grew their family. Marie's parents also moved to Kansas City, Kansas.

John's occupation is unknown and Marie was a homemaker. Marie Wood was the daughter of Marion and Lillian V. Dobson

Marie died at the age of 39 years ole, and was buried on 3 Feb 1941 in Kansas City, Wyandotte County, Kansas.

Photo of John Birdsong & Marie (Wood) Birdsong

John & Marie Birdsong's children's known health history:

Harry Birdsong was born in 1919. Harry died of a heart attack, he was only 22 years old at his mother's death.

Violet Birdsong was born in 1921, died in 2009 from lung cancer, age at mother's death 20 years old.

Floyd Birdsong was born in 1923, Floyd had complication of diabetes, age at mother's death 18 years old.

Fern (Lula) Birdsong was born in 1925, MIA age at mother's death 16 years old. Last place heard from her was when she was in St. Louis.

Elena (Helena) Birdsong was born in 1927, died of cirrhosis of the liver, age at mother's death 14 years old.

Eloise (Goldie O) Birdsong was born in 1929, died August 27th 1976 of breast cancer, age at mother's death 12 years old.

John Patrick Birdsong was born February 25th 1931 died December 15th 1988 of colon cancer, age at mother's death 10 years old.

Eugene Birdsong was born in 1933. Had complications from diabetes. Age at mother's death 8 years old.

David Birdsong was born in 1935. Age at mother's death 6 years old.

Geraldine Birdsong was born in 1937, died in 2007 buried in Kansas City, Ks of complications of diabetes. Breast cancer survivor, age at mother's death 4 years old.

Gerald Birdsong was born in 1937, died in 1937 from whooping cough, and was buried in 1937.

After Marie (Wood) Birdsong death, her children had to take care of themselves until the state stepped in and the story goes something like this Harry, Violet, Floyd & Fern were old enough to live independently.

Photo of Harry Birdsong

Photo includes Elena, Eloise, Geraldine & Betty Sue

After Marie (Wood) Birdsong death, her children had to take care of themselves until the state stepped in and the story goes something like this Harry, Violet, Floyd & Fern were old enough to live independently. John & Eugene lived in the St John's Orphanage. David & Geraldine was put into foster care and later adopted by 'Frank X"

John & Eugene story by St John's Orphanage Sisters

St Johns Orphanage

In 1918, an influenza epidemic raged throughout the United States. St. John the Baptist Parish recorded 51 deaths that year and 71 in 1919. Many children of the parish were left without one or both parents. Msgr. Martin D. Krmpotic, Pastor of St.John's was determined to remedy this situation. He asked the Sisters of St.Fransis of Christ the King to open an orphanage. Mr. John McFadden a neighbor of Msgr. Krmpotic expressed his desire to sell his residence, located north of the parish house.

On August 15, 1919, Sister Mary Bonaventure, the superior, visited the McFadden home and purchased it for $15,400. The Sisters supplied the $3,000 down payment and the sum of $12,400 was raised in the parish. It was decided that the orphanage was to open to the children of all nationalities, creeds and races. Along with the sheltered care for the children, the Sisters operated a day care and nursery school program. Within a few years there was a great increase in the number of orphans. Over the course of eight years, four additions were made to the original house but always leaving the main facade and ornate interiors intact.

By 1931, the orphanage was caring for 68 children. In 1940, the orphanage received its first license from the State Board of health and was authorized to care for 70 children. In 1950's, the Sisters started attending workshops on nursery care and become caseworkers. The Orphanage was changing.

The Orphanage operated through the Catholic Charities of the Archdioceses of Kansas City, Kansas, during the 1960's. At that point they cared for only 35 children. In 1973, the name was changed to St. John Children's home. During the 1970's and 1980's the focus changed from a children's home to a long-term residential treatment facility.

In 1988, the Sisters closed the Home. Thru its lifetime the orphanage cared for more then 3,000 children who called it "Home".

In 1996, my research took me searching for the Sisters at the St John's Orphanage now a museum. St John's gave me the number to the Sister's retirement home. Sister Barbara answered; I shared the Birdsong story and explained how it was so sad that my father had to be raised in an Orphanage. She too was raised there and they were always good to her. After hanging up, I felt bad and called back to apologize. She said it did not offend and she was glad I called, because some of the sisters had remembered my dad.

First, I spoke with Sister Claire a teacher, she said dad was a good child always wanted to pitch in and help. She remembered Eugene and Geraldine. She said that dad was there for about 7 years, then his older sister (Violet) came and took the entire kids home with her. Sister Benedict got on the phone and shared a story about the boys going to dinner with Father. The restaurant owner mentioned it was nice that the boys cleaned up after their selves and how he wished all customers did that. Sister Benedict said; "She knows dad is in heaven with our Lord, she could feel it. She always prayed for him and he is smiling down on us for trying to figure out more about his past. It hurt him too much to talk about it. Sister Benedict was the house keeper and barber for Eugene and John Patrick Birdsong. She talked about how dependable the boys were and how it was incredible that they carried that throughout their lives.

Sister Ester, remembered Eugene really well and that the boys were very pleasant. Sister Theodore shared dad came for a visit and he was doing really well and turned out nicely but Eugene had not been doing to good. She always' liked it when they came to visit her. I received a letter short time after speaking to the sisters it's located under

St John's Sisters letter

December 1, 1996

Dear Cheryl,

I am one of the Sisters who lived at St. John's at the time your father John and your uncle Eugene were brought to St. John's Home. As you must know their mother died of cancer and the boys needed care.

John and Eugene were well liked by their teachers, classmates and by their "housemother". Both were willing to help - especially John. John became attached to one of the Sisters who worked in the kitchen and if we wanted to find John we didn't have to look far.. he was with Sr. Asumpta giving her a helping hand and pouring out his heart to her. John worked hard in school and there were no complaints that I ever heard as far as his teachers were concerned. All in all he was a very good boy.

The last time I saw John was some years later when I was again assigned to the Home. He dropped by for a visit and he was now a young man of about eighteen. He said things were fine with him but he did worry about Eugene who was having some problems.

I wish I could tell you nore but I was sent
to another school while John and Eugene
were still at St. John's.

I hope this little bit of information will be
of some help. The family background was not d
discussed - all I know is that their mother died
and the boys needed care. Just tell your
children that your dad was a fine man.

I am enclosing a post card picturing St. John;s
Home where your father lived for some years.
The original part of the house was a mansion
and wings were added on to accommodate all
the Sisters who lived there - the school
sisters, the housemothers, the working staff
and the children. The Home is now a
cultural center and a museum. Perhaps some
day you might want to visit .

The Christmas season is here, so let me wish
you and your family a Blessed Christmas.

                Sincerely yours,

                Sister Theodora

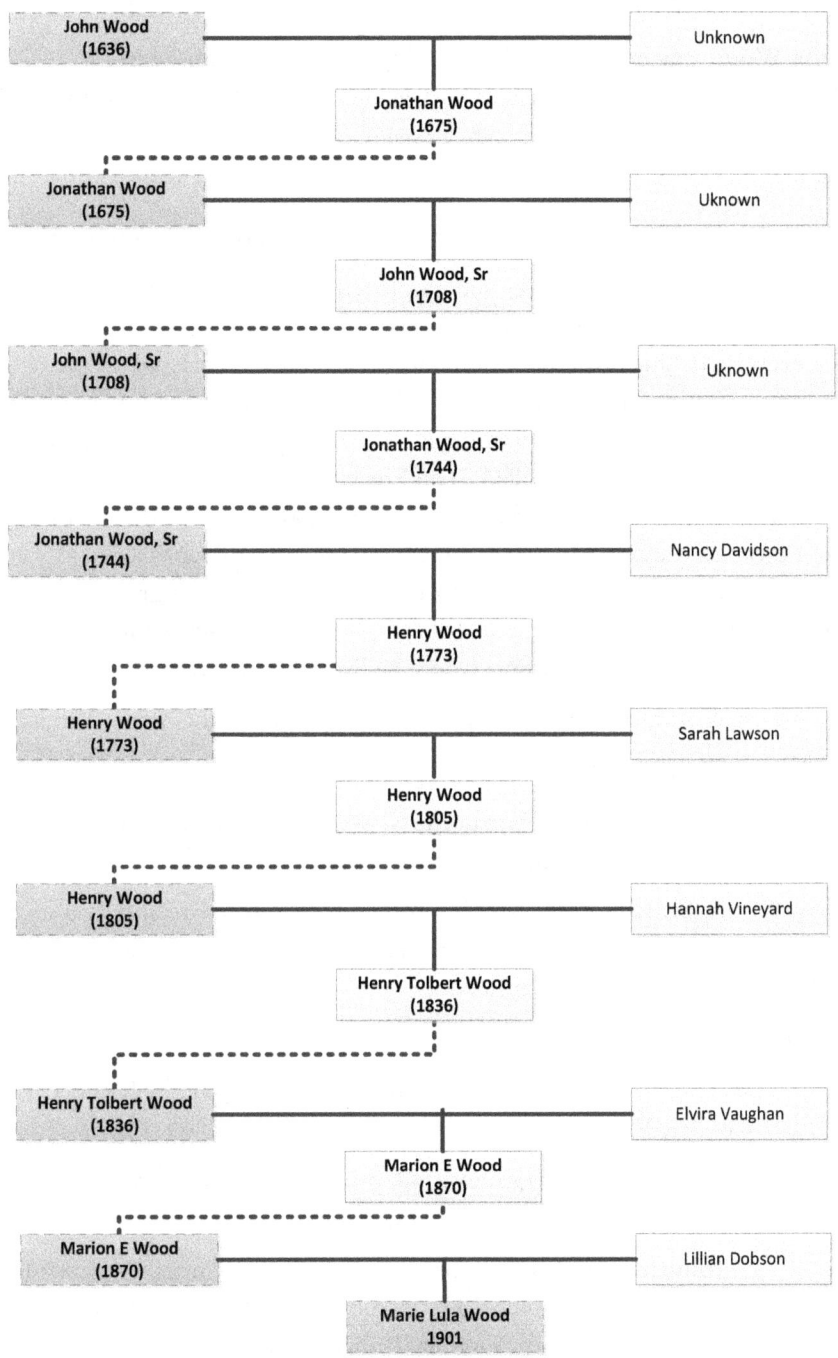

THE ANCESTRY OF MARIE WOOD, WIFE OF JOHN P BIRDSONG (1882)

John Wood was born about 1636 in England and died about in Westmoreland County, Virginia, He was married in 1662 in Westmoreland County, Virginia.

Children of John Wood are:

    1. **Jonathan Wood**, born in 1675 in Westmoreland County, Virginia.

John was educated as a lawyer and employed by London capitalists to locate lands for them in the Colony of Virginia. He was also a good surveyor and the exercise of this profession gave him an accurate knowledge of the country. After completing the surveys for his London employers, he decided to live in Virginia. He moved there in 1655 and settled on the south side of the Potomac, in what was called "The Freshes." He took out patents for several valuable tracts of land in that section: 1,000 acres on the south side of the Potomac granted on January 14, 1656, one grant of 1,200 acres in Northumberland County dated October 12, 1658 and a last grant dated March 4, 1662. In about the year 1662, he married and settled in Westmoreland County, Virginia where he lived until his death.

Jonathan Wood, (John[1]) born in 1675 in Westmoreland County, Virginia.

Children of Jonathan Wood are:

    1. **John Wood, Sr.** born in 1708 Westmoreland County, Virginia; died 1770 Loudoun County, Virginia.

John Wood, Sr. (Jonathan[2],John[1]), born in 1708 Westmoreland County, Virginia; died 1770 Loudoun County, Virginia. He probably married in 1738 in Westmoreland County, Virginia.

Children of John Wood, Sr. are:

    1. Isaac Wood born in 1742, probably near, Potomac River, Loudoun County, Virginia; died probably, Pennsylvania.

    2. John Wood, Jr. born in 1740, probably near, Potomac River, Loudoun County; died probably in New York.

    3. **Jonathan Wood, Sr.** born in 1744, probably near, Potomac River, Loudoun County, died 13 November 1804 Near, Big Moccasin Creek, Scott County, Virginia. Burial in the Jonathan Wood Cemetery, Near, Fort Houston State Marker, Scott County, Virginia.

John was born in Westmoreland County, Virginia in 1708. Soon after his marriage he settled in Loudoun County, Virginia near where Leesburg now stands. Here he accumulated a large estate for that day but for some reason his descendants did not long enjoy possession of it. He had three sons: Isaac, John, and Jonathan. On the first two sons, one settled in Pennsylvania and the other settled in New York. The youngest son, Jonathan, remained at the paternal

Jonathan Wood, Sr. (John^3,Jonathan^2,John^1) born in 1744, probably near, Potomac River, Loudoun County, died 13 November1804 Near, Big Moccasin Creek, Scott County, Virginia, USA. He married **Nancy Davidson** in 1767 in Loudoun County, Virginia.

The burial Buried at the Jonathan Wood Cemetery, Near, Fort Houston State Marker, Scott County, Virginia, USA.

Children of John Wood, Sr. and Nancy Davidson:

> 1. Jonathan Wood, Jr. born 23 April 1778 in Scott County, Virginia; died 9 April 1848 in Scott County, Virginia. Buried at the Jonathan Wood Cemetery, Near, Fort Houston State Marker, Scott County, Virginia.

> 2. Mary Jane Wood, born 1 January 1780 in Moccasin Creek, Scott County, Virginia; died 8 December 1827.

> 3. **Henry Wood,** born 18 May 1773 near, Fort Houston, on, Big Moccasin Creek, Scott County, Virginia, USA; died 4 February 1859 Big Moccasin Creek, Scott County, Virginia, USA buried Mount View School House Cemetery, Scott County, Virginia.

> 4. John Wood born 25 March 1771 Big Moccasin Creek, Scott County, Virginia; died 29 December 1821 Scott County, Virginia.

The Jonathan Wood Cemetery is located on Route #613 in Scott County, Virginia. From gate City, go 6.6 miles to Route 613 and go 3.4 miles to the Warren Stallard place on the left side of the road. This is past the Fort Houston State Marker. The Stallard house is white block and the cemetery is on the hill to the left as you face it. The cemetery is about 70 feet by 110 feet with a chain link fence. Source: Thomas B. and Yvonne Wood Hamrick.

The original land that James Osborn and Jonathan Wood Sr obtained is adjacent to the parcel belonging to William Houston where he built his fort.

Jonathan Wood was born near the Potomac River in eastern Virginia. He married the widow Osborn in 1767.

Nancy Davidson's parents lived somewhere on the South Branch of the Potomac River. At the age of 18, Nancy married Solomon Osborn. They had a son named James. A short time after their marriage the Indians made a raid on the settlement where they lived, and in the encounter her husband was killed (Another source has Solomon killed while on a hunting trip in Rowan County, North Carolina). This terrible circumstance along with the other Indian encounters must have made a great impression on her, for when her mind was enfeebled with old age and her grandchildren or great-grandchildren would go to her home on a visit, she would ask them if they had seen any Indians. She would ask this in a whisper, as if she was fearful that the savages were lurking near the house.

About two years after the death of Solomon Osborn, Jonathan Wood became acquainted with this young widow, and was at once enamored of her. In due time they were married. In about the year 1770 Jonathan with his wife and step-son, James Osborn, immigrated to southwest Virginia and located on Big Moccasin Creek, within the present limits of Scott County. (Originally Russell County) Big Moccasin Creek, it is said, was so named because early explorers, on first coming to the creek, found many tracks made in the soft mud of its banks by Indians who wore moccasins. Judge M. B. Wood, in his book "History Of The Wood Family In Virginia", attributes the naming of the creek to Daniel Boone and his companions, who came through Big Moccasin Gap in 1769.

Jonathan Wood was one of the earliest settlers in Big Moccasin Valley near Fort Houston where he went for safety in time of threatened Indian attack. One hundred, eighty-five acres were surveyed for him December 15, 1774. His home was built on the site known today as the Skillern Wood Farm.

Several stories are told about Jonathan in the History of Scott County: A three-day Indian siege was in progress, and one of the men determined to go home for some purpose. He had proceeded but a short distance from the fort gate when he was fired on by the Indians and mortally wounded. Seeing this, Jonathan Wood, in great danger to his own life, rushed out to the rescue of his wounded neighbor. Several shots were fired at him but fortunately none of them struck him. Jonathan succeeded in bringing the wounded man into the fort although the man died that night.

At another time the Indians made a raid into the settlement of Fort Houston. By this time, Jonathan Wood had built a very large smokehouse upon which he had placed a round roof. The roof gave the building a peculiar and striking appearance which at once attracted the attention of the Indians. Observing it curiously from a distance they fired several shots into it. But soon departed without doing any damage whatever. However, the smokehouse seemed to have lost its novelty, for the next time the Indians came they burned Jonathan's dwelling and all of its contents.

On still another occasion, Indians came to his home. The only ones at home were Nancy and a Negro slave who had only recently been imported from Africa. The slave, who was frightened, sat on the fence making queer gestures and jabbering his unintelligible language. For whatever reason, the Indians went away without attacking or doing any other damage. This was the last visit of the Indians to the neighborhood of Fort Houston.

Jonathan Wood's name appears on a list of Botetourt County Militia, in Captain Mills' Company, the 56th district.

Jonathan Wood was a soldier in the Revolution. He was present at, and participated in, the battle of King's Mountain fought on October 7, 1780 in Tryon County in the western part of North Carolina. The British were totally routed and their commander, Colonel Ferguson, was killed. Jonathan always believed that he fired the fatal shot at Colonel Ferguson in that battle. It is said that standing by his horse, and resting his gun upon the saddle, he fired seven times taking deliberate aim each time. He had a bearskin cover for his saddle and near the close of the battle one of the enemy's bullets struck the bearskin close to his head, throwing hair and dust into his eyes. Thus blinded, he stumbled and fell. It was reported by some of his comrades who preceded him on their return home, that he had been killed in battle. When he returned home a few days later, he was asked where he had been. He replied, "I decided to do some hunting on the way home." Upon the disbandment of the soldiers after the war he returned to his home, where he continued to live in undisturbed peace and happiness for the remainder of his life. He devoted his time to the cultivation of his farm. He gave his children the best education that could then be obtained in this new and unsettled country. They did not receive a classic education, but learned the common English branches. This procured for them the notoriety of being fine scholars in that age and country.

Jonathan joined the Methodist Church a short time before his death, and gave evidence of his hopes of happiness in the future state. He died at his home on Big Moccasin Creek. His personal estate was appraised on January 25, 1805 and amounted to $3,568.22 which was a large sum of money at that time for this new country. His wife Nancy survived him more than twenty years. They are buried in the oldest cemetery in the Wood community of Scott County, Virginia. It is located one half mile northeast from the Fort Houston historical marker. This was taken from the book, Scott County, Virginia and its people 1814-1991. It was one of those created by the county. "Following William Houston into Moccasin Valley was Jonathan Wood who came from Loudon County, Virginia, and his brother-in-law James Davidson."

Henry Wood, (Jonathan[4],John[3],Jonathan[2],John[1]) born 18 May 1773 near, Fort Houston, on, Big Moccasin Creek, Scott County, Virginia, USA; died 4 February 1859 Big Moccasin Creek, Scott County, Virginia, USA buried Mount View School House Cemetery, Scott County, Virginia. He married Sarah Sally Lawson 14 August 1794 Scott County, Virginia

Children of Henry Wood, and Sarah Sally Lawson:

> 1. Elizabeth Wood born 27 January 1797 Moccasin Creek, Scott County, Virginia; died 18 December 1882 Scott County, Virginia.
>
> 2. Nancy Wood born 20 July 1795 Moccasin Creek, Scott County, Virginia; died 12 May 1797 Scott County, Virginia.
>
> 3. Mary Polly Wood born 19 February 1799 Moccasin Creek, Scott County, Virginia; died 3 December 1837 Hawkins County, Tennessee.
>
> 4. James Osborn Wood born 13 December 1806 Near, Fort Houston, On, Big Moccasin Creek, Scott County, Virginia; died 22 July 1874 Estillville, Scott County, Virginia.
>
> 5. William Milligan Wood born 18 April 1803 Moccasin Creek, Scott County, Virginia; died 9 October 1881 Scott County, Virginia.
>
> 6. Jonathan R Wood born 16 February 1801 Moccasin Creek, Scott County, Virginia; died 25 February 1885 Scott County, Virginia.
>
> 7. **Henry Wood** born 7 January 1805 Moccasin Creek, Scott County, Virginia; died 19 March 1888 Miller County, Missouri buried at Tolwood Cemetery, Eldon, Miller County, Missouri.

The place where Henry was born is now in Scott County, Virginia, which was formed by portions of Russell, Washington, and Lee Counties in 1814. Henry was born on May 18, 1773 Near, Fort Houston, on, Big Moccasin Creek, Russell County, Virginia.

Henry Wood and five generations of his family are buried about three miles East of Gate City, Virginia, near Moore Memorial Church.

Here is a quote from a different book: "Henry Wood, another son of Jonathan Wood I, represented Russell County, Virginia in the legislature, and after the formation of Scott County was also one of the early sheriff's, and one of its gentlemen justices. Clintwood, Virginia, the county seat of Dickerson County, was named for a grandson of Henry Wood, Major Henry Clinton Wood." Henry Wood and Sallie Lawson settled in Moccasin Valley, Scott County, Virginia, about three miles East of Gate City. Ref. 1 page 80.

1820 Scott County Virginia Census: [Name of Head of Household - free white males 0-10, 10-16, 16-18, 16-26, 26-45, over 45, free white females 0-10, 10-16, 16-26, over 45]

Henry Wood (Henry^5,Jonathan^4,John^3,Jonathan^2,John^1) born 7 January 1805 Moccasin Creek, Scott County, Virginia; died 19 March 1888 Miller County, Missouri buried at Tolwood Cemetery, Eldon, Miller County, Missouri. He married **Hannah Vineyard** on 1 May 1831 Scott County, Virginia.

Children of Henry Wood and Hannah Vineyard:

1. Mary Wood born 18 March 1838 Scott County, Virginia; died 9 February 1909 Pocahontas, Randolph County, Arkansas.

2. George V Wood born 1834 Scott County, Virginia; died 1884 Miller County, Missouri.

3. Emily Wood born 1841 Scott County, Virginia; 18 October 1890 Missouri.

4. Sarah C Wood born 1832 Scott County, Virginia.

5. Margaret Wood born April 1843 Scott County, Virginia.

6. **Henry Tolbert Wood** born 28 July 1836 Scott County, Virginia; died 15 September 1902 Eldon, Miller County, Missouri buried at Tolwood Cemetery, Eldon, Miller County, Missouri.

Henry Tolber Wood (Henry[6],Henry[5],Jonathan[4],John[3],Jonathan[2],John[1]) born 28 July 1836 Scott County, Virginia; died 15 September 1902 Eldon, Miller County, Missouri buried at Tolwood Cemetery, Eldon, Miller County, Missouri. He married **Elvira Jane Vaughan** 27 August 1854 Eldon, Miller County, Missouri.

Children of Henry Wood and Elvira Jane Vaughan:

    1. Sarah Jane Wood born 15 October 1855, Miller County, Missouri; died 26 November 1929 Miller County, Missouri.

    2. Elisha Henry Wood born January 1860, Eldon, Miller County, Missouri; died 24 December 1937 Miller County, Missouri.

    3. James Sterling Wood born 6 April 1862, Miller County, Missouri; died 24 June 1948 Miller County, Missouri.

    4. Tabitha C Wood born 1857 Eldon, Miller County, Missouri; died 1901.

    5. Henrietta Wood born 17 July 1866 Eldon, Miller County, Missouri; died 17 July 1866 Eldon, Miller County, Missouri.

    6. Emily Elizabeth Wood born 11 March 1864 Bagnell, Miller County, Missouri; died 23 April 1935 Equality Township, Miller County, Missouri.

    7. Anna M Wood born 1867 Miller County, Missouri; died 1949 Miller County, Missouri

    8. William Wesley Wood born 1868 Miller County, Missouri; died 1920.

    9. **Marion E Wood** born January 1870 Miller County, Missouri; died 1920.

Henry Tolbert Wood, George V. Wood, and Mary Smith Wood were of Henry Wood, Jr. and his wife, Hannah (Vineyard) Wood. This family came from Scott County, Virginia and were in Miller County when the 1850 census was taken. Henry Tolbert and his brother George V. Wood served in the Civil War in 1861 with Alvin Kemp Vaughan who married in 1862 to Mary Smith Wood. As Confederate soldiers, they served with Company A, Col. William Brown's Regiment, Calvery, Missouri State Guard Volunteers. Company A was also known as Captain James Johnson's Osage Tigers.

Henry Tolbert's signature is on his father's, Henry Wood, Jr's Probate Record, File Number 77, of Miller County, Missouri. The document was dated October 18, 1890. Henry Tolbert signed, "H. T. Wood." At the top of the document Henry Tolbert's name was written, "Henry T. Wood."

A newspaper article entitled, "Tol Wood Family Meets" dated a few days after May 31, 1981, tells of Tol Wood's death. It reads, "He died on Sept. 15, 1902, when a threshing machine fell on him on a hill side, crushing his body and breaking his leg." The article in its entirety follows... From a newspaper clipping sent by Ezma Maust to my mother, Imogene Smith, it reads: "Tol Wood descendants and friends gathered for a family reunion of Sunday, May 31, in Eldon at the Rock Island Park.

In the afternoon Mrs. George Heldstab read aloud some interesting family history: Tol Wood was born July 23, 1836. He came from here. He started several schools and churches in this area. He was the first one to bring a threshing machine to this area and also was the first with a steamer. He died on Sept. 15, 1902, when a threshing machine fell on a hillside, crushing his body and breaking his leg.

Marion E Wood (Henry[7]Henry[6]Henry[5]Jonathan[4]John[3]Jonathan[2]John[1]) born January 1870 Miller County, Missouri; died 1920. Marion married **Lillian V Dobson** 5 January 1893 Miller County, Missouri. Lillian is the daughter of Thomas Dobson and Nancy Carol.

Children of Marion E Wood and Lillian Dobson:

    1. Lena V Wood born in 1895 in Eldon, Miller County, Missouri.

    2. Willard R Wood born in 1896 in Eldon, Miller County, Missouri.

    3. **Marie Lula Wood** born 6 March 1901 Eldon, Miller County, Missouri; died 31 January 1941 Kansas City, Wyandotte County, Kansas.

    4. Roy M. wood born in 1900 Eldon, Miller County, Missouri.

Photo of Marion Wood and Lillian (Dobson) Wood

CHAPTER SEVEN

SEVENTH GENERATION

JOHN BIRDSONG & DELLA RHYNERSON
Includes related families the Rhynerson, Bennett, & Anderson

John Patrick Birdsong (John [I], John [II], William, Sr., [III], William, Jr. [IV], Peter [V], John [VI]) born 25th February 1931 Kansas City, Kansas; died 15th December 1988 in Kansas City, Kansas married **Della Lorene Rhynerson** born 5 February 1936 Lynn County, Kansas; died 17 August 2009 Shawnee Kansas. She was the daughter of Harry Rhynerson and Vera Bennett.

Children of John Birdsong and Della Rhynerson:

    1. John Michael Birdsong, born in Kansas City, Kansas.

    2. Teresa Birdsong, born in Kansas City, Kansas.

    3. James Birdsong, born in Kansas City, Kansas.

    4. Jeffrey Birdsong, born in Kansas City, Kansas.

    5. Jerome Birdsong, born in Kansas City, Kansas.

    6. Joseph Birdsong, born in Kansas City, Kansas.

    7. Johanna Birdsong, born in Kansas City, Kansas.

    8. Cheryl Birdsong, born in Kansas City, Kansas.

John worked at Colgate Palmolive and at retirement was a boiler room fireman or better known as an environmental engineer Della was a home maker and volunteered at St John's to pay for part of the kid's tuition at for school. She also ironed clothes for spending money for the kid's lunches.

John Patrick Birdsong's Story

Photo left to right: Jim Waldo, Paul Briggs & John Patrick Birdsong

John born in Kansas City, Kansas and mother passed at the age of 40 years old. John was only 10 years old and went to live at Saint John's Orphanage. His mother died of cervical cancer and he had 11 siblings. Father abandon the children and the state came in and took the children after they was caught stealing from the local grocery store to feed their siblings.

John Birdsong, Jr passed in 1988 and at that time all I knew was the names of his sibling's and that his mother passed away when he was only 10 years old. At that time he went to live at Saint John's Orphanage with his brother Eugene. His two younger siblings, David & Geraldine were adopted by a man named "Frank Mae" and that his other siblings Harry, Violet, Floyd, Lula, Elena, Eloise lived on their own. I had so many unanswered questions like, "Why didn't his father (John, Sr.) raise the kids.

The story goes something like this; Marie (Wood) Birdsong passed of cancer in 1941 at 40 years old. The eleven kids were trying to care for themselves without much food or supervision and their sister Lula called social services. This is when social services got involved and took the kids under the age of

18 and placed them in both foster care and the orphanage.

John Birdsong, Jr lived in at St. Johns orphanage from the age 10 years old until he went to the Marine Boot Camp March 4th 1948, only seven days after his 17th birthday and was discharged 3 Mar 1952 (1 year voluntarily extended for service in Korea).

John Patrick Birdsong served in the Korean War he was part of the Inchon landing, the liberation of Seoul and the Chosin Reservoir Campaign. It is said that service man died from being frozen more than by combat. The marines are known for this War because they did not leave any of their members behind even though the weather conditions. They were also heavily outnumbered by the Koren's and surrounded.

John Patrick Birdsong received an Honorable Discharge after three years of service he decided to go back for one more year. Although, John never mentioned the challenges he faced during his time in Korea we do not have to look far to better understand what our service man and women went through. It was one of the most recognized wars in the United States history.

John Patrick Birdsong participated in the decisive Inchon amphibious landing. As well as, the liberation of Seoul, which is now the capital of modern South Korea. He also, participated in the Chosin campaign, known as the Frozen Chosin.

John Patrick Birdsong was a member of the 1st Marine Division was the most decorated military units in the Korean War.

Some additional notes about the 1st Marine Division in the Chosin campaign:

"On 25 June 1950, eight divisions of the North Korean People's Army, equipped with Soviet tanks, mobile artillery, and supporting aircraft, crossed the 38th Parallel and invaded the Republic of Korea. On 27 June, the United Nations Security Council proclaimed the North Korea attack a breach of world peace, and requested member nations to assist the Republic of Korea.

On 30 June, President Harry S Truman ordered a naval blockade of the Korean Coast and authorized the Commander in Chief Far East, General Douglas A. MacArthur, to send U.S. ground troops into Korea. On 2 July, General MacArthur requested that a regimental combat team be deployed to the Far East. The Joint Chiefs approved his request on the following day.

On 7 July, the 1st Provisional Marine Brigade was activated at Marine Corps

Base, Camp Pendleton, California. The primary core of the ground element was the 5th Marines, while Marine Aircraft Group 33 constituted the air element of the brigade. Just five days after its activation, the 1st Provisional Marine Brigade, with a strength of 6,500, sailed on 12 July from San Diego, California, enroute to Pusan, Korea.

The first elements of the brigade came ashore at Pusan on 2 August. The next day, the first Marine aviation mission against North Korea was flown from the USS Sicily by gull-winged Corsairs of Marine fighting Squadron 214 (VMF-214) in a raid against North Korean installations. They were subsequently joined by fighter-bomber from Marine Fighting squadron 323 (VMF-323), flying from the USS Badoeng Strait, as the two squadrons harassed enemy positions and installations. Marine ground forces first engaged the enemy on 7 august at Chindong-ni, some miles west of Pusan. In twelve days of hard fighting, the North Koreans were driven back with heavy losses, and the Pusan Perimeter defense was stabilized.

During the grim opening weeks of the Korean War, while American forces fought desperately in defense of the Pusan Perimeter, General MacArthur was already conceiving a bold stroke that would crush the North Korean People's Army. He planned an amphibious assault behind North Korean lines at Inchon, the port for the city of Seoul, and close to both the 38th Parallel and North Korean Army supply lines. The 1st Marine Division would spearhead the assault. The attacking force would have to navigate a narrow channel with swift currents, islands, and coastal defense battery sites. Final approval for the operation, code-named "Chromite," was not given until 8 September.

On 15 September, the 1st Marine Division, under the Command of Major General Oliver P. Smith led the first major United Nations strike in North Korean territory, with an amphibious assault at Inchon that completely caught the enemy by surprise. In five days of textbook campaigning, the division closed on the approaches of Seoul, the South Korean Capital, and in house to house fighting, wrested the city from its communist's captors on 27 September. On 7 October 1950, with North Korean forces in fully retreat, the Inchon-Seoul campaign was formally declared closed.

In late October, the 1st Marine Division made an unopposed landing at Wonsan, on the East Coast, which initiated U.N. operations in northeast Korea, and established security for the operations in northeast Korea, and established security for the port Wonsan. The division was then ordered to advance northwest of Hungnam along a mountain road to the Chosin Reservoir, the site of an important hydroelectric plant; the Marines would then advance to the Yalu River and the border between North Korea and the People's Republic of China.

Despite intelligence in early November that Chinese Communists forces were massing in force across the Yalu River, the 1st Marine Division was ordered to continue its progress northwest from Hungnam to the Chosin Reservoir. Elements of the division reached Hagaru-ri, at the southern tip of the Reservoir, on 15 November. The brief autumn weather was almost over, and the temperatures were turning bitterly cold. On 27 November, elements of the Chinese Communists People's Liberation Army struck, eight Chinese divisions charged down from surrounding mountains with the express mission of destroying the 1st Marine Division.

Over the next four weeks, the Chinese and Marine Forces engaged in some of the fiercest fighting of the Korean War. In an epic movement, the 1st Marine Division completed a successful fighting withdrawal through 78 miles of mountain road in northeast Korea that ended in mid-December with the amphibious evacuation of the 4,000 battle casualties, and uncounted numbers of frostbite, Marine air and ground units had inflicted nearly 25,000 casualties on Chinese Communist forces.

During the first three months of 1951, the 1st Marine Division participated in several United Nations offensive operations, first against North Korean guerrillas, and later participating in an advance through the mountain of east-central Korea. From late April to early July, the division took part in the United Nations defense against a Chinese Communist spring offensive, in which the enemy committed almost 500,000 men against U. N. forces. This Chinese offensive ended in mid-May with heavy enemy losses.

The 1st Marine Division then participated in the Eighth Army drive northward past the eastern tip of the Hwachon Reservoir. By 20 June 1951, the division had taken its portion of the X Corps objective, a ridgeline over looking a deep Circular valley in the Korean mountains nicknamed the "Punchbowl." Truce negotiations now began, and the UN forces settled down into a defensive line.

In early September, the division was directed to take the remainder of the

Punchbowl. Hampered by rains, poor roads, and a well-entrenched enemy, the Marines nevertheless gained their initial objectives in hard fighting, when X Corps suspended offensive operations.

The first Marine mass helicopter resupply mission took place during operations at the Punchbowl on 13 September 1951, when Marine Helicopter Transport Squadron 161 successfully executed Operation Windmill I. Eight days later, the same squadron landed 224 Marines of the division reconnaissance company and 17,772 pounds of cargo on an isolated hilltop at the Punchbowl. In November, the squadron would conduct the first frontline relief of a Marine battalion in Operation Switch.

The winter of 1951 found the 1st Marine Division deployed along eleven miles of front just north of the Punchbowl. In mid-March, the division was reassigned from the X Corps' eastern position in Korea, to the I Corps area at the Far Western end of Eighth Army line. On 24 March, the division assumed responsibility for approximately 35 miles of frontline, which Seoul corridor. The pace of the war now slowed, with small, localized actions, replacing the earlier large-scale offensives.

In mid-August 1952, in the first major Marine ground action in western Korea, the 1st Marine Division began its successful defense of Outpost Bunker Hill. Two months later, during the Battle of the "Hook," the division again defended a segment of the United Nations Main Line of Resistance (MLR). A winter lull during January-February 1953 brought some relief to Marines at the front, while cease-fire talks at Panmunjom remained suspended.

The relative quiet on the front was rudely shattered in late March 1953, when Chinese force mounted a massive offensive across the United Nations front line that hit 1st Marine Division outposts in their right sector. On 26 March, enemy forces attacked outposts "Reno," "Vegas," and Carson" (the so-called Nevada Cities campaign), all manned by the 5th Marines. In particularly bitter fighting, Outpost Reno fell to the enemy, but the stubborn 5th Marines maintained control of Outposts Vegas and Carson. Marine casualties totaled over 1,000, with Communist losses at least twice as high.

In late April, truce talks resumed at Panmunjom, which again did not present a renewed outbreak of savage fighting in western Korea, while truce details were worked out by negotiators, communist forces launched a regimental-strength attack against the I corps sector. Heavy fighting took place in the

Nevada Cities and Hook area outposts.

During the first week of July, the command outposts Berlin and East Berlin in the 7th Marines right regimental sector came under attack during the Marines' relief of the US 25th Infantry Division. The Marines did not concede a key terrain, and at 2200 on 27 July, the truce argued out at Panmunjom finally went into effect, ending three years of fighting in Korea.

The price of liberty in human costs is always high, and the Korean War was no exception. Marine causalities totaled over 30,000; just over 4,500 Marines gave their lives in Korea. Forty-two Marines were awarded the Medal of Honor for heroism above and beyond the call of duty in Korea; twenty-seven of these were posthumous. Though sometimes viewed as an "indecisive" conflict, the Marine Corps can truly be proud of its role in stemming the tide of Communist aggression during the Korean War."

President Ronald Reagan said "Some people spend an entire lifetime wondering if they made a difference. The Marines don't have that problem." Another famous quote; "Those that were there will never forget! Those who were not will never know!"

John Patrick Birdsong lived with the pain of the War his entire life. He never forgot even up to just before his death he shared painful memories with his daughter Teresa and wondered if the Lord in Heaven would understand. That speaks volumes of the character have this man. Some would call him "Jr" for his small statue. His five sons thought he was tough on them. He was a stern man to them often good was not good enough when it came to his children.

Yet, John Patrick Birdsong was the best story teller around. Often, he shared "funny" stories to make people laugh yet rarely did he we hear about the horrors he experienced during his time in the Korean War.

John Patrick Birdsong discharge papers stated his rank at discharge was Sergeant and the weapons qualifications "Marksman - M1 Rifle" his specialty was "Rigger". He was also a combat Engineer in the Korean War. He was discharged from the Engineer School Battalion, at Camp Lejeune, NC. Camp Lejeune is known as the world's largest amphibious training base.

After his Honorary Discharge from the service John came back to Kansas City, Kansas to find his missing sister Geraldine Birdsong that was in foster care. Once he found her and learned she had been abused by her foster parents and he managed to remove her from their home. Geraldine moved in with their sister Violet until marrying.

John Patrick Birdsong met Della Rhynerson while she was in the city with her father during a wrestling match. Della's father came to the city to wrestle for money.

John developed colon cancer at the age of 56 years old he was diagnosed with the cancer in July 1988 and passed 6 months later.   John had lost many siblings to cancer and when he was diagnosed with colon cancer he knew death was near and decided not to seek much treatment.

Della Rhynersong's story

Della Rhynerson was a small town girl for the country. She was born in a barn in Linn County, Kansas and raised in LaCygne, Kansas. She went to school at a small school house that had school kindergarten through 8th grade.

Della married John Patrick Birdsong at 17 years old and moved to the city to much her mother's dismay. Della loved her father dearly. Her father would leave for weeks at a time and once came home with a horse for Della. Her father Harry Rhynerson passed of a server heart attack at 56 years old.

Vera Rhynerson (Bennett) born May 28th 1915, married Harry at the age of 18 on May 4th 1933 she was an entrepreneur. She worked in the factory and also had a barn behind her house where she raised rabbits for sale. She also had a large garden of vegetables and fruit trees. She was a Baptist and lived until she was 86 years old.

Della was a home maker and volunteered at St John's to pay for part of the kid's tuition at for school. She also ironed clothes for spending money for the kid's lunches. John worked at Colgate Palmolive and at retirement was a boiler room fireman or better known as an environmental engineer.

Della had had a massive stroke at 71 years of age on her left side of her brain (she surprised the Drs and survived). The stroke compromised her right side she could not form words and she could not eat at first by herself.

Here is the eulogy written by Karla Woodward a minster at the Church of the Resurrection. She was Della's minister later in life.

Photo's of Della (Rhynerson) Birdsong

Reflections of Della (Rhynerson) Birdsong

"For the past two years, I've had the opportunity to visit Della, to get to know her, to witness her great strength and determination. We had wonderful conversations and her smile lit up the room. Family was often with her, and they mirrored all that she was. Della let me know what she liked, and she let me know what she didn't like. At first she moved little, then she moved more, and then she was a bundle of unbridled energy despite a body that didn't always cooperate with her will. It rarely occurred to me that in our many conversations, she didn't verbally speak. She was simply one of those people who had such great presence, such great drive for going forward, that clearly spoken words were simply unnecessary.

As many of Della's children gathered Wednesday to share stories with me, the words to an old poem began playing through my mind. Titled *The Weaving* by Ron Ekloff (adapted), it reads: "On a loom we are created and have our breadth of days. Our web is fashioned by unseen weaver's hands, as deftly spun we become the woof, then the warp, slowly turned into tapestry. The filaments of our lives entwine with each strand touching others. They are of soft wool, hard jute, supple linen, and have a spectrum of color and feel. Amid the rough fibers is a gold thread blended with those of common mettle. Each sees their texture but dimly, for we busy ourselves in being the yarn. Yet, in heaven's time an artful plan is revealed in a fabric woven from laughing hearts and joy; and of sorrow's tears on the humble trail we have trod."

Della's life has been a weaving of simple, rough threads and beautiful golden strands, which today we celebrate as a tapestry of a life well lived.

Her life began as it ended, with a thread of the simple. She was born at home on a farm near Butler, Missouri in a time when enough was as good as a feast. Her parents were hard working and provided a good life for Della and her sister Roberta. The farm formed Della – she loved the outdoors, the nature around her, the bounty of the crops, the animals. She loved to ride horses, fish and go morel mushroom hunting in the spring. She watched the soaring hawks and reveled in their freedom of flight, developing the attitude that nothing could contain her either. She was a tomboy, a "daddy's girl", a young, free spirit.

Photo of Della (Rhynerson) Birdsong

In this simple thread, she learned to rely on what she had and the importance of family and love. She learned well the values of hard work, strength and determination; that you did what you had to do when times were hard.

She began weaving a thread of faith in her tapestry as her family worshipped at their community Baptist church, singing *Amazing Grace* and *Jesus Loves Me*, being baptized into a community of believers; learning of forgiveness and grace, salvation and eternal life.

Della went to a one room school house, but learned all she needed to know. One day when she was 16, she met a kindred spirit who came riding by on his motorcycle.

He had just returned from service in Korea, and a new thread began weaving in Della's life tapestry, that of her husband John. He had grown up in an orphanage, and brought with him the values of discipline and strictness; wanting everything to be "just so". Together they moved to the Kansas City, Kansas area, and wove a life together.

Their family began to grow, and grow, as children John Michael, Teresa, James, Jeffrey, Jerome, Joseph, Joanna and Cheryl wove their threads deep into Della's life. All of you were her love, her focus, her reason for living. It was all about the kids, and Della was described as a "professional mother, grandmother and great-grandmother." She was a very good mother, continuing to make the most from what she had. In addition to John's hard work, 24/7 with lots of coffee I heard, Della also became a provider, ironing and taking in laundry to give her kids the extras she wanted them to have. She hung the ever-present diapers on the line, even when they freeze dried. She became a counselor, apparently with her own "Birdsongology".

But clearly, Della's life was never about what she didn't have. It WAS about the blessings and joy she found everywhere she turned. She loved to read, especially romance novels in later life, and her love of nature continued to weave as she read of the Native Americans and their horses, and watched Animal Planet on television. Every year the family piled into the station wagon and they took off on great adventures seeing the country – viewing the great American landscape in California, Yellowstone and Colorado. Sometimes they'd travel thousands of miles, stopping infrequently – not an easy task I'm sure with eight children in the car, but they didn't often slow down.

Della's thread wove through her children's lives in many ways. She didn't abide by cussing, and many described mouthfuls of soap when they verbally went astray. She modeled faith by converting to her husband's Catholic religion, getting the family up, dressed and to Mass every Sunday morning for years. She taught the older kids how to be parents as they cared for the younger children. When the girls had their own children, Della taught them how to do what they had to do to become parents who fought through adversity.

Della taught her own that children are a gift from God and it's a privilege given to us to raise them.

She coached, watched and taught, managed with firmness, held her children accountable, and helped them grow up right; although apparently she was MUCH easier on the boys than she was on the girls. She rose above the tough times, and taught others how to do that as well.

She was straightforward and loyal. You always knew where you stood. She was independent, trusting, and worked really hard all the time.

Della loved life. She always looked on the bright side and was a good friend. All she had she gave to her kids.

She also gave all she had to others as she wove a thread of mercy into her tapestry. The children described how a train track ran behind their home, and occasionally people who had nothing would come to their door asking for help. Della didn't always have much more, but she never turned anyone away. Despite there being 10 people in a two bedroom house, there was always space on the floor, food, or love to share with those in need.

One of the girls said this in part was because Della believed that you never knew when it was really Jesus who was asking. Ironically enough, the following story was forwarded to me right after the family and I met on Wednesday. It says:

One day Ruth went to her mail box and there was only one letter. She picked it up and looked at it before opening it. There was no stamp, no postmark, only her name and address.

Dear Ruth:

I'm going to be in your neighborhood Saturday afternoon and I'd like to stop by for a visit.   Love Always, Jesus. Her hands were shaking as she placed the letter on the table. "Why would the Lord want to visit me'? I'm nobody special. I don't have anything to offer."

With that thought, Ruth remembered her empty kitchen cabinets. "I really don't have anything to offer. I'll have to run down to the store and buy something for dinner." She reached for her purse and counted out its contents. Five dollars and forty cents.

"Well, I can get some bread and cold cuts, at least." She threw on her coat and hurried out the door.

A loaf of French bread, a half-pound of sliced turkey, and a carton of milk, leaving Ruth with grand total twelve cents to last her until Monday. Nonetheless, she felt good as she headed home, her meager offerings tucked under her arm. "Hey lady, can you help us, lady?"

Ruth had been so absorbed in her dinner plans, she hadn't even noticed two figures huddled in the alleyway. A man and a woman, both of them dressed in little more than rags. "Look lady, I ain't got a job and my wife and I have been living out here on the street. It's getting cold and we're hungry. If you could help us, we'd really appreciate it." They were dirty and they smelled bad. "Sir, I'd like to help you, but I'm a poor woman myself. All I have is a few cold cuts and some bread, and I'm having an important guest for dinner tonight." "Yeah, well okay lady, I understand. Thanks anyway." Ruth said, "Wait! Take this food, I'll figure out something else to serve my guest." She noticed that the woman was shivering and said, "I've got another coat at home. Take this one" and she slipped the jacked over the woman's shoulders.

She was chilled when she reached her front door, and worried too. The Lord was coming to visit and she didn't have anything to offer Him. But then she noticed another envelope in her mailbox. It read, "Dear Ruth: It was so good to see you again. Thank you for the lovely meal. And thank you, too, for the beautiful coat. Love always, Jesus."

Della modeled the thread of generosity, Christian service, and humbleness for others in profound and powerful ways; but perhaps never more than in the past two years. Della began weaving a thread of great physical adversity into her life tapestry; yet as always, she did so with strength, grace and determination. She fought hard to keep going with a joy that was astounding. It was "make it or break it" time, and she made it. She rolled with it as she always had. She never gave up. She fought, and she loved.

This past Saturday, Della began weaving one final thread. This one, as always, was twisted together with God's thread. As I sat at her bedside on Monday, reading scripture, anointing her, and praying with her, I had no doubt whatever that Della's faith was her rock and her salvation. She believed in Christ's love for her, of the place prepared for her in heaven, of forgiveness and grace and God's infinite love. She was not afraid. She often said to her children that she was a simple woman, and probably wouldn't be one that would be right next to Jesus when she saw him face to face. She figured she'd be at the back of the bus, on the back row of God's concert, maybe just getting to see him for a moment. I wonder. We began with the Beatitudes, let's look at them again.

"[3] God blesses those who are poor and realize their need for him, for the Kingdom of Heaven is theirs.

[4] God blesses those who mourn, for they will be comforted.

[5] God blesses those who are humble, for they will inherit the whole earth.

[6] God blesses those who hunger and thirst for justice, for they will be satisfied.

[7] God blesses those who are merciful, for they will be shown mercy.

[8] God blesses those whose hearts are pure, for they will see God.

[9] God blesses those who work for peace, for they will be called the children of God.

[10] God blesses those who are persecuted for doing right, for the Kingdom of Heaven is theirs."

Della embodied each of these blessings. I can imagine God saying right to her, "well done, good and faithful servant; welcome, welcome home."

A beautiful life tapestry, of threads that are woven into each of you, a legacy, a gift, a blessing.

Della's Obituary, in the Kansas City, Star:

Della L. Birdsong, 73, of Shawnee, Kansas passed away on August 17, 2009 at Shawnee Mission Medical Center.

Della was preceded in death by her parents Harry and Vera (Bennett). She is survived by her sister, Roberta Sparks and eight children Mike (Diana Lea) Birdsong, Grapevine, Texas; Terri (Carl Ray) Crump, Lenexa, Kansas; Jim (Gina) Birdsong, Murrieta, California; Jeff Birdsong, Lenexa, Kansas; Jerome

Birdsong, Kansas City, Kansas; Joe Birdsong, Kansas City, Kansas; Johanna (Dan) Dickman, Shawnee, Kansas; Cheryl Birdsong-Dyer (Sean Dyer), Leawood, Kansas;

26 grandchildren:

Bridgett Yeldell, Amy Birdsong, Angie Birdsong, Dana Jones, Meagan Riley, Steven Dickman, Jenna Dickman, Tyler Dickman, Justin Birdsong, Julie Hansett, Bill Hansett, Sarah Birdsong, Nellie Dyer, Webster Dyer Melissa Birdsong, Brett Birdsong, Bambi Birdsong, Brooke Birdsong, Jerome Birdsong, Jessy Birdsong, Samantha Birdsong, Chris Birdsong, Tyler Birdsong, Ashlynn White, Joseph Birdsong, Dylon Birdsong, Niki Birdsong, Brandy Birdsong

31 great-grandchildren:

Aaliyah Yeldell, Dominic Yeldell, Paul Guerrero II, Kaitlyn Birdsong, Alyssa Toth, Tait Torset, Dominick Herrera, Heaven Herrera, Rogelio Herrera, Michael jr Herrera, Marissa Herrera, Kennidy Birdsong, Jayden Hansett, Jordan Hansett, Jeremy Daniels, Jayden Daniels, Delaino Loya, Anthony Loya, Alexis Pena, Juleonna Pena, Amiliyana Birdsong, Alycia Pena, Jerome Birdsong, Jaiden Birdsong, Jasmine Birdsong, Jessy Birdsong, Jerome Birdsong, Joseph James Birdsong, Joseph David Birdsong, Jessalyn Birdsong, Haylee Birdsong; and nieces and nephews.

Poem Della's granddaughter wrote for her eulogy:

"When you first think of Della Birdsong you think of a strong, loved, unique, wise, comforting, honest, gorgeous, independent, loving, amazing woman. Della Birdsong has been through a lot in her life, and through all of it she's been amazingly strong, some of us just don't understand how she does it. She always had a way to amaze us all, many of her family members looked up to her, and I'm not talking about a small family. Della has a very big family that loves her and adores her. It's funny because she had 2 things she loved to do, playing solitaire and reading, and she would do both a lot. Della was always a very comforting person; she always had a way to make you feel loved. No matter what she always gave the best advice, and would always tell you her honest opinion. She also had something you can't find in many places these days, she wasn't judgmental, and no matter what you've done she would make you feel equal to everyone else. She was very beautiful and gorgeous inside and out, honestly I don't think anyone will ever fill her shoes because she was just that great. Even in heaven I believe she'll be sharing her greatness forever and ever. You will be loved and missed. God bless.

"Authored by: Sarah Jade Birdsong"

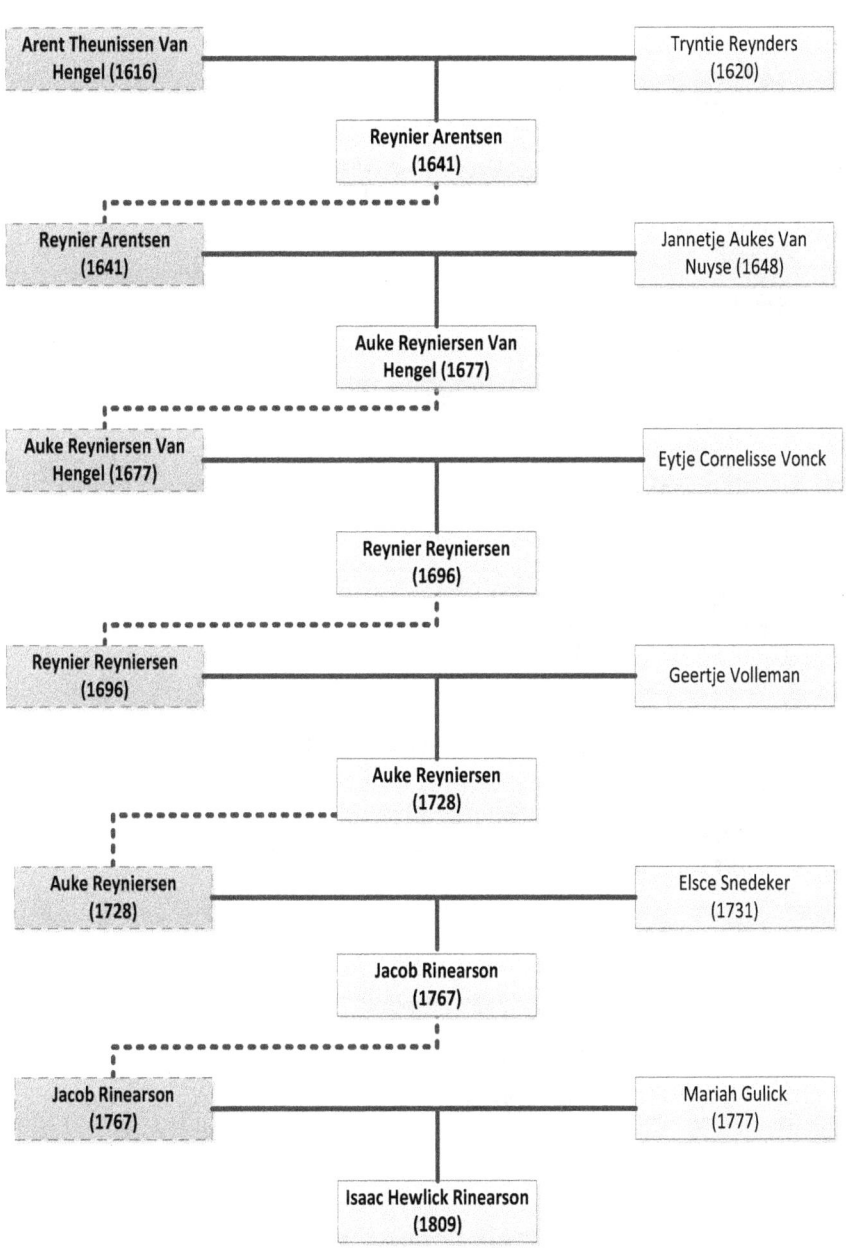

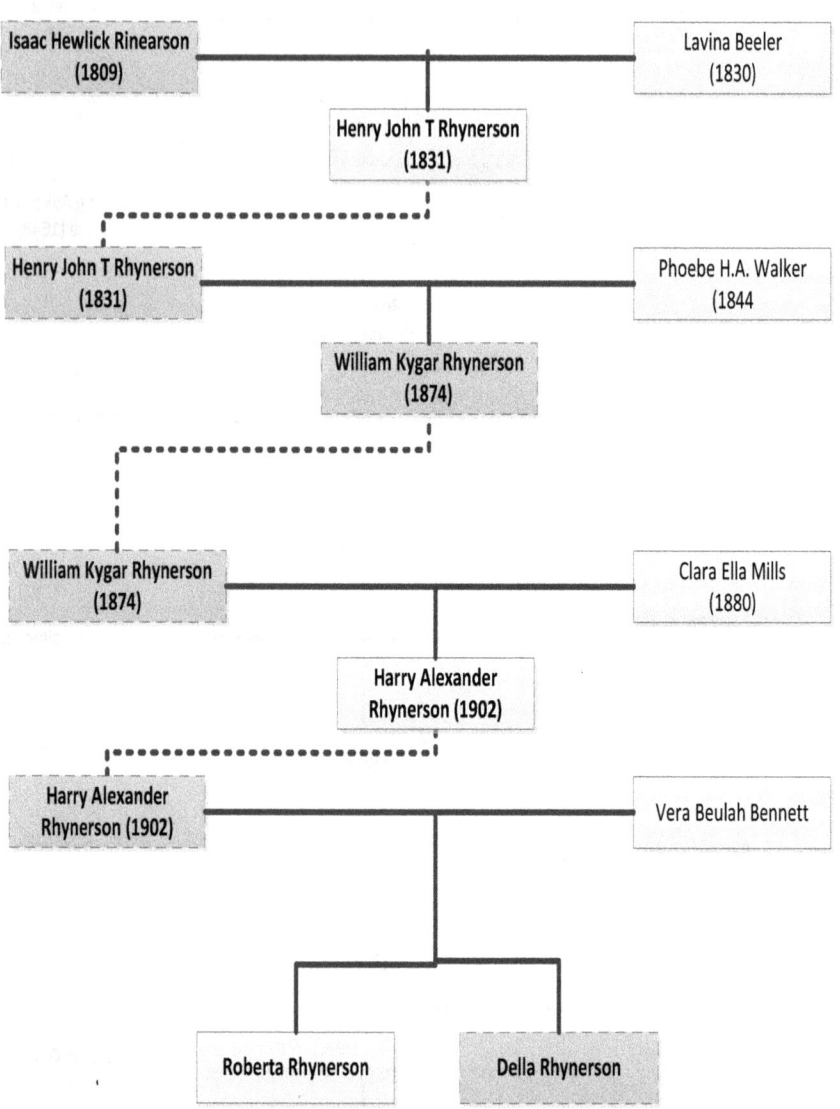

THE ANCESTRY OF DELLA RHYNERSON, WIFE OF JOHN BIRDSONG (1931-1988)

Arent Theunissen Van Hengel, was born about 1616 in Hengelo, Geld, Netherlands, and died Sep 1655 in Staten Island, New York, and was buried in Sep 1655 in Staten Island, New York. He married **Tryntie Reynders.**

Surname: Van Anglen and the origins is Dutch

Arent married Tryntie Reynders abt. 1638, Netherlands

Children of Arent Theunissen Van Hengel and Tryntie Reynders:

> 1. **Reynier Arentsen**, born about 1641, Hengelo, Geld, Netherlands; died 17 Sep 1721, New York.
>
> 2. Arentsen, born about 1648, Hengelo, Geld, Netherlands; died about 1655, Staten Island, New York.
>
> 3. Hendrick Arentsen, born about 1643, Hengelo, Geld, Netherlands; died 14 Jun 1689.
>
> 4. Mary Arentsen, born about 1640, Hengelo, Geld, Netherlands.
>
> 5. Van Hengel Arentsen, born about 1646, Of Helgel, Holland, Netherlands.

Tryntie Reynders was born in 1620 in Hengelo, Gelderland, Holland, died on 5 Aug 1671 in Kings County, New York at age 51, and was buried in Aug 1671 in Kings County, New York.

Surname of Immigrant: Van Hengel; Given name(s) of Immigrant: Arent Theunissen

Name of Ship: Unknown; Arrival Date: about 1653

Origin of Immigrant: Hengel, Holland

Immigrant's Date & Place of Birth: about 1616

Immigrant's Date & Place of Death: 1655, Staten Island

Immigrant's Spouse: Tryntie Reynders

Source of Information: Somerset County Historical Quarterly

Immigrant's Children: Reynier Arentsen Van Hengel and Mary Arents Van Hengel, Hendrick Arentsen Van Hengel Resided in Staten Island then moved to New Jersey.

Arent Theunissen was (sup) killed in the Indian Uprising of 1655. Tryntie Reynders remarried to Severyn Laurenszen abt. 1656/57. The children and ancestors used surnames Van Hengel, Van Hengelen, Vanhengel, etc, Reyniersen, Reynierson, Rinearson, Rhynerson.

Note from Lorine: The marriage of Severyn Laurenszen to the widow of Arent Teunissen Van Hengel is online at The Olive Tree Genealogy at Marriages of the Reformed Dutch Church New York, New York for 1656 as: 25 May Severyn Laurenszen, Van Rootsisil, in Deenmarcken, en Tryntje Reynderts, Wede. Van Arent Teemszen.

As well, Arent's widow is listed among the list of survivors dated 4/14 Nov., 1657, as: "The wife of Aerent van Hengel, now married to one Severyn, with three children, lives at the Manhatans. He has stepped into the contract of Aerent van Hengel, whose widow has a son doing all kinds of farm labor.

Records of the Reformed Dutch Church in New Amsterdam/New York – Marriages.

New York was New Amsterdam until 1674

Researchers in this time period should also familiarize themselves with common Dutch phrases used in Baptismal, Marriage and death records. The serious researcher will also need to be very familiar with Dutch naming systems and patronymics.

The names are for the most part, in patronymic form. The actual surname the family may have taken, would not have developed for some years. If known, I have indicated the family name which this individual or his/her descendants eventually took. Remember that spelling was largely phonetic in this time period - and your ancestor may be found under a variety of names (patronymics) and spellings. So... be creative! In these early records the use of "Van" is not usually part of the surname, but is intended as "from" showing the place of origin of the individual.

Spellings:

Arent Theunissen Van Hengel "Van" means from and "Hengel" is the location Holland "Van Hengel" 2. Reynier Arentsen, 3. Reyniersen, 4 Rinearson, 5 Rhynerson

Reynier Arentsen Van Hengel and Jannetje Aukes Van Nuyse

Reynier Arentsen Van Hengel (Arent Theunissen[1]), son of Arent Theunissen Van Hengel and Tryntie Reynders, was born in Hengelo, Gelderland, Holland, died after 17 Sep 1721, and was buried after 17 Sep

1721. **Jennetje Aukes Van Nuyse**, daughter of Aucke Janse Van Nuyse and Magdalena Pieterse, born 12/10/1648 New Amsterdam, New York, married 4/28/1666 New York. Jannetje Aukes Van Nuyse was born in 1645 in Nuis, Groningen, Netherlands, died after 17 Sep 1721, and was buried after 17 Sep 1721. This is when the name "Reynier Arentsen" changed to "Reyniersen"

Children of Reynier married Annetje Hermans

    1. Aermout Arentsen Van Hengel was born on 26 Apr 1666.

Reynier next married Jannetje Aukes Van Nuyse

Children of Reynier next married Jannetje Aukes Van Nuyse

    1. **Auke Reyniersen Van Hengel** born 17 Apr 1677, Flatbush, Queens, New York; died 20 Jan 1739/40, Somerset, New Jersey.

    2. Tryntie Arentsen Van Hengel was born in 1671 in Flatbush, Long Island, New York.

    3. Maghdaleetie (Helena Arentsen Van Hengel was born in 1667 in Flatbush, Long Island, New York.

    4. Hendrick Arentsen Van Hengel was born in 1675 in Flatbush, Long Island, New York.

    5. Marytie Arentsen Van Hengel was born in 1677 in Flatbush, Long Island, New York.

    6. Barbara Arentsen Van Hengel was born on 14 Dec 1679 in Flatbush, Long Island, New York.

    7. Adriantje Arentsen Van Hengel was born on 12 Mar 1682 in Flatbush, Long Island, New York.

    8. Gertruyd Arentsen Van Hengel was born on 27 Jun 1684 in Flatbush, Long Island, New York.

    9. Barbara Arentsen Van Hengel was born on 6 Sep 1685 in Flatbush, Long Island, New York.

    10. Tunis Arentsen Van Hengel was born on 22 Sep 1689 in Flatbush, Long Island, New York.

    11. Teunis Arentsen Van Hengel was born 29 Mar 1696 in Flatbush, Long Island, New York.

Auke Reyniersen Van Hengel, (Reynier Arentsen[2], Arent Theunissen[1]) son of Reynier Arentsen Van Hengel and Jannetje Aukes Van Nuyse, was born 17 Apr 1677 in Flatbush, Long Island, New York. Auke married **Eytje Cornelisse Vonck**.

Children of Auke Reyniersen Van Hengel and Eytje Cornelisse Vonck:

    1. **Reynier Reyniersen** born in 1696 in Brooklyn, New York.

    2. Magdalen Reyniersen Van Hengel was born on 23 Oct 1698 in Brooklyn, New York.

    3. Hedrick Reyniersen Van Hengel was born on 11 Aug 1700 in Brooklyn, New York.

    4. Catherine (Tryntie) Reyniersen Van Hengel was born in 1702 in New York.

    5. Cornelius Reyniersen Van Hengel was born in 1705 in New Brunswick, New Jersey.

    6. Ida Reyniersen Van Hengel was born in 1710.

    7. Alida Reyniersen Van Hengel was born in 1715 in Montgomery Twp., Somerset County, New Jersey.

    8. Aernout Reyniersen Van Hengel

    9. Mary Reyniersen Van Hengel

    10. Ariaentje Reyniersen Van Hengel

    11. Fenny Reyniersen Van Hengel

    12. Ouke (Auke) Reyniersen Van Hengel was born on 8 Oct 1721 in New Utrecht, Kings County, New York.

Reynier Reyniersen, (Auke Reyniersen[3], Reynier Arentsen[2], Arent Theunissen[1]) son of Auke Reyniersen Van Hengel and Eytje Cornelisse Vonck, was born in 1696 in Brooklyn, New York. Reynier married **Geertje Volleman**.

Children of Reynier Reyniersen and Geertje Volleman:

    1. **Auke Reyniersen** born on 27 Jan 1728 in New Utrecht, Long Island, New York.

    2. Geertie Reyniersen was born 19 Apr1730 in New Brunswick, Misddlesex County, New Jersey.

    3. Eydae Reyniersen was born on 9 May 1734 in Harlingen, New Jersey.

4. Barent Reyniersen was born in 1738 in Neshanic, New Jersey.

5. Catherine Reyniersen

6. Magdalena Reyniersen

7. Sarah Reyniersen

Auke Reyniersen, (Reynier[4],Auke Reyniersen[3],Reynier Arentsen[2],Arent Theunissen[1]) son of Reynier Reyniersen and Geertje Volleman, was born on 27 Jan 1728 in New Utrecht, Long Island, New York, died on 2 Oct 1778 in Somerset County, New Jersey at age 50, and was buried on 4 Oct 1778 in Somerset County, New Jersey. Auke married **Elsce Snedeker.** Elsce Snedeker was born on 6 Jun 1731 in New Utrecht, Long Island, New York.

Children of Auke Reyniersen and Elsce Snedeker:

1. Rynier (Rynard, Reynard) Reyniersen was born on 3 Jun 1752 in Harlingen, Montgomery Township, Somerset County, New Jersey.

2. Gerret Reyniersen was born on 25 Jul 1754 in Somerville, Somerset County, New Jersey 3. Barent Reyniersen was born on 2 Oct 1756 in Six Mile Run Somerset County, New Jersey.

4. Eysak (Isaac) Reyniersen was born on 8 Sep 1758 in Harlingen, Montgomery Township, Somerset County, New Jersey.

5. Ouken Reyniersen was born on 9 Nov 1760.

6. Yan (John) Reyniersen was born on 17 Feb 1763 in Harlingen, Montgomery Township, Somerset County, New Jersey.

7. Cornelius Reyniersen was born on 27 Apr 1765.

8. **Jacob (Yacob) Rinearson**

9. Christoffel (Christopher) Reyniersen was born 11 Jun1769 in Somerset County, New Jersey.

10. Joachem (James, Joseph?) Reyniersen was born on 2 Jun 1771 in Somerset County, New Jersey.

11. Reyniersen was born on 21 Jan 1774, died on 20 Aug 1777 at age 3, and was buried in Aug 1777.

12. Geertie (Charity) Reyniersen was born on 26 Jan 1775, died on 19 Feb 1775, and was buried in Feb 1775.

Jacob (Yacob) Rinearson, (Auke[5],Reynier[4],Auke Reyniersen[3],Reynier Arentsen[2],Arent Theunissen[1]) son of Auke Reyniersen and Elsce Snedeker, was born on 20 Jun 1767 in Harlingen, Montgomery Township, Somerset County, New Jeresy, died on 15 Aug 1845 near Berlington, Iowa at age 78, and was buried in Aug 1845 in Hawkeye, Windsor Township, Fayette County, Iowa. He is buried in the Hawkeye Cemetery Location, Hawkeye, Windsor Township, Fayette County, Iowa. He married **Mariah Gulick**.

Children of Jacob (Yacob) Rinearson and Mariah Gulick

    1. Rinearson was born in 1802.

    2. Elsey Rinearson was born in 1803 in Butler County, Ohio.

    3. John J. Rinearson was born in 1804.

    4. **Isaac Hewlick Rinearson** was born in 1809

    5. Eleanor Rynearson was born on 18 Apr 1810 in Butler County, Ohio and died on 25 Aug 1840 in Butler County, Ohio at age 30.

    6. Jacob S Rinearson was born in 1814 in Butler County, Ohio, died on 2 Mar 1900 in Clackmas County, Oregon at age 86, and was buried in Mar 1900 in Oregon City, Oregon.

    7. Abraham Voorhees Rinearson born in 1817 Butler County, Ohio.

    8. Peter Mills Rinearson was born on 7 Feb 1819 in Hamilyon, Butler County, Ohio.

    9. Sarah Rinearson was born in 1821, died on 12 Dec 1838 at age 17, and was buried in Dec 1838 in Huron Township, Des Moines, Iowa.

Mariah Gulick daughter of Tunis Gulick and Mariah Voorhees, was born on 20 Jul 1777 in Somerset Co., IA, died on 23 Apr 1836 in Des Moines, Iowa at age 58, and was buried in Apr 1836 in Hawkeye, Windsor Township, Fayette County, Iowa.

Isaac Hewlick Rinearson, (Jacob Rinearson[6], Auke[5], Reynier[4],Auke Reyniersen[3],Reynier Arentsen[2],Arent Theunissen[1]) son of Jacob (Yacob) Rinearson and Mariah Gulick, was born in 1809. Isaac married **Lavina Beeler** on 12 Apr 1830 in Butler County, Ohio.

Children of Isaac Hewlick Rinearson and Lavina Beeler

    1. Amanda E Rynearson was born in 1830 in McClean County, Illionis.

2. **Henry John T. Rhynerson** was born in 1831 in McClean County, Illionis.

3. Jacob Rinearson was born in 1834.

4. Rinearson was born in 1835.

5. Rinearson was born in 1835.

6. Rinearson was born in 1840.

7. Adeline Rinearson was born in 1842 in Illionis.

Isaac next married Mary Ann Daniels on 15 Oct 1846 in Des Moines County, Iowa. Lavina Beeler, daughter of Samuel Beeler and Mary Graveswas born in 1810. Lavina married Isaac Hewlick Rinearson on 12 Apr 1830 in Butler County, Ohio.

Isaac Rinearson, served in the America Civil War 1861-1865. He was a private part of the Union, 85th Regiment, Indian Infantry

Henry John T. Rhynerson (Isaac ^{7} Jacob Rinearson ^{6}, Auke^5, Reynier^4, Auke Reyniersen^3, Reynier Arentsen^2, Arent Theunissen^1) son of Isaac Hewlick Rinearson and Lavina Beeler, was born in 1831 in McClean County, Illionis. Rhynerson, Henry T married 12 Jan 1867 in Mc Lean County, Illinois, a bride named **Phoebe H A Walker**. Phoebe H. A. Walker was born in Sep 1844 in North Carolina.

Children of John T Rhynerson and Phoebe H.A. Walker:

> 1. James Henry Rhynerson was born on 24 Dec 1866 in Bloomington, Bloomington Township., Mcclean County, Illionis, died on 9 Jan 1961 in Warrensburg, Warrensburg Township, Johnson Co., MO at age 94, and was buried in Jan 1961 near Warrensburg, Warrensburg Township, Johnson County., Missouri.

> 2. Ada E. Rhynerson was born on 18 Nov 1869 in Bloomington, Bloomington Township, Mclean County, Illionis.

> 3. Mary Amelia Rhynerson was born on 2 Nov 1871 in Henry County., Missouri, died on 16 Dec 1907 in Lacygne, Lincoln Township, Linn County, Kansas at age 36, and was buried on 17 Dec 1907 in Lacygne, Lincoln Township, Linn County, Kansas.

> 4. **William Kygar Rhynerson** born on 22 Nov 1874 in Cass County,

Missouri, died on 13 Oct 1952 near La Cygne, Lincoln Township, Linn County, Kansas.

5. John Theodore Rhynerson was born on 8 Aug 1876 in Burtville, Jefferson Township, Johnson County., Missouri, died in 1919 near La Cygne, Lincoln Township, Linn County, Kansas at age 43, and was buried in 1919 in La Cygne, Township, Linn County, Kansas.

William Kygar Rhynerson (John T. Rhynerson[8], Isaac [7], Jacob Rinearson[6], Auke[5], Reynier[4], Auke Reyniersen[3],Reynier Arentsen[2],Arent Theunissen[1]) son of Henry John T. Rhynerson and Phoebe H. A. Walker, was born on 22 Nov 1874 in Cass Coounty, Missouri, died on 13 Oct 1952 near La Cygne, Lincoln Township, Linn County, Kansas at age 76, and was buried in Oct 1952 in La Cygne, Lincoln Township, Linn County, Kansas.

General Notes: Served in World War I, He is buried in the Oak Lawn Cemetery Location. William married Clara Ella Mills on 9 Feb 1899 in La Cygne, Township, Linn County, Kansas.

Children of William Rhynerson and Ella Clara Mills:

1. Frank Theodore Rhynerson Sr. was born on 22 Dec 1899 near La Cygne, Lincoln Township, Linn County, Kansas, died on 1 Dec 1983 in Fort Scott, Scott Township, Bourbon County, Kansas at age 83, and was buried on 3 Dec 1983 in La Cygne, Lincoln Township, Linn County, Kansas.

2. Ethel Pearl Rhynerson was born on 13 Dec 1900 near La Cygne, Lincoln Township, Linn County, Kansas, died on 5 Dec 1943 in Mound City, Mound City Township, Linn County, Kansas at age 42, and was buried in Dec 1943 in Lucas, Fairview Township., Russell County, Kansas.

3. **Harry Alexander Rhynerson** born on 23 Jun 1902, near La Cygne, Lincoln Township, Linn County, Kansas, died on 5 Dec 1961 near La Cygne, Lincoln Township, Linn County, Kansas.

4. Laura Edna Rhynerson was born on 10 Mar 1904 near La Cygne, Lincoln Township, Linn County, Kansas, died on 3 Feb 1937 near La Cygne, Lincoln Township, Linn County, Kansas at age 32, and was buried in Feb 1937 east of La Cygne, Township, Linn County, Kansas.

5. Goldie Mae Rhynerson was born on 27 Oct 1905 near La Cygne, Lincoln Township, Linn County, Kansas, died on 18 Nov 1989 in El Cajon, El Cajon Twp., San Diego County, California at age 84, and was buried in Nov 1989 in El Cajon, El Cajon Township, San Diego County, California.

6. Infant Rhynerson was born in 1906 near La Cygne, Lincoln Township, Linn County, Kansas, died in 1906 near La Cygne, Lincoln Township, Linn County, Kansas, and was buried in 1906 in La Cygne, Lincoln Township, Linn County, Kansas.

7. Oscar William Rhynerson was born on 11 Nov 1908 near La Cygne, Lincoln Township, Linn County, Kansas, died on 9 Sep 1943 near Leesville, Ward 1-4, Vernon Coounty, Louisiana at age 34, and was buried in Sep 1943 in La Cygne, Lincoln Township, Linn County, Kansas.

8. Harold Henry Rhynerson was born on 5 Sep 1912 near La Cygne, Lincoln Township, Linn County, Kansas, died on 22 Dec 1986 in Overland Park, Country Side Township, Johnson County, Kansas at age 74, and was buried on 24 Dec 1986 in La Cygne, Lincoln Township, Linn County, Kansas.

9. Ernest Edgar "Ernie" Rhynerson was born on 10 Oct 1914 near La Cygne, Lincoln Township, Linn County, Kansas, died on 14 Feb 1988 in South East Of La Cygne, Lincoln Township, Linn County, Kansas at age 73, and was buried on 17 Feb 1988 near La Cygne, Lincoln Township, Linn County, Kansas.

10. Clara Fern Rhynerson was born on 5 Feb 1918 near La Cygne, Lincoln Township, Linn County, Kansas, died on 15 Aug 1990 near Pleasanton, Potosi Township, Linn County, Kansas at age 72, and was buried on 17 Aug 1990 in Pleasanton, Potosi Township, Linn County, Kansas.

11. Freda Mabel Rhynerson was born on 9 Aug 1924 near La Cygne, Lincoln Township, Linn County, Kansas.

Clara Ella Mills daughter of Alexander Mills and Mary Frances Remington, was born on 2 Dec 1880 near La Cygne, Lincoln Township, Linn County, Kansas, died on 20 Jan 1968 in Butler, Mount Pleasant Township, Bates

County, Missori at age 87, and was buried in Jan 1968 in La Cygne, Lincoln Township, Linn County, Kansas.

Clara Rhynerson, 87, passed away January 20, 1968 at the hospital in Butler, Missouri, where she had been a patient since December 21, following a fall at Swan Manor in. La Cygne where she had lived for the past two years. Born December 2, 1880, in Linn County, she was the daughter of Alexander and Mary Mills. On February 8, 1899, she was united in marriage to William K. Rhynerson, and they were the parents of ten children, seven of whom survive: Pearl, wife of Vardie Jackson, Lucas; Goidie, wife of Albert Zimmerman, Escoidtdo, Calif.; Fern, wife of Harold Carpenter, Pleasanton Freda, wife of Dee Perine, Marshall, Mo.; Harold Rhinestone, Blue Mound. Frank and Ernest Rhynerson, La Cygne. Also surviving are 33 grandchildren, 69 great-grandcluldren and 4 great- great-grandchildren. Preceding her in death were her husband in 1952; a daughter, Laura Miller, 1937; sons Oscar, 1943, and Tarry in 1961.

Mrs. Rhynerson was a member of the La Cygne Methodist church and the Royal Neighbor Lodge. Funeral services were held Monday afternoon: at 2:00 o'clock at the La Cygne Methodist church with Rev. William De Laughder officiating. Donald Burnett sang "Beautiful Garden of Prayer" and "The Lard's Prayer," with Mrs. Dan Ross as accompanist. Casket bearers were Lawton Stoker, Walter Rose, Bill Massey, Elmer Beckuau, Layton Murr and Bud Miller. Burial was in Oak Lawn cemetery. - She is buried in the Oak Lawn Cemetery.

Photo of William Kygar Rhynerson

The Ancestry of Clara Ella Mills, Wife of William Kygar Rhynerson (1847)

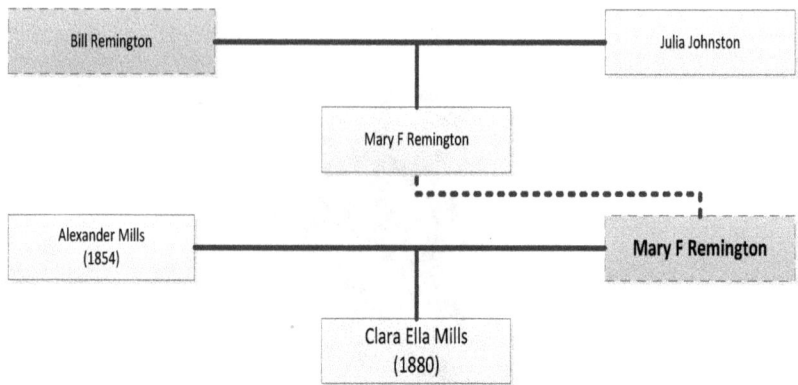

Alexander Mills and Mary Frances Remington

Alexander Mills was born on 18 Sep 1854 in Madison County, Kentucky, died on 6 Mar 1928 near La Cygne, Lincoln Township., Linn County, Kansas at age 73, and was buried on 8 Mar 1928 in La Cygne, Lincoln Township., Linn County, Kansas. Mary married Alexander Mills on 8 Jul 1879 in Clinton, Clinton Township, Henry County, Missouri.

Mary Frances Remington daughter of Bill Remington and Julia Johnston, died on 23 Nov 1889 near La Cygne, Lincoln Township, Linn County, Kansas and was buried in Nov 1889 in La Cygne, Lincoln Township, Linn County, Kansas.

Children of Alexander Mills and Mary Francis Remington:

> 1. **Clara Ella Mills** born on 2 Dec 1880 near La Cygne, Lincoln Township., Linn County, Kansas, died on 20 Jan 1968 in Butler, Mount Pleasant Township, Bates County, Missouri.

> 2. George Mills; birth unknown date

> 3. Frank D. Mills was born in 1885 east of La Cygne, Lincoln Township, Linn County, Kansas and died on 29 Oct 1965 at age 80.

Bill Remington and Julia Johnston

Bill married Julia Johnston

The child from this marriage was:

> 1. **Mary** Frances Remington; birth unknown date.

> 2. Julia Johnston daughter of Unknown and Unknown.

LaCygne Journal March 16, 1928 Alexander Mills passed away March 6, 1928 at the age of 73Y, 7m & 25days. He was born in Kentucky September 10, 1854 and came to Kansas when he was a small boy and has since lived on a farm in Miami and Linn Counties. He was united in marriage to Mary Frances Remington on July 8, 1879. To this union three children were born: Mrs Ella Rhynerson, George who died in infancy, and Frank of Cedar Point, Kansas. He was married to Mary A. Rhynerson July 28, 1890 and to this union six children were born: Mrs Ethel Hoyt who lives on a nearby farm; John of Kansas City; Elra of Paola; Earl of La Cygne; Hazel Harvey who died in 1920 and Amie who died in infancy. (The second wife died Dec. 1907) He was next married to Unie Orndoff Nov. 11, 1908 and six children were born to this union., twin girls Ida & I ra died in infancy; Jesse; James; Rosa of the home and Oscar who died in infancy. Funeral services were held at the Christian Church on Thursday and burial was in Oak Lawn Cemetery. He is buried in the Oak Lawn Cemetery.

Alexander married Mary Frances Remington on 8 Jul 1879 in Clinton, Clinton Twp., Henry County, Missouri.

Photo: Harry, Oscar, Ernie & Frank Rhynerson

Harry Alexander Rhynerson, (William[9], John T. Rhynerson[8], Isaac [7], Jacob Rinearson[6], Auke[5], Reynier[4], Auke Reyniersen[3], Reynier Arentsen[2], Arent Theunissen[1]) born on 23 Jun 1902, near La Cygne, Lincoln Township., Linn County, Kansas, died on 5 Dec 1961 near La Cygne, Lincoln Twp., Linn Co., KS at age 59, and was buried in Dec 1961 in South East Of La Cygne, Lincoln Township., Linn County, Kansas. He was the son of William Kygar Rhynerson and Clara Ella Mills.

Vera Beulah Bennett born on 21 May 1915 near La Cygne, Lincoln Township., Linn County, Kansas, died on 17 Dec 1997 in La Cygne, Lincoln Township., Linn County, Kansas at age 82, and was buried on 20 Dec 1997 in South East of La Cygne, Lincoln Township., Linn County, Kansas.

Harry married Vera Beulah Bennett on 4 May 1933 in Butler, Mount Pleasant Township., Bates County, Missouri.

Both are buried in the Star Valley Cemetery Location

Children of Harry Alexander Rhynerson and Vera Beulah Bennett:

    1. Roberta Maxine Rhynerson born on 12 Oct 1933 in La Cygne, Lincoln Township., Linn County, Kansas.

    2. **Della Lorine Rhynerson** born on 5 Feb 1935 near La Cygne, Lincoln Township., Linn County, Kansas.

Harry Rhynerson worked many jobs to support his family. He worked as a coal miner in Butler Missouri and worked on the road as part of the Workforce Labor Association. He would also go to Kansas City, Kansas to wrestle in tournaments to make additional money.

Left to right: Harry Rhynerson, 2nd photo; Harry Rhynerson, Teresa & Michael Birdsong

Vera (Bennett) Rhynerson lived in La Cygne all of her life. Her father passed away when she was only four years old. She had an older brother Donald Bennett that was a big part of her life. Her mother Cora (Anderson) Bennett remarried after the death of Vera's father to Presley Jacob Stump. Vera was an entrepreneur and found many ways to support her family. She worked at Simmons the mattress factory for a while as well as raised rabbits and tended a garden to have additional money to support her family. She was a strong Baptist women. She lover her daughters and her grandchildren dearly. She developed Parkinson's and suffered from mini strokes which caused her to develop dementia later in life. She spent the last few months of her life at a nursing home in Ottawa, Kansas.

Left to right: Roberta (Rhynerson) Sparks, Michael Birdsong, Teresa Birdsong, Vera (Bennett) Rhynerson, John Birdsong & Della (Rhynerson) Birdsong

The Ancestry of Vera Bennett, Wife of Harry Rhynerson (1902-1961)

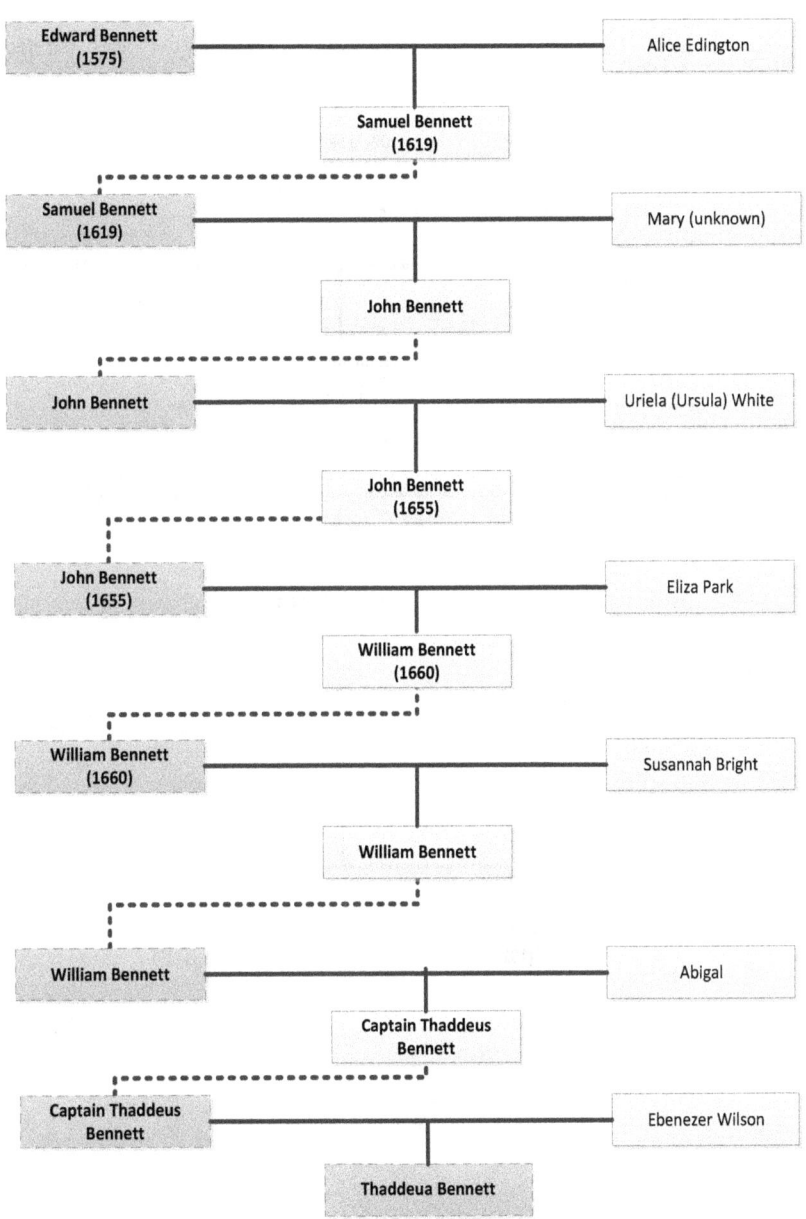

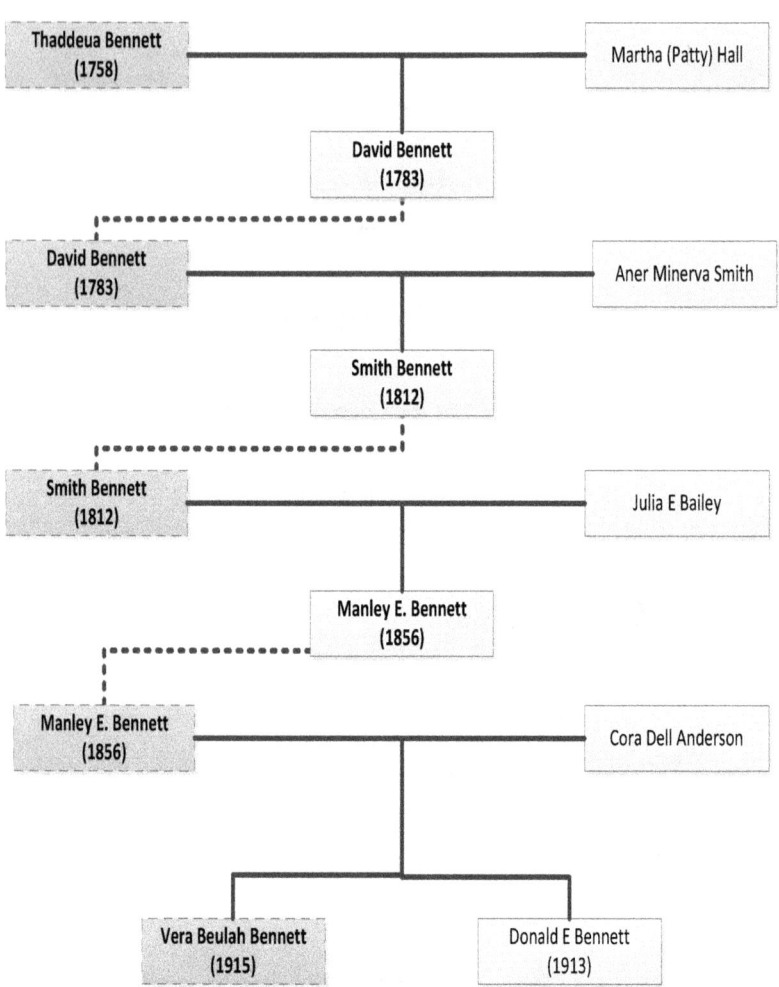

THE ANCESTRY OF VERA BENNETT, WIFE OF HARRY RHYNERSON

Edward Bennett was born Bet. 1575 - 1607 in Wiltshire, England, and died 1645 in Rehoboth, Bristol, Massachusetts. (Buried in Proprietor's cemetery). He married **Alice Edington** 27 Oct 1622 in England. She was born between 1584 - 1609 in England, and died between 1633 - 1698.

Children of Edward and Alice:

> 1. **Samuel Bennett** born about 1619, Wiltshire, England or Dorset, England; died 04 Sep 1684, East Greenwich, Kent, Rhode Island (will proven).
>
> 2. John Bennett, born about 1630, Wiltshire, England or Dorset, England; died 22 Oct 1691, Stonington, New London, Connecticut.
>
> 3. Priscilla Bennett, born about 1632, Weymouth, Dorset, England; died 20 Oct 1663, Rehoboth, Bristol, Massachusetts.
>
> 4. Edward Bennett, born about 1634, Weymouth, Dorset, England.

Edward Bennett sailed from Weymouth, Malcombe-Regis Dorset, England to Weymouth MA with his wife and 4 children in 1636. There he took up as he was entitled to thirty-six acres of public land. He was made a freeman in 1636. After a residence there for seven years he became an original proprietor in the company that founded Rehoboth, to which place he removed in 1643 with a certain Rev. Newman. He died at Rehoboth in 1645, an original proprietor wealthy, and was buried in Proprietor's cemetery."

Referring to the children of Edward Bennett upon his death prior to Feb. 18, 1646, Ralph Bennett

Writes:

"The older sons were old enough to run the widow's farm. Samuel Bennett was 18; John Bennett, 16. But the farm came into the possession of Richard Bowen Jr., whose name appears instead of hers in an allotment list drawn up in 1658."

"By then, son Samuel had moved to Rhode Island and son John, to Connecticut. Daughter Priscilla married William Carpenter on October 5, 1651, and died on October 20, 1663, the day their son Benjamin was born. Edward and Richard Bennett, the younger sons, stayed in Rehoboth but later the Bennett name fades from town records."

Samuel Bennett (Edward[1]), born about 1619, Wiltshire, England or Dorset, England; died 04 Sep 1684, East Greenwich, Kent, Rhode Island (will proven) Samuel arrived by the ship Mary Rose at Lynn, Massachusetts, in 1637.

Samuel Bennett, who was a house carpenter, came to this country by way of London, England, in the "James," and William Bennett of Salem, Mass., testified before a justice court that Samuel and he both came together in the "James" in 1630. Samuel settled in Iynn, Massachusetts, when he was nineteen years old and in 1639 he settled in Chelsea, Massachusetts, where he owned a large farm, shop, windmill, etc. His wife's name was Mary.

Children of Samuel Bennett and Mary (unknown):

    1. Samuel Bennett; birth unknown.

    2. Richard Bennett; birth unknown.

    3. Klisha Bennett; birth unknown.

    4. Lydia Bennett; birth unknown.

    5. **John of Boston Bennett;** birth unknown. He married Uriela White and died Stonington, Connecticut on September 22, 1691.

John Bennett (Samuel[2], Edward[1]) married **Uriela White** (Ursula?), daughter of William and Elizabeth White. He was at Mystic, CT. as early as 1658. He died at Stonington, Connecticut on September 22, 1691.

Children of John Bennett and Uriela White

    1. **John Bennett**, born about 1655.

    2. William Bennett, born about 1660.

    3. Thomas Bennett, unknown birth date.

    4. Isaac Bennett, unknown birth date.

    5. Elizabeth Bennett, born about 1672.

    6. Cornelius Bennett, unknown birth date.

    7. Joseph Bennett, born about 1681.

    8. Ursula Bennett, unknown birth date.

    9. Susanna Bennett, unknown birth date.

John Bennett (John[3], Samuel[2], Edward[1]) born in 1655 and married **Eliza Park**

Children of John Bennett and Eliza Park

    1. Eliza Patty Bennett, unknown birth date.

    2. John Bennett, born February 24, 1650 and died in 1654.

    3. **William Bennett**, born about 1660.

    4. John Bennett again, born about 1666.

    5. Joseph Bennett, born about 1671.

    6. Samuel Bennett; unknown birth date.

    7. Anthony Bennett, born November 12, 1679; died September 22, 1691.

William Bennett and **Susannah Bright**

Children of William Bennett and Susannah Bright:

    1. **William Bennett**; unknown birth date.

    2. Henry Bennett; unknown birth date.

    3. Samuel Bennett; unknown birth date.

    4. Daniel Bennett; unknown birth date.

William Bennett and Abigal

Children of William Bennett and Abigal:

    1. Deliverance Bennett; unknown birth date.

    2. Joseph Bennett; unknown birth date.

    3. Stephen Bennett; unknown birth date.

    4. **Thaddeus Bennett;** unknown birth date.

    5. Sarah Bennett; unknown birth date.

    6. Abigal Bennett; unknown birth date.

Will of William Bennett.

I give to my wife, Abigal, so much, to my son. Deliverance, to my son, Joseph, to my son, Stephen, to my son, Thaddeus, and daughter, Sarah, to my daughter, Abigal, to my four sons and my two daughters to share and share alike. I appoint my brothers, Samuel and Daniel, as executors of my Will.

Captain Thaddeus Bennett and **Ebenezer Wilson**

Children of Captain Thaddeus Bennett and Elizabeth Wilson:

    1. Joseph Wilson Bennett; born unknown.

    2. **Thaddeus Bennett**; born unknown.

    3. Grizell Bennett, married Isaac Odell, who was a sergeant in the army.

    4. Sarah Bennett, Nathan Fairchild.

Will of Thaddeus Bennett

Captain Thaddeus Bennett was the son of William and Abigal Bennett, having three brothers, Deliverance, Joseph and Stephen, and two sisters, Sarah and Abigal. William, the father, had two brothers, Samuel and Daniel, as he named them as executors of his will, which is on the probate records at Fairfield, (Jonn, where it can be found of August 5, 1772.)

Probate Record of Fairfield, Conn., A. D. 1772.

Captain Thaddeus Bennett, a shoemaker and farmer, was Captain of the trained band at the commencement of the Revolutionary War and went to New York with his Company in August, 1776, to defend the city against the British troops. His Company suffered considerable loss by death and the Captain died soon after returning home from the campaign. He died on January 21, 1777, aged 52 years.

Thaddeus Bennett II, was born in Stratford, Conn., August 23, 1758, and there, on February 28, 1782, married **Martha Patty Hall**, daughter of David and Lydia Hall, who was born Dec. 3, 1760. Thaddeus 2ik1 was a soldier of the Revolutionary War, serving as a private in his father's company of Militia at Stratford, Conn., in the fall of 1776 served two months in New York City in Regiment commanded by Col. Jchabod Lewis; in the autumn of 1777, three weeks at White Plains in the same company under Capt. Abijah Sterling ; in 1778 served eight months at Black Rock in the company of G. Ward, under

Ensign Samuel Still man ; in 1779 served twelve months at Mutton Lane in the company commanded by Lieut. William Hall. (For copy of the original record in the Bureau of Pensions at Washington, see page 10.)

When he was discharged and returned home he settled down and raised a large family — six boys and three girls.

Children of Thaddeus Bennett and Martha Hall:

    1. **David Bennett**, born January 20, 1783; died August 8, 1868.

    2. George Bennett, born July 15, 1785.

    3. Elijah Bennett, born June 25, 1787.

    4. Betsy Bennett, born March 7, 1789.

    5. Thaddeus Bennett, born October 17, 1790.

    6. Lydia Bennett, born July 30, 1794.

    7. Eli Bennett, born June 30, 1799.

    8. Minerva Bennett, born January 13, 1802; died December 28, 1823.

    9. Wildman Bennett, born July 20, 1804.

Thaddeus was in the Revolutionary War in Washington, D. C, December 17, 1907

In reply to your request of 7th inst. received 9th inst., for a statement of the military history of Thaddeus Bennett, a soldier of the Revolutionary War, you will find below the desired information as contained in his widow's application on His in this Bureau.

Dates of Enlistment or Appointment Summer or Fall of 1776, Fall of 1777, May 1, 1778, Jan. 1, 1779 Length of Rank Service 2mos. 3wks. Private 8 mos. 12 mos.

Officers under whom service was rend'd Thaddeus Bennett his father' Ichabod Lewis Abijah Sterling Ens. Sam'l Silliman Lieut. Wm. Hall Sam'l Whiting Soldier's father Thaddeus died January 21, 1777, and is mother Elizabeth, who afterwards married Ebenezer Hall, died November 16, 1815, aged 87 years.

Battles engaged in Residence of soldier at enlistment, Parish of Stratford, Fairfield, Fairfield County, Conn. Dale of application for pension, July 2,

1840. Her claim was allowed: Residence at date of application, Monroe, Fairfield Co., Ct. Age at date of application; she was born December 3, 1760, at Weston, Eairlield County, Conn. Remarks. Soldier was born August 23, 1758, in Stratford Parish, Conn, and there married on February 28, 1782, Martha (or Patty), daughter of I.ydia and David Hall. Soldier died in Newton, Fairfield County, Connecticut, January 8, 1831. Children: David, born Jan. 20, 1783; George, born July 15, 1785; Elijah, born June 25, 1787; Betsy, born Mar. 7, 1789; thaddeus, born October 17, 1790; Lydia, born July 30, 1794; Eli, born June 30, 1799; Minerva, borii Jan. 13, 1802, died Dec. 28, 1823; Wildman, born July 20, 1804."

David Bennett, son of Thaddeus and Martha Hall Bennett, and grandson of Captain Thaddeus Bennett, was born in New- town, Fairfield County. Conn., on January 20, 1783. Here he received such education as was pro curable at tliat time and learned the scythemaker's trade. All of his spare time was made use ofwith his books until he became qualified for the ministry and followed tlie Baptist faith, alsoteaching both district and private schools. He preached in Monroe, Newtown, Ashford aud at Manchester Green, Conn.

He was married about 1805 or 1806 to **Aner Minerva Smith**

Children of David Bennett and Aner Minerva Smith

    1. **Smith Bennett**; unknown birth date.

    2. Mary Ann Bennett; unknown birth date.

    3. William Henry Bennett; unknown birth date.

    4. Minerva Bennett; born unknown birth date.

    5. Lioomis G. Bennett; unknown birth date.

Aner Minerva died about 1831. David married again, about 1832, Clarissa Farnham of Ashford, Conn. She was a school teacher and was born November 21, 1793. There were two boys by this union: Farnliam O. and Maurice B., who became noted physicians at Manchester Green.

David kept a store for quite a while, but sold out and on May 18, 1842, purchased a farm in Burlington, Conn., where he moved his family and resided there until 1864. Here he became school visitor and registrar of births, marriages and deaths and was also a judge of probate for a number of years. In 1864 he sold his farm to George Case of Burlington, Conn., and moved to Ashford and Westford, Conn., where he died on August 8, 1868. His wife died at Westford, Conn, on January 6, 1869, aged 76 years

Smith Bennett born in 1812 in Rhode Island; died on 19 Aug 1873 married **Julia E Bailey** on 21 Oct 1851, Carroll County, Illinois daughter of Elijah Bailey and Polly Patchin.

Children of Smith Bennett and Julia E Bailey:

    1. Granville J. Bennett, died 24 February 1925 York, Carroll, Illinois.

    2. **Manley E. Bennett**, born 1856; died 1918.

    3. Emiline Bennett; unknown birth date.

    4. Julia Bennett; unknown birth date.

    5. Amy Bennett; unknown birth date.

    6. Della Bennett; unknown birth date.

    7. Infant Bennett; unknown birth date.

Smith Bennett was a farmer and resided in Carroll County, Illinois in 1860.

Julia Bailey was born between 1814 and 1819, Warren County, Illinois and she moved Aug 1845, with her parents, to Carroll County, Illinois and resided in 1889, on own 167 acre farm, with son Granville, in York, Carroll County, Illinois.

Manley E. Bennett was born in 1856, died in 1918 at age 62, and was buried in 1918 in Southeast La Cygne, Lincoln Township, Linn County, Kansas. Manley married **Cora Dell Anderson** on 4 Apr 1912.

Both are buried in the Star Valley Cemetery Location,

Children of Manley Bennett and Cora Anderson:

    1. Donald E. Bennett was born on 10 Nov 1913 near La Cygne, Lincoln Township, Linn County, Kansas, died on 2 Nov 1978 at age 64, and was buried in Nov 1978 in S.E. Of La Cygne, Lincoln Township, Linn County, Kansas.

    2. **Vera Beulah Bennett** born on 21 May 1915 near La Cygne, Lincoln Township, Linn County, Kansas, died on 17 Dec 1997 in La Cygne, Lincoln Township, Linn County, Kansas.

Cora Dell Anderson daughter of Solomon Anderson and Osea Miles, was born on 26 Mar 1896 in Darlington, Cooper Township., Gentry County,

Missouri, died on 21 Dec 1978 in Olathe, Johnson County, Kansas at age 82, and was buried on 23 Dec 1978 in Southeast of La Cygne, Lincoln Township, Linn County, Kansas.

Donald Bennett did not marry and never had children. Donald served in the World War II. He lived with his mother Cora (Anderson-Bennett) Stump until his death.

Photo: Manley Bennett

Photo left to right; back to front: Vera (Bennett) Rhynerson, Cora (Anderson-Bennett) Stump, Teresa Birdsong, and Jerome Birdsong

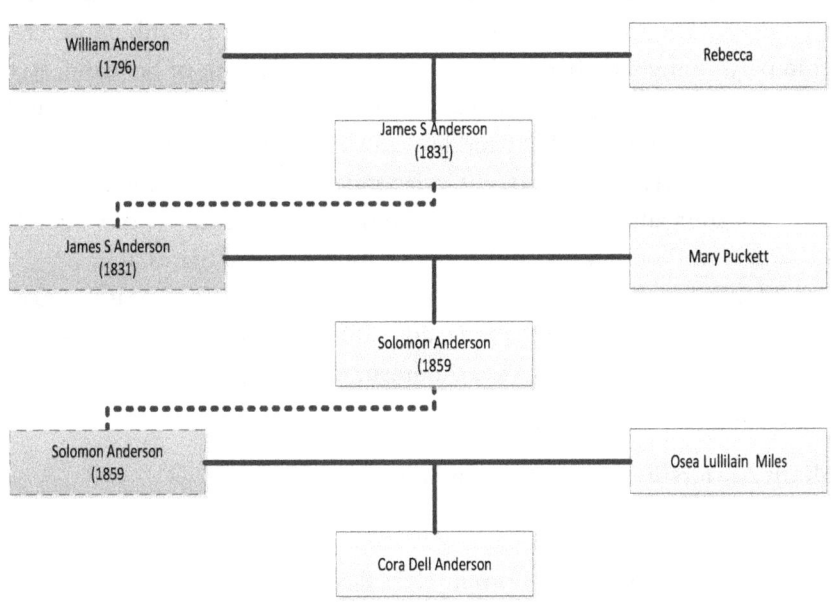

THE ANCESTRY OF CORA ANDERSON, WIFE OF MANLEY E BENNETT (1856)

Anderson - Scottish and northern English: very common patronymic from the personal name Ander(s), a northern Middle English form of Andrew. See also Andreas. The frequency of the surname in Scotland is attributable, at least in part, to the fact that St. Andrew is the patron saint of Scotland, so the personal name has long enjoyed great popularity there. Legend has it that the saint's relics were taken to Scotland in the 4th century by a certain St. Regulus. The surname was brought independently to North America by many different bearers and was particularly common among 18th-century Scotch-Irish settlers in Pennsylvania and Virginia. In the United States, it has absorbed many cognate or like-sounding names in other European languages, notably Swedish Andersson, Norwegian and Danish Andersen, but also Ukrainian Andreychyn, Hungarian Andrásfi, etc.

William Anderson and Rebecca

William Anderson born in 1796 and died in 1858

Children of William Anderson and Rebecca

    1. **James Anderson** born in 1831 died in 1885.

James Anderson born in 1831 died in 1885 married **Martha Puckett.**

Children of James Anderson and Martha Puckett:

    1. **Solomon Anderson** born on about 1859 Illinois.

Solomon Anderson born on about 1859 Illinois, and died in 1920, his father was James Anderson and Martha Pucket. Solomon married **Osea Miles**

Children of Solomon Anderson and Osea Mills:

    1. **Cora Dell Anderson** was born on 26 Mar 1896 in Darlington, Cooper Township, Gentry County, Missouri, died on 21 Dec 1978 in Olathe, Johnson County, Kansas.

AMERICAN SERVICE

Treasurer of Virginia for Life

WILLIAM CLAIBORNE

Deputy Governor

WILLIAM CLAIBORNE

The Virginia Company Of London

WILLIAM HANOCK, SR   CAPT THOMAS HARRIS

Berkeley Hundred

WILLIAM HANOCK, SR

House of Burgess

RANDALL HOLT, JR.

Bacon's Rebellion

RANDALL HOLT, JR

English Civil War

RANDALL HOLT, JR

MATHEW SWAN

Bacon's Rebellion

MATHEW SWAN

French and Indian war

NICHOLAS ALLEE

American Revolutionary War

DAVID ALLEE
ENOCH JOBE
JACOB (YACOB) RINEARSON
CAPTAIN THADDEUS BENNETT

War of 1812

WILLIAM BIRDSONG, SR.
JAMES BIRDSONG

American Civil War

HENRY TOLBERT WOOD
PETER BIRDSONG
ISAAC HEWLICK RINEARSON

World War One

WILLIAM RHYNERSON (DRAFT REGISTRATION)

World War Two

DONALD BENNETT   OSCAR RHYNERSON

Korean War

JOHN P. BIRDSONG

Vietnam

JOHN MICHAEL. BIRDSONG

Gulf War

JAMES BIRDSONG

BIRDSONG FAMILY CRESTS

NOTES

For further details about the sources listed in these notes, please refer to the Bibliography, which begins on page and chapter. Use the refence and chapter to find the refernecne section.

REFERENCE

Introduction

German immigrants was in 1683 to the colony named Germantown in Pennsylvania Encyclopedia of Immigration, published December 19, 2011. http://immigration-online.org/519-german-immigrants.html

Birdsong Family Genealogy, http://www.birdsongfamily.com/genealogy/resources.htm

Carlton Hugo Le Bird: http://familytreemaker.genealogy.com/users/b/y/r/Wayne-A-Byrd/WEBSITE-0001/UHP-0737.html

"The surname 'Byrd' originates from England. English Noble families, http://english.araldica.info/tag/byrd/

Chapter one

Charles Parish, Viginina - The Virginia State Library Board. Includes brief history, list of ministers, parish register births (1648-1789) and deaths (1665-1787) Bell, Landon C. Charles Parish, York County, Virginia. History and Registers. Richmond, Va.: The Virginia State Library Board. Includes brief history, list of ministers, parish register births (1648-1789) and deaths (1665-1787).

Charles Church - Inscription. About one mile east, on north (left-hand) side of road et.al. The Historical Marker Database, http://www.hmdb.org/marker.asp?marker=34008 n,

Charles Parish on the Birdsong family; Bell, Landon C. Charles Parish, York County, Virginia.History and Registers. Richmond, Va.: The Virginia State Library Board.

Charles Parish, Viginina -Site of Charles Church in George Carrington Mason, Colonial Churches of Tidewater Virginia (Richmond, Va.: Whittet and Shepperson, 1945) et.al; Charles Parish, Virginia: Family Search https://www.familysearch.org/learn/wiki/en/Charles_Parish,_Virginia

New Poquoson's name was change in 1692 to Charles Parish et.al; Kinard, June. Charles Parish Records, York County, Virginia, 1648-1789 [database on-line]. Provo, UT, USA: The Generations Network, Inc., 1998

211. 16 January 1711/1712—Richd Craford is hereby bound an apprentices to serve Jno Birdsong three years from this time forward in the occupation & trade of a Tayler [tailor], in consideration were of ye sd John Birdsong doth herby oblige himself during the said term to find & allow ye sd Richard sufficient apparel, diet, washing & lodging, to do an honest

endeavor to teach him ye trade and that he will not confine the sd Richd to work about any other labour but the trade of Tayor only in tending corn (to wit) no other labour with a hoe but otherwise to perform such necessary services as are suitable to his circumstances." et.al; "Northumberland County, Virginia Apprenticeships order"

Site of Charles Church in George Carrington Mason, Colonial Churches of Tidewater Virginia (Richmond, Va.: Whittet and Shepperson, 1945). Digital version at Family History Archives, https://www.familysearch.org/learn/wiki/en/Charles_City_County,_Virginia

Chapter two

338 acres on the South side of Blackwater swamp. Beginning and extending his own corner tree thence and extending to a pine in snake branch; Publication 3 November 1750. Other Format Available on microfilm. Virginia State Land Office. Patents 1-42, reels 1-41. Location: Surry County.

1820 Census this is likely Miles - John & Daramis son; 1820 Census Sussex Co. VA, 1820 American Community Survey/prepared by the U.S. Census Bureau, 1820

John and Daramis artifacts; Pg 15. Source: Land Office Patents No. 30, 1750-1752, p. 430 (Reel 28). Part of the index to the recorded copies of patents for land issued, by the Secretary of the Colony serving as the colonial Land Office. The collection is housed in the Archives at the Library of Virginia.

Publication 3 November 1750. Other Format Available on microfilm. Virginia State Land Office. Patents 1-42, reels 1-41. Location: Surry County.

1820 Census Sussex Co. VA, 1820 American Community Survey/prepared by the U.S. Census Bureau, 1820

Daramis (Hancock) Birdsong's Will; Ye Olde Cooper Clan, Moniteau Co. Historical Society, Author: E.M. Richards

Part I - Daramis Hancock

The story of our English, French & Scottish ancestry is not complete without including the ancestries of at least nine of our "great" grandmothers; (1) Family charts by Luther Pryor Harris; (2) 15th Edition, Encyclopedia Britannica - 1975.; (3) Virginia Settlers and English Adventurers, 3 Vols. in one, by Currer-Briggs.; (4) Historical Families of Southern United States, Vol. 10, Pgs.164-165, by John Boddie.; (5) The Genesis of the United States, Vols. 1 and 2, by Alexander Brown. Vol. 1, pp. 465-469

William Hancock (1580)

Shortly after 1630, three of William's sons came to America. Augustine, Simon and William became prominent planters in Virginia and established a family line that today includes many thousands of their descendants. From Virginia, their descendants migrated throughout the southeastern and midwestern states and today are living in all parts of the country.(1)Hancock Genealogy & Descendants of Georgia, South Carolina and Virginia, http://hancockgenealogy.ucan.us/ hann03.htm#284, e-mail: ucanusa@yahoo.com (2) William Hancock 1580 – 1621 came on the"Margaret" from Devonshire, England; (3) Descendants of

William Hancock,s ubmitted by JamesReid Hancock, http://www.kykinfolk.com/henry/hancock.htm

Jane Holt; Ancestors of Barbara Ann Bryant
http://familytreemaker.genealogy.com/users/e/n/f/Jerry-A-Enfield-Richmond/GENE2-0025.html

The progenitor of this Hancock family line was William Hancock who was born about 1580 in England. He was a member of The Virginia Company Of London which was created by King James I for the purpose of colonizing in America. The first settlement was established at Jamestown in 1607. As an investor in the Virginia Company, William traveled to Jamestown in 1619 aboard the"Margaret" of Bristol. He was a member of a group that founded Berkeley Hundred. On 22 March 1622 the settlement was attacked by Indians and William, along with many others, was massacred. et.al; (1) Hancock Genealogy & Descendants of Georgia,

WILLIAM HANCOCK (Jane Holt, Randall, Randall) left will 11 Aug. 1764-18 April 1765. He married Elizabeth Phillips, daughter of William and Mary (Swann) Phillips." Ref. table 2.2 & 2.3

JANE [Jean] HANCOCK (John , Jane Holt, Randall , Randall), born 15 Aug. 1741, married, (bond 24) Feb. 1762, Hartwell Phillips, son of John and Martha (Crafford) Phillips, of Edgecombe Co., N.C., who married (2), b 1772, Feraby Jones and left will about 1807." Ref. table 2.2 & 2.3; Adventurers of Purse and Person, Virginia, 1607-1624/5, Families G-P By John Frederick Dorman.

South Carolina and Virginia, http://hancockgenealogy.ucan.us/hann03.htm#284, e-mail: ucanusa@yahoo.com

Marriage of William Hancock & Elizabeth Philips; The Next Generation of Genealogy Sitebuilding, Version 9.1.1 ©, written by Darrin Lythgoe 2001-2013. http://www.riverwye.us/getperson.php?PersonID=I11015&tree=Watkins

A list of Tithables in Hogg Island Lawnes Creeke p(ar)ish taken June the 10th 1678 - Mr. Rand: Holt; (1)Surry County, Virginia Tithables, 1668-1703, page. 37, by Edgar E. MacDonald, Richard Slatten (2) Bacon's Rebellion, http://www.pbs.org/wgbh/aia/part1/1p274.html (3) Lineage Of John Stone, Blockmaker, By Spessard Stone, Appendix C- The Hansford Family

Randal Holt; Line of Descent from Colonist Henry Randolph of Virginia, By Rosemary E. Bachelor on Jun 5, 2010 1) http://suite101.com/article/line-of-descent-from-colonist-henry-randolph-of-virginia-a245247; 2) Jamestown City, VA Census – 1624 http://files.usgwarchives.net/va/jamestown/census/jameship.txt

John was not the famous John Hancock but they are likely related back in England or where the Hancock's originally came from, et.al This John Hancock was in Virginia about the same time as the other famous John Hancock's grandfather was in Massachuetts.; Olde Cooper Clan, Moniteau Co. Historical Society, Author: E.M. Richards

Mary's executor, Carter Crafford is her brother-in-law who married her sister Sarah Swann. (Carter Crawford).; Surry County, Virginia Book 7, page. 697. - from "Wills and Administration of Surry County, Virginia 1671-1750", p. 129.

WILLIAM HANCOCK (Jane Holt, Randall, Randall) left will 11 Aug. 1764-18 April 1765. He married Elizabeth Phillips, daughter of William and Mary (Swann) Phillips. (1) Adventurers of Purse and Person, Virginia, 1607-1624/5: Families G-P by John Frederick Dorman http://www.lfeldhaus.com/philipsofearlyvirginia/id2.html

William Philips, dated 2-14-1721, probated 4-19-1721; Wills and Administrations of Isle of Wight County, Virginia: 1647, Books 1-3

Mathew Swann was part of the Nathanial Bacon crew for the Bacon's Rebellion, he also rebelled against taxation. Et.al. Matthew Swan, the ringleader of this protest against high taxes, has many descendants in Virginia and the South. In 1675 he married Mrs. Mary Spiltimber, widow of Anthony Spiltimber and daughter of Robert Harris. His will was dated December 14, 1702 and probated Jan. 5, 1702. He mentioned daughter, Elizabeth, wife of John Drew, daughter, Sarah; Elizabeth, daughter of John Drew; son-in-law, John Drew; daughter, Mary, wife of William Phillips; and grandson, John Phillips."; Colonial Surry, By John Bennett Boddie, First published in 1948, AMERICA'S FIRST TAX STRIKE pages 106 and 107. http://www.lfeldhaus.comphilipsofearlyvirginia/id3.html

Will of Mary (Swann) Phillips, 1727. PHILLIPS, Mary. Leg - To daughter, Mary Edwards, wife of John Edwards, my Plantation where I live for her life, then to my daughter, Ann Phillips. Et.al; Wills and Administrations of Surry County, Virginia 1671-1750.Abstracted and compiled by Eliza Timberlake Davis, 1955 Page 129

William Swann married his second wife Mary Harris in 1675 and had Mary Swann who married William Phillips; Colonial Surry, By John Bennett Boddie, First published in 1948, AMERICA'S FIRST TAX STRIKE, pages 106 and 107, Southside, By John Bennett Boddie, published in 1956,

Mathew Swann made his will on December 14th 1702 and it was probated on January 5th 1703 so we know he died within that three weeks. His will listed his three daughters and their husband's names, but named no sons, so they evidently all died in the Bacons' Rebellion or hung after it.; Philips of Early Virginia, Larry Feldhaus, http://www.lfeldhaus.com/philipsofearlyvirginia/id3.html

William Philips last name with one "L". I will do the same on this page, having no reason to spell it otherwise as I have not seen the hand written copies of either William or Mary's wills or the deeds shown on this page.; Southside Virginia Families, Volume 2, By John Bennett Boddie, Published 1956, pages 350-356.

Henry Randolph (1665-1693) was born at the Henrico settlement and spent his life there. He married Sarah Swann of Surrey Co. In 1687; Line of Descent from Colonist Henry Randolph of Virginia, By Rosemary E. Bachelor on Jun 5, 2010 http://suite101.com/article/line-of-descent-from-colonist-henry-randolph-of-virginia-a245247

Part II - Elizabeth Philips/Hansford

John Hansford's will, dated 9 May 1654, was proved on 24 June 1661 and was recorded in York County Records No. 3 1657/62, page 122. It showed his wife was Elizabeth, sons were John, William, Thomas, and Charles, and daughters were Elizabeth, Mary, and Margaret; also he possessed over 2,170 acres of land and livestock. (1) 1658-1758 Charles County MD Families "The first 100 years", http://wc.rootsweb.ancestry.com/cgi-bin/igm.cgi?op=GET&db=mrmarsha&id=I68496

Title Hansford, John. Publication 1661. Gen. note Part of index to York County Wills and Administrations (1633-1811); p. 67. Guardian accounts rec. 25 Apr. 1666. p. 92. Estate division rec. 24 Aug. 1698. p. 94. Guardian account rec. 21 June 1666. p. 111. Guardian account [12 Nov. 1666]. p. 96. Estate division rec. 24 Aug. 1698.Note Deeds, Orders, Wills, etc. [Records no. 11], 1698-1702 (Reel 5a); p. 112. Guardian accounts rec. [12 Nov. 1666]. p. 120. Exors. bond rec. 24 June 1661. ; p. 121. Will pro. 24 June 1661.p. 173. Estate division ordered [10 Sept. 1662]. p. 179. Estate division rec. [20 Oct. 1662]. Note Deeds, Orders, Wills, etc. [Records No. 3], 1657-1662 (Reel 2a); p. 194. Inv., appr., accounts rec. [24 June 1668].;p. 214. Guardian accounts rec. 7 Dec. 1668. Note Deeds, Orders, Wills, etc. [Records No. 4], 1665-1672 (Reel 2a)

Title Hansford, Elizabeth.Publication 1678.Gen. note Part of index to York County Wills and Administrations (1633-1811); p. 35 Exors. bond rec. 24 Apr. 1678.;p. 39. Will pro. 24 Apr. 1678.p. 87. Codicil to will rec. 24 Mar. 1678/9.; p. 315. Guardian account rec. 24 Aug. 1696. Note Deeds, Orders, Wills, etc. [Records No. 10], 1694-1697 (Reel 4 a); p. 397. Accounts rec. 24 Mar. 1681/2.Note Deeds, Orders, wills, etc. [Records No. 6], 1677-1684 (Reel 3 a)

Elizabeth made her will 4 Mar 1708/9; probated 3 May 1709 in Surry Co., VA. Leg: to grandson Charles, son of John, Dec'd; Tax Record: Quit Rent, Surry Co., VA 1450 acres;

John Holt, born about 1664 in Surry Co., VA; died 1705 in Surry Co., VA; married Mary Binns before 1685; born about 1666 inprobably Surry Co., VA. ; Ancestors of Barbara Ann Bryant http://familytreemaker.genealogy.com/users/e/n/f/Jerry-A-Enfield-Richmond/GENE2-0025.html

15th Edition, Encyclopedia Britannica - 1975., 2.Virginia Settlers and English Adventurers, 3 Vols. in one, by Currer-Briggs., 4. Historical Families of Southern United States, Vol. 10, Pgs. 164-165, by John Boddie., 5. The Genesis of the United States, Vols. 1 and 2, by Alexander Brown. Vol. 1, pp. 465-469

Lineage Of John Stone, Blockmaker, By Spessard Stone, Appendix C- The Hansford Family

On 6 Aug 1650, Randall Holt re patented Hog Island and the adjacent tract of his father's, amounting to 1022 acres. It is assumed that Randall Jr had reached his majority at this time. In 1679 he patented 1450 acres in Surry Co. Member of House of Burgesses 1656; appointed Justice for Surry Co., 22 Dec 1668. ; Olde Cooper Clan, Moniteau Co. Historical Society, Author: E.M. Richards

A transcription follows: John Hansford of Cheesecake, York. To my eldest sons John Hansford and William Hansford 600 acres of land lying upon Claybanke Creek on the north side of York river to be equally divided between them 3 cows apiece etc; Lineage Of John Stone, Blockmaker, By Spessard Stone, Appendix C- The Hansford Family

Maryland Land Records, Liber 2, fo. 254; Records Provincial Court, Liber B, fo. 224. This John Hansford or Handford (father of Col. Thomas Hansford who was educated {executed in Accomac Co. Va) for his share in Bacon's Rebellion) was perhaps the principal creditor of Weston; though he may have been a connection, for the court record seems to show that Weston, in his will, had named him as executor. He was probably the son of Sir Humphrey

Handford of London, one of the Virginia Company, and descended from the armorial family of Handford of Cheshire and Worcestershire. Mr. Tyler says that the Virginia Hansfords had seventy acres of land in York County, which had originally belonged to Weston. The Maryland land, Westbury Manor, passed to the Conants; Proceedings of the Massachusetts Historical Society By Massachusetts Historical Society 1922, pg 171

In a list prepared by Sir William Berkeley, and preserved among the Harleian MSS. in the British Museum, enumerating the persons who were executed by him in the seventeenth century for participating in Bacon's Rebellion, occurs the name of one Thomas Hansford, who is described by Sir William as "a valiant, stout man," and "a most resolved rebel."1 The few other references to Hansford in the current accounts2 of the times are in harmony with this description, and justify a natural desire to be still further acquainted with him; Thomas Hansford: The First Native Martyr to American Libety, http://www.newrivernotes.com/old_nrn/va/hansford.htm, Thomas Hansford: A tale of Bacon's Rebelion, published by Geo. M. West, Richmond, Va., 1857; republished after the war by a Philadelphia firm, under the title "The Devoted Bride."

Part III –Mary Swan/ Part IV – Mary Harris

Major Robert Harris married to Mary "Mrs. Rice" Claiborne and he was the son of Captain Thomas Harris; [S062128] Gedcom File of Lawson, Stephen M. [steve/@/Lawson.net], (2 OCT 1998); http://gawtwotwinmen.familytreeguide.com/getperson.php?PersonID=I06310&tree=T1&PHPSESSID=abc17f587b377f8f255d21b4226bff2e,

Mary Harris that married Mathew Swann was Robert Harris & Mary Claiboorne first born child; 'Harris Genealogy' by Gideon Dowse Harris, 1914., http://familytreemaker.genealogy.com/users/g/o/e/F-Goebel-FL/GENE1-0021.html

Major Robert Harris I, born ABT 1615 in Wales; died ABT 1701 in New Kent Co., VA. He was the son of 576. Thomas Harris and 577. Adria Gurganey. He married 289. Mary Claibourne 1650 in Yorktown, York Co., VA.; Gedcom File of Lawson, Stephen M. [steve/@/Lawson.net], (2 OCT 1998), 'First Families of America', Vol 1.,http://gawtwotwinmen.familytreeguide.com/getperson.php?personID=I06310&tree=T1&PHPSESSID=abc17f587b377f8f255d21b4226bff2e

Mary Claibourne, born 1630 in Elizabeth City, King Co, VA, British Colonies; died 9 Feb 1709/10 in Glen Cairn, Doswell, Hanover Co., VA. She was the daughter of 578. William Claibourne and 579. Elizabeth Jane Butler. ; Ancestors of Frances Lenora Berry, http://familytreemaker.genealogy.com/users/g/o/e/F-Goebel-FL/GENE1-0021.html

Suite101: Line of Descent from Randall Holt of Virginia | Suite101 http://suite101.com/article/line-of-descent-from-randall-holtof-virginia-a181274#ixzz2GBZFmaMT, By Rosemary E. Bachelor, on Dec 19, 2009, Olde Cooper Clan, Moniteau Co. Historical Society, Author: E.M. Richards

Bacon's Rebellion; http://www.pbs.org/wgbh/aia/part1/1p274.html

Philips of Early Virginia, Mathew Swann; http://www.lfeldhaus.com/philipsofearlyvirginia/id3.html

In 1702 when Mathew Swann wrote his will, he left his daughter Mary, who is the wife of

William Philips, and her son John Philips his "house and plantation where I now live". It's likely that John was the only son of William and Mary Philips born at that time and that was the reason he was named in the will. (1)Hancock Genealogy & Descendants of Georgia, (2)South Carolina and Virginia, http://hancockgenealogy.ucan.us/hann03.htm#284, e-mail: ucanusa@yahoo.com, (3) Descendants of William Hancock, http://www.kykinfolk.com/henry/hancock.htm, email: HANSER5@aol.com, (4)Ye Olde Cooper Clan, Moniteau Co. Historical Society, Author: E.M. Richards

Part V – Mary Claireborne

Olde Cooper Clan, Moniteau Co. Historical Society, Author: E.M. Richards

Lineage Of John Stone, Blockmaker, By Spessard Stone, Appendix C- The Hansford Family

Part VI –Alice Smythe

Andrew was born at Tonbridge (about 40 miles from London) in Kent County, England. He was the son of Margaret Chichle of Canterbury and John Judd (also spelled Judde). , The had a daughter name Alice who married Thomas Smythe (b. 1520; d. 1591).; The Plantagenet Ancestry of King Edward III and Queen Philippa, by George Andrew Moriarty., The Plantagenet Ancestry, by W. H. Turton., History and Antiquities of Essex and the History of the County of Essex, both by Morant.

Alice Judd & Thomas Smythe had 13 children, one named Alice who married Sir William Harris of Creeksea; The Plantagenet Ancestry of King Edward III and Queen Philippa, by George Andrew Moriarty., The Plantagenet Ancestry, by W. H. Turton., History and Antiquities of Essex and the History of the County of Essex, both by Morant.

Alice Smythe, wife of Sir William Harris of Creeksea and the mother of our immigrant ancestor, John Harris; Dorothy Waldegrave, wife of Arthur Harris who died in 1597 and the mother of Sir William Harris of Creeksea; and Johanna Percy, wife of Arthur Harris, who was born about 1476 and the great-grandmother of Sir William Harris of Creeksea.; From Essex England to the Surry Southern USA by: Robert E. Harris Chapter 7 OUR OTHER ENGLISH AND EUROPEAN ANCESTORS AND RELATIVES Pages 909-925; Virginia Settlers and English Adventurers, 3 Vols. in one, by Currer-Briggs. , The Genesis of the United States, Vols. 1 and 2, by Alexander Brown. Vol. 1, pp. 465-469. "Adventurers of Purse and Person, Virginia, 1607-1624/5: Families G-P by John Frederick Dorman.

Pepin II, seigneur de Peronne & de S. Quentin (b. 815, d. Aft. 840); The Plantagenet Ancestry of King Edward III and Queen Philippa, by George Andrew Moriarty., The Plantagenet Ancestry, by W.H. Turton.; http://familytreemaker.genealogy.com/users/f/l/e/Debbie-Fletcher-DE/WEBSITE-0001/UHP-0198.html. The branch back through Poppa goes through the seigneures and comtes of various French provinces, to the famous St William of Gellone (b. 755), in the following documented line: 33. "Poppa" was daughter of: Cunegundis des Francs (b. 855) and Wido, comte de Senlis; 34. Cunegundis des Francs (b. 855) was the daughter of: Pepin II (b. ca. 815), seigneur de Peronne and N. N. de Vermandois; 35. Pepin II (b. ca. 815) was the son of: Cunigundis of Francs (b. 800) and Bernard, roy d'Italie; 36. Cunigundis of Francs (b. 800) was the daughter* of:; 37. St. Guilhem de Gellone (b. 755), comte de Toulouse and Kunigunde des Francs; Our Line Back to St William of

Gellone.,http://alignment2012.com/StWilliam.html

Sir William Harris died on 20 November 1616 at Crixse, County Essex. He married Alice Smythe, daughter of Sir Thomas Smythe of Weston Hangar, County Kent; Will, P. C. C. - 119 Cope - 1616; Brown, Genesis, p. 912-13; Vis. Essex I:213, 414; Will of Sir Thomas Smythe the Younger in Va. Nag. of History & Biography XXVI:267-70; Records of the Virginia Company of London III:84, 326; IV:553; Will. P. C. C. - Savile 42-1622.

Part VII –Dorothy Waldegrave

Dorothy Waldegrave; Peerage of Enland, by Arthur Collins pg 309.

Dorothy Waldegrave married Arthur Harris, Esquire, of Woodham Mortimer and Crixse, County Essex. He died on 30 June 1597, Vis. Essex I: 60, 213; Morant, History of Essex, I: 363; Will, Prerogative Court of Canterbury (50 Cobham) 1597

Sir William Waldegrave of Waltham-Stow, County Essex and Smallbridge, Count Suffolk, died on 2 May 1554. He married Juliane, daughter of Sir John Rainey ford; Vis. Suffolk I: 94; Vis. Essex I:96, 121

Anne Drury married Sir George Waldegrave of Smallbridge, County Suffolk. He V born in 1483 and died in 1528. Muskett, Suffolk Manorial Families I:313-4,354; II:241, 256, 354; Vis. Suffolk 1:93-95; Vis. Essex I:120

Anne Calthorpe died ca. 1494. She married Sir Robert Drury of Hawstead, Count Suffolk. He died on 2 March 1535/6 at St. Edmunds. He is buried at St. Marys; Dictionary of National Biography 6:57-8; Muskett, II: 354

30. Elizabeth Stapleton was born ca. 1440 and died on 18 February 1504/5. She married Sir William Calthorpe, the Sheriff of Norfolk, of Burnham Thorpe, Count Norfolk before 7 March 1463/4. He was born on 30 January 1409/10 and died on 1 November 1494. He is buried at White Friars, Norwich, 29. Sir Miles Stapleton of Ingham and Bedale was born ca. 1408 and died on 30 Sept ber-1 October 1466. He is buried at Ingham Priory. He married (his second Katherine de la Pole of Grafton Regis. She was born ca. 1415 and died on 13/1 October 1488. She is buried at Rewley Abbey, Cecily Bardolf died on 29 September 1432. She married Sir Brian Stapleton of Ingham and Bedale. He was born before 1380 and died in August 1438. They are buried at Ingham Priory; New Complete Peer age, V: 397

William Bardolf, Lord Bardolf of Wormegay, County Norfolk was born 21 October 1349 and died on 29 January 1385/6. He is buried at Friar Carmelites, Lynn County Norfolk. He married Agnes, daughter of Michael, Lord Poynings. She died on 12 June 1403. She is buried at Trinity Priory, Aldgate, London; NCP 419

Elizabeth Damory was born before 23 -May 1318 and died after 1360. She marries John Bardolf, Lord Bardolf, before 25 December 1327. He was born at Wormegay County Norfolk on 13 January 1313/14 and died on July-August 1363 at Assisi, Italy; NCP I: 418-19; IV:45-46; V:715 note d

Elizabeth de Clare was born at Tewkesbury on 16 September 1295 and died on 4 November 1360. She is buried at St. Marys, Ware. She married Sir Roger Damory, Lord Damory (her third) of Bletchingdon, Oxon. He died at Tutbury Castle m 13/14 March 1321/2; NCP V: 736t; IV: 42-43

Sir Gilbert de Clare, Earl of Hertford and Gloucester, was born 2 September 1245: at Christ Church, Hampshire and died on 7 December 1295 at Monmouth Castle. He married (his second) Joan Plantagenet on April-May 1290. Joan, the daughter W Edward I, King of England, was born ca. 1272 at Acre, Holy Land, and died on 2! April 1307 at Clare, County Suffolk (England). NCP V:736+, 702-710; III:244; IV:670 Chart III; Turton, The Plantagenet Ancestry, p. 73.

Sir Richard de Clare, Earl of Clare, of Hertford and Gloucester, was born on 4 August 1222 and died on 15 July 1262. He married (his second) Maude de Lacy, Countess of Lincoln, ca. 25 January 1237/8. She died before 10 March 1288/9; NCP IV: 670 Chart III; V: 696-702, 736+; III: 244; Turton, p. 73, 94

Isabel Marshall died on 17 January 1239/40 at Berkhamstead. She married Sir Gilbert de Clare, Earl of Clare, of Hertford and Gloucester on 9 October 1217. He was born ca. 1180 and died on 25 October 1230 at Penros, Brittany; NCP IV: 670 Chart III; V: 694-5, 736+; 1II:244; Turton, p. 94.)

Isabel de Clare died in 1220. She married Sir William Marshall, Earl of Pembroke and Regent of the Kingdom in August, 1189 in London. He was born ca. 1146 and died on 14 May 1219. They are buried at Temple Church.; NCP IV: 670 Chart III; V:736+; 1:358-364; Turton, p. 94.

Richard de Clare "Strongbow", Earl of Pembroke, Striguil, Justiciar of Ireland, was born ca. 1130 and died ca. 20 April 1176. He married ca. 26 August 1171 to Eva, daughter of Dermot MacKurrough, King of Leinster, at Waterford, Ireland. He was living in 1186. ; IV: 670 Chart III; V: 736+; X:352-357; Turton, p. 114

Isabel de Beaumont married Gilbert de Clare, Earl of Pembroke. He was born ca. 1100 and died on 6 January 1147/8. ; NCP IV: 670 Chart III; V:736+; VII:520; 1:348-352; Turton p.114.

Isabel de Vermandois, Countess of Leicester, died in February 1131. She married Sir Robert de Beaumont, Count of Meulan and companion of William the Conqueror. Re was born ca. 1046 and died on 5 June 1118. They were married in 1096; NCP X:351; IV:670 Chart III; VII:520, 523-526, 737; Turton, p. 100, 114.

Adelaide de Vermandois, Countess of Vermandois and Valois, died ca. 1120. She married Hugh Magnus, Duke of France and Burgundy, Crusader. He died in 1101; NCP X:351, Herbert IV, Count de Vermandois, was born ca. 1032 and died ca. 1080. He married Adele de Vexin, daughter of Raoul III, the Great, Count of Valois and Vexin, Eudes (Otho), Count de Vermandois, was born ca. 1000 and died on 25 May 1045. He married Parvie, Herbert III, Count of Vermandois, was born ca. 955 and died ca. 1000. He married (her second) Ermengarde, daughter of Reinald, Count of Bar, Albert I, the Pious, Count of Vermandois, was born in 920 and died in 987/8. He married Gerberga of Lorraine, daughter of Giselbert, Duke of Lorraine; Turton, p. 112; Moriarty, The Plantagenet Ancestry, p. 134.

Herbert II, Count of Vermandois and Troyes, was born 880-890 and died ca. 943 at St. Quentin. He married Hildebrante (Liegarde), daughter of Robert I, Duke of France., Herbert I de Vermandois, Count of Vermandois, Siegneur of Senlis, Peronne and St. Quentin, was born ca. 840 and died ca. 902. He married Beatrice de Morvois',Pepin, Count of Senlis, Peronne and St. Quentin, was born in 818 in Vernandois, Normandy and died in 848 in Milan, Italy, Pepin,

King of Italy and Lombardy, was born on 12 April 781 and died on 8 July 810 at Milan. He was baptized at Rome by Pope Adrian I., Charlemagne, King of the Franks, and Emperor of the West - expanded the Carolingian Empire also known as "Charles the Great" was born on 2 April 747 and died on 28 January, 813/4. He married (probably, his third) Hildegarde, daughter of Count Geroud of Swabia. She died on 30 April 783.; Moriarty, p. 5; Turton, p. 112

Cunegundis des Francs & Herbert I de Vermandois, Count of Vermandois, Popie de Valois ("Poppa") & Rollo Rognvaldsson, William the Longsword & Espriota de Bretagne, Richard I, Duke of Normandy & Gunnora of Denmark Duchess of Normandy, Richard II, "The Good" Duke of Normandy & Judith de Bretagne (Judith Brittany), Robert I, "The Magnificent" Duke of Normandy & Herleva, William I, "William the Conqueror" & Matilda (Maude) of Flanders, Henry I Beauclerc, King of England & Matilda (Edith) Cammore of Scotland, Empress Matilda & Geoffrey Plantagenet of Anjou, France, Henry II King of England & Eleanor of Aqutane, John of England & Isabella, Countess of Anqouleme, Henry III of England & Eleanor of Provence, Edward I of England &Eleanor of Castile, Edward II of England & Isabella of France, Edward III of England & Philippa of Hainault., Lionel of Antwerp, 1st Duke of Clarence & Elizabeth de Burgh, Philippa Plantagenet & Edmund de Mortimer, 3rd Earl, Lady Elizabeth Mortimer & Sir Henry Percy, Mary of Lancaster, Henry Percy, 1st Earl of Northumberland and Margaret Neveille, daughter of Ralph Neville, 2nd Baron Neville and Maud Neville, Lady Elanor Neville, Ralph Neville, 2nd Baron Neville, Henry Percy, 3rd Earl &Eleanor, Lady Poynings, Richard Poynings & Eleanor, Countess of Arundel., Henry Percy, 4th Earl & Maude Herbert, Henry Algernon Percy & Catherine Spencer; "Christian Settipani & Patrick van Kerrebrouck, La Prehistoire des Capetiens 481-987, Premiere partie: Merovingians, Carolingians et Robertiens (Villeneuve d'Ascq: Editions Christian, 1993), tableau 8. Hereinafter cited as Capetiens 481-987. http://familytreemaker.genealogy.com/users/f/l/e/Debbie-Fletcher-DE/WEBSITE-0001/UHP-0198.html, http://alignment2012.com/StWilliam.html & the LDS"

72 Sir Thomas Percy & Eleanor Harbottle; Thomas Percy, Sir Knight at geni.com (citing as sources (1) Adams, Arthur, and Howard Horace Angerville. Living Descendants of Blood Royal London: World Nobility and Peerage, 1959. Vol. 4 page 417; (2) Charles Mosley, Burke's Peerage and Baronetage, 106th edition), Essex England to the Surry Southern USA by: Robert E. Harris Chapter 7 OUR OTHER ENGLISH AND EUROPEAN ANCESTORS AND RELATIVES Pages 909-925., This article incorporates text from a publication now in the public domain: Herbermann, Charles, ed. (1913). "Bl. Thomas Percy". Catholic Encyclopedia. Robert Appleton Company. (Author Burton, Edwin}, Sir Bernard Burke. A genealogical and heraldic history of the landed gentry of Great Britain & Ireland , Volume 2. Harrison, 1871. pg 1153.; Thomas Percy, Sir Knight at geni.com (citing as sources (1) Adams, Arthur, and Howard Horace Angerville. Living Descendants of Blood Royal London: World Nobility and Peerage, 1959. Vol. 4 page 417

Olde Cooper Clan, Moniteau Co. Historical Society, Author: E.M. Richards, The Plantagenet Ancestry, Lt.-Col. W. H. Turton
http://www.genealogical.com/products/The%20Plantagenet%20Ancestry/5850.html, House of Plantegenet Family tree, http://www.britroyals.com/plantagenet.htm

Part VIII –Joanna Percy

Joan (Joanna) Percy & Arthur Harris; Peerage of England, 1812, by Sir Egerton Brydges pg 309, 15th Edition, Encyclopedia Britannica - 1975.,The Plantagenet Ancestry of King Edward III and Queen Philippa, by George Andrew Moriarty., The Plantagenet Ancestry, by W. H. Turton., History and Antiquities of Essex and the History of the County of Essex, both by Morant.

Johanna Percy; Christian Settipani & Patrick van Kerrebrouck, La Prehistoire des Capetiens 481-987; Premiere partie: Merovingians, Carolingians et Robertiens (Villeneuve d'Ascq: Editions Christian, 1993; tableau 8. Hereinafter cited as Capetiens 481-987; Charles Mosley, Burke's Peerage and Baronetage, 106th edition), Essex England to the Surry Southern USA by: Robert E. Harris Chapter 7 OUR OTHER ENGLISH AND EUROPEAN ANCESTORS AND RELATIVES Pages 909-925; This article incorporates text from a publication now in the public domain: Herbermann, Charles, ed. (1913); Peerage of England, 1812, by Sir Egerton Brydges pg 309, 15th Edition, Encyclopedia Britannica - 1975

Alfred "The Great", King of England, & Ealhswith of Gaini (daughter of Aethelred "Mucil" Ealdormand of the Gaini), Edward I "The Elder", King of the Anglo Saxons & Eadgifu (daughter of Sigehelm Ealdor mand of Kent, Olde Cooper Clan, Moniteau Co. Historical Society, Author: E.M. Richards, The Plantagenet Ancestry, Lt.-Col. W. H. Turton http://www.genealogical.com/products/The%20Plantagenet%20Ancestry/5850.html, House of Plantegenet Family tree, http://www.britroyals.complantagenet.htm

Edmund I "The Magnificent", King of England & Saint Aelfgifu, Olde Cooper Clan, Moniteau Co. Historical Society, Author: E.M. Richards, The Plantagenet Ancestry, Lt.-Col. W. H. Turton http://www.genealogical.com/products/The%20Plantagenet%20Ancestry/5850.html, House of Plantegenet Family tree, http://www.britroyals.com/plantagenet.htm

Edgar "The Peaceful", King of England & Ealfthyrth "the Fair" (Elfrida), Ethelred II "The Unready", King of England & Elgifa Gunnarsson (daughter of Thored Ealdorman Gunnarsson, Earl of Wessex), Edmund II Ironside, King of England & Ealdgyth of Northumbria; Olde Cooper Clan, Moniteau Co. Historical Society, Author: E.M. Richards, The Plantagenet Ancestry, Lt.-Col. W. H. Turton http://www.genealogical.com/products/The%20Plantagenet%20Ancestry/5850.html, House of PlantegenetFamily tree, http://www.britroyals.com/plantagenet.htm

Part IX – Matilda Of Scotland

Edward "The Atheling", "The Exile" of Scotland & Agtha von Braunschweigh of Hungary (daughter of King of Hungary Stephen I)a, Malcom III Cammore, King of Scotland; & Margaret "Atheling" Saint of Scotland, Matilda (Edith) Cammore Of Scotland & Henry I Beauclerc; Olde Cooper Clan, Moniteau Co. Historical Society, Author: E.M. Richards, The Plantagenet Ancestry, Lt.-Col. W.H. Turton http://www.genealogical.com/products/The%20Plantagenet%20Ancestry/5850.html, House of Plantegenet Family tree, http://www.britroyals.com/plantagenet.htm

Additional references cited:

The Grasty Families of America; Dolores Merritt

History and Registers of Charles Parish, York Co., VA, Births 1648-1789, Deaths 1665-1787, pp 51, 2 & 204, Landon C Bell, Published by the VA State Library Board

Register of Charles Parish, York County, Colonial VA

Parish Lines, Diocese of Souther Virginia; Colonel Withers G. Birdsong

Sussex County VA Records

Procession orders by the Anglican Church 1759 and 1771, against the land of Charles Birdsong in Nasemond County, VA; Mary Duvall

Head of Families - Virginia 1582

Head of Families - Virginia 1783

Head of Families - Virginia 1784

Head of Families - Virginia 1790

Brunswick Co., VA marriag records

Brunswick Co., VA Deed bl 14 p 297 11 jul 1787

Marriage Records, sussex co., Va 1754-1810

Virginia Marriage Records, Viriginia Magazine of History and Biography, William an dMary College Quarterly 1984

1787 census of Virginia

Sussex County VA index to wills (1754-2948) LDS #034.1 55

Albemarle Register

Anglican Church

Virginia settlers and English adventuress; Noel Briggs; pg 1347

The descendants of four members of the first colony of virginia ini 1609,Rev. Francies Campbell Symonds, D.D.

William Hubbard; http://books.google.com/books?id=REJVAAAAMAAJ&pg=PA294&lpg=PA294&dq=william+hubbard+abigail+dudley&source=bl&ots=OnJp7ZcCMi&sig=elpFGa49HwWEiHkKYs42d3RK4KE&hl=en&sa=X&ei=NPYsUbWQKePq2QWprYGgAw&ved=0CDMQ6AEwAA#v=onepage&q=william%20hubbard%20abigail%20dudley&f=false; norse king hubba

Thomas Hubbard Hobart; http://www.royalblood.co.uk/D1241/I1241413.html

Christian Settipani & Patrick van Kerrebrouck, La Prehistoire des Capetiens 481-987, Premiere partie: Merovingians, Carolingians et Robertiens (Villeneuve d'Ascq: Editions Christian, 1993), tableau 8. Hereinafter cited as Capetiens 481-987. http://familytreemaker.genealogy.com/users/f/l/e/Debbie-Fletcher-DE/WEBSITE-0001/UHP-0198.html, http://alignment2012.com/StWilliam.html & the LDS

Thomas Percy, Sir Knight at geni.com (citing as sources (1) Adams, Arthur, and Howard Horace Angerville. Living Descendants of Blood Royal London: World Nobility and Peerage, 1959. Vol. 4 page 417; (2) Charles Mosley, Burke's Peerage and Baronetage, 106th edition),

Essex England to the Surry Southern USA by: Robert E. Harris Chapter 7 OUR OTHER ENGLISH AND EUROPEAN ANCESTORS AND RELATIVES Pages 909-925., This article incorporates text from a publication now in the public domain: Herbermann, Charles, ed. (1913). "Bl. Thomas Percy". Catholic Encyclopedia. Robert Appleton Company. (Author Burton, Edwin}, Sir Bernard Burke. A genealogical and heraldic history of the landed gentry of Great Britain & Ireland, Volume 2. Harrison, 1871. pg 1153.

Wives and Daughters: The Women of Sixteenth-Century England (1984), compiled by Kathy Lynn Emerson. Retrieved on 05 January 2013, http://www.kateemersonhistoricals.com/TudorWomenH-He.htm Peerage of England, 1812, by Sir Egerton Brydges pg 309, 15th Edition, Encyclopedia Britannica - 1975.,The Plantagenet Ancestry of King Edward III and Queen Philippa, by George Andrew Moriarty., The Plantagenet Ancestry, by W. H. Turton., History and Antiquities of Essex and the History of the County of Essex, both by Morant.

Olde Cooper Clan, Moniteau Co. Historical Society, Author: E.M. Richards, The Plantagenet Ancestry, Lt.-Col. W. H. Turton http://www.genealogical.com/products/The%20Plantagenet%20Ancestry/5850.html, House of Plantegenet Family tree, http://www.britroyals.com/plantagenet.htm

The Plantagenet Ancestry of King Edward III and Queen Philippa, by George Andrew Moriarty., The Plantagenet Ancestry, by W.H. Turton.

Chapter Three

Thomas Tomlinson, Jr and Elizabeth Cooke; Olde Cooper Clan, Moniteau Co. Historical Society, Author: E.M. Richards

John Tomlinson, Sr and Mary Chappell, Thomas Tomlinson and Mary Cotton; Olde Cooper Clan, Moniteau Co. Historical Society, Author: E.M. Richards

Chapter Four

William Birdsong & Winaford Allee; Olde Cooper Clan, Moniteau Co. Historical Society, Author: E.M. Richards; Probate; Personal files

Birdsong William -- 1798 Jan 14 - 1863 Sep 11,.Birdsong Winaford -- 1886 Jul 25 -- Aged 85y 6m 10d ; Olde Cooper Clan, Moniteau Co. Historical Society, Author: E.M. Richards

Duvrai emploi des Peres", which was translated into English by Thomas Smith under the title, "A Treatise concerning the right use of the Fathers 1651; A Treatise concerning the right use of the Fathers 1651)

Jean d'Allee Sr. was educated at Poitiers and Saumur; and in 1626 became the Huguenot minister at the great church at Charenton. He was the president of the last national synod held in France in 1659, which met at Loudun. Of his works, the best known is the treatise; H.M Baird: The Huguenots and the Revocation of the Edict of Nantes", 1895, Vol. 1, p. 412); Allee Genelogical Study, Compiled by Raymond Allee Circa 1932.)

Notes for Nicholas John Allee; Halifax VA voting records before 1764; Pittsylvania land entries, 1750s area with Jeremiah Stover

Ann Stephens was born 1738 in Halifax County, Virginia, and died Bef. 1797 in Virginia. It is thought that Ann Stephens was a Powhatan Indian. This according to Court Proceedings 5 April 1787, p.818. Our own family legend was that she was Spanish; Olde Cooper Clan, Moniteau Co. Historical Society, Author: E.M. Richards

On August 27, 1772 he and Ann sold land to Robert Stockton of Pittsylvania County, Virginia. Land Records show that as of May 31, 1774 he owned 546 acres on the Little Branch of New River. On April 5, 1774 a survey was made in Fincastle County on the South side of Little River, a branch of New River for Thomas Allee.; Pittsylvania County, Virginia. Land Records, August 27, 1772

On January 1756 Nicholas Allee was on the private payroll of Captain Robert Steward's Company, Troop of Light Horse, Cumberland Fort, Virginia, commanded by General George Washington.; Murtie June Clark, Colonial Soldiers of the South 1732 - 1774, BEN PUB Company, Inc.1983, pp. xvii, 346, 348. Clayton Library, Houston, Texas GEN 975.C594

Nicholas Allee; tax list of Pittsylvania County, Virginia in 1767

Thursday, September 28, 1758 he presented a petition to the Virginia House of Burgesses stating that he ought to be paid for a disabling wound he received last year in June; Virginia House of Burgesses to request payment for provisions which he had provided in 1757

The Last Will and Testament of Nicholas Allee; wills, Montgomery County, Virginia July Court 1808

David Allee, of French and English descent, was born on April 25, 1762 in Pittsylvania co., VA. His parents were Nicolas and Ann Allee et.al; Moniteau Co. MO Family History Book p 94 Rev David Allee

David Allee served in the American Voluntary War; VIRGINIA MILITIA IN THE REVOLUTIONARY WAR PART II/ Virginia's Share in the Military Movements of the Revolution page 129; Daughter American Revolution War (DAR), http://www.dar.org/library/online_research.cfm

Moniteau Co. MO Family History Book p 94, Published by Taylor Publishing, David Allee's Childrenhttp://tthompsonmedia.com/west/showmedia.php?mediaID=185&medialinkID=269; 2) 108 ALLEE, DAVID.--Cooper County, Mo., May 6, 1833. Born in Pittsylvania, Va., April 25, 1762. Served in Henry, Spring of 1777, under Capt. Peter Herston; VIRGINIA MILITIA IN THE REVOLUTIONARY WAR PART II, Virginia's Share in the Military Movements of the Revolution page 129

David was granted 200 acres for his service during the American Revolutionary War.; THE KENTUCKY LAND GRANTS, CHAPTER IV GRANTS SOUTH OF GREEN RIVER (1797-1866); Volume 1, Part 1, CHAPTER IV GRANTS SOUTH OF GREEN RIVER (1797-1866), THE COUNTIES OF KENTUCKY;page 262, Grantee: Allee, David, Acres: 200, Book: 23, Page: 147 Date Survey: 11-14-1804, County: Barren,Watercourse

Allee Genelogical Study, Compiled by Raymond Allee Circa 1932.

Murtie June Clark, Colonial Soldiers of the South 1732 – 1774.

Olde Cooper Clan, Moniteau Co. Historical Society, Author: E.M. Richards, A Treatise concerning the right use of the Fathers 1651). (H.M Baird: The Huguenots and the Revocation of the Edict of Nantes", 1895, Vol. 1, p. 412). (Allee Genelogical Study, Compiled by Raymond Allee Circa 1932.)

David allee William Birdsong, & James Birdsong The war of 1812; http://www.gatewayno.com/history/War1812.html

David Allee's Children, http://tthompsonmedia.com/west/getperson.php?personID=I02977&tree=West

Ye Olde Cooper Clan, Moniteau Co. Historical Society, Author: E.M. Richards

William & Winsford Ancestor #: A001329 http://www.lfthompson.com/davidcharity_allee.htm

THE KENTUCKY LAND GRANTS, Volume 1, Part 1, CHAPTER IV GRANTS SOUTH OF GREEN RIVER (1797-1866)
THE COUNTIES OF KENTUCKY, page 262, Grantee: Allee, David, Acres: 200, Book: 23, Page: 147, Date Survey: 11-14-1804, County: Barren, Watercourse

Chapter Five

Jobe Abraham -- 1836 Jul 25 - 1923 May 01; Old Salem Cemetery http://www.moniteau.net/cemetery/oldsalem/oldsalem.htm

Peter Birdsong, it appears he had family members living with him et.al; 1850 American Community Survey Moniteau County, Missouri/prepared by the U.S. Census Bureau, 1850

Marriage certificate of Peter Birdsong & Elizabeth Jobe; researcher personal files

Peter Birdsong Civil War documents; researchers personal files

1850 American Community Survey Moniteau County, Missouri/prepared by the U.S. Census Bureau, 1850.

Peter Birdsong, 54 years old et.al; 1880 American Community Survey Moniteau County, Missouri/prepared by the U.S. Census Bureau, 1880. page 15, #140

Peter Birdsong Age 73 et.al; 1900 American Community Survey Moniteau County, Missouri/prepared by the U.S. Census Bureau, 1900.

Peter Birdsong Age 82 et.al; 1910 American Community Survey Moniteau County, Missouri/prepared by the U.S. Census Bureau, 1910.

Peter and Elizabeth attended Salem Baptist Church Members through 1883 (by date joined); Salem Baptist Church Members through 1883 (by date joined), retrieved on December 28th 2012, from http://www.moniteau.net/salemmem.htm.

Elizabeth Jobe daughter of Abraham Jobe and Clarinda Chandler, was born in 1840 in Moniteau Co.,MO, died on 14 Jan 1912 et.al; Missouri Death Certificates, http://www.sos.mo.gov/archives/resources/deathcertificates/; Moniteau County Missour,Jobe/Birdsong Cemetery listings, retrieved on December 28th 2012, from http://www.moniteau.net/cemetery/jobe/birdsong-elizabeth-peter.JPG

The name Jobe has origins in both English and French et.al; Jobe Family History, by Emma Katherine Katschman Bommell, 2000pg. 11-17, Moniteau County Missour, Jobe/Birdsong Cemetery listings, retrieved on December 28th 2012, from http://www.moniteau.net/cemetery/jobe/jobe-abraham-clarinda.JPG; Jobe Family Crest and Name History; http://www.houseofnames.com/jobe-family-crest

Joshua Jobe; Dell, Cecil, Pioneers of Old Frederick County, Virginia (1995), Marceline, MO: WalsworthPublishing Company, 1995, pp. 411-420

A resident of Shenandoah City, Virginia enlisted February 18, 1776 in Capt. William Croghan's Co et.al; Jobe Family History, by Emma Katherine Katschman Bommell, 2000 pg. 11-17 Reference: Jobe Family History, by Emma Katherine Katschman Bommell, 2000 pg. 11-17, Dell, Cecil, Pioneers of Old Frederick County, Virginia (1995), Marceline, MO: Walsworth Publishing Company, 1995, pp. 411-420

Thomas Scott, born in Barren County, KY in 1810 et.al; History of Moniteau County", page 318; Olde Cooper Clan, Moniteau Co. Historical Society, Author: E.M. Richards

Elizabeth (Jobe) Birdsong; ref. January 18, 1912 California Democrat newspaper

Census on Abraham S Jobe & Clarinda Chandler; 1840 American Community Survey Cole County, Missouri/prepared by the U.S. Census Bureau, 1840.page 86, Line 28

Census on Abraham S Jobe & Clarinda Chandler; 1850 American Community Survey Moniteau County, Missouri/prepared by the U.S. Census Bureau, 1850. Page 40

Census on Abraham S Jobe & Clarinda Chandler; 1860 American Community Survey Moniteau County, Missouri/prepared by the U.S. Census Bureau, 1860 Page 769

Census on Abraham S Jobe & Clarinda Chandler; 1870 American Community Survey Moniteau County, Missouri/prepared by the U.S. Census Bureau, 1870 Moniteau Co, Mo Census - Walker Township, page 479; 1880 American Community Survey Moniteau County, Missouri/prepared by the U.S. Census Bureau, 1880. page 15, #140

Abraham Jobe's death certificate; personal files

Salem Baptist Church Members through 1883 (by date joined), retrieved on December 28th 2012, from http://www.moniteau.net/salemmem.htm,, Moniteau County Missour, Jobe/Birdsong Cemetery listings, retrieved on December 28th 2012, from http://www.moniteau.net/cemetery/jobe/birdsong-elizabeth-peter.JPG

Jacob served in the American Revolutionary War
https://familysearch.org/pal:/MM9.1.1/N9KM-Z38

Chapter Six

John Birdsong; 1910 American Community Survey Moniteau County, Missouri/prepared by the U.S. Census Bureau, 1910; 1920 American Community Survey Kansas City, Kansas /prepared by the U.S. Census Bureau, 1920; 1930 American Community Survey Kansas City, Kansas /prepared by the U.S. Census Bureau, 1930; 1940 American Community Survey Kansas City, Kansas /prepared by the U.S. Census Bureau, 1940

Marie Wood Birdsong death certificate; researchers personal files

Eugene "Gene" Birdsong death; Kansas City Star, personal files

Marion Wood & Lillian; 1940 American Community Survey Kansas City, Kansas /prepared by the U.S. Census Bureau, 1940

Strawberry Hill Museum & Cultural Center; https://www.wycokck.org/InternetDept.aspx?id=16224&banner=15284

Personal Interview Sister Claire from St John's Orphanage

Letter from Sister Theodora from St John's Orphanage

John Wood was educated as a lawyer and employed by London capitalists to locate lands for them in the Colony of Virginia, The first of this Wood family to be in America was Thomas Wood, who came over from England at age 16 in the 1600's to Missouri and others of the Wood family went to Arkansas to settle; The Wood Family in Virginia, by M. B. Wood (written 1892).

Jonathan Wood; LDS - Ancestral File Number AFN: 1WMQ-MQP

Jonathan Wood (1675) & John wood (1708); LDS - Ancestral File Number AFN: 1WMR-H37

Jonathan, Isaac, John Wood; LDS - Ancestral File Number AFN: 1WMR-MM3

Jonathan Wood's name appears on a list of Botetourt County Militia, in Captain Mills' Company, the 56th district.; Botetourt County Militia, in Captain Mills' Company, the 56th district.

John Wood & Nancy Davidson; LDS - Ancestral File Number AFN: QLF5-VH

Jonathan Sr. WOOD (AFN: 1WMQ-MM3) Sex: M Event(s): Birth: 1745 Leesburg, Loudoun Co., Virginia Death: 13 Nov 1804 Moccasin Creek, Scott Co., Virginia, Fort Houston Burial: Fort Houston, Big Moccasin Crk, Scott Co.

John WOOD Sex: M Event(s): Birth: Abt. 1708 Westmoreland, Virginia Parents: Father: Jonathan WOOD Mother:; The Wood and Related Families of Southwest Virginia, by James I Wood.

Nancy Davidson's parents lived somewhere on the South Branch of the Potomac River. Et.al; Judge M. B. Wood, in his book HISTORY OF THE WOOD FAMILY IN VIRGINIA Henry Wood, Sr (1773); LDS - Ancestral File

Henry Wood, Sr (1773); LDS - Ancestral File; Number AFN: 1LSJ-8BD & 1WMQ-MKN, & 24LB-0K

221

Both Henry and Sarah (Sally) were buried at: Cemetery Big Moccasin, Valley 4 mi E., Gate City, Scott County, Virginia. Henry Wood and five generations of his family are buried about three miles East of Gate City, Virginia, near Moore Memorial Church.; The Wood and Related Families of Southwest Virginia, page 86.

Henry Wood, another son of Jonathan Wood I, represented Russell County, Virginia in the legislature, and after the formation of Scott County was also one of the early sheriff's, and one of its gentlemen justices. Clintwood, Virginia, the county seat of Dickerson County, was named for a grandson of Henry Wood, Major Henry Clinton Wood."; The Wood and Related Families of Southwest Virginia, by James I. Wood. Henry Wood's birth/death; LDS Family History Center (AFN: 1LSJ-8BD

The place where Henry was born is now in Scott County, Virginia, which was formed by portions of Russell, Washington, and Lee Counties in 1814. Henry was born on May 18, 1773 Near, Fort Houston, on, Big Moccasin Creek, Russell County, Virginia.; The Wood Family in Virginia, by M. B. Wood, Page 34 and 54.

Henry's family can be found at the LDS Family History Center (AFN: 1LSJ-8BD). The LDS file contains this information: Henry's birth is listed as August 14, 1773. His death date as February 4, 1859.; LDS Family History Center (AFN: 1LSJ-8BD)IGI Record Henry WOOD Sex: M Marriage(s): Spouse: Sally LAWSON Marriage: 14 Aug 1794 Big Moccasin Creek, Scott, Virginia; Source Information: Batch number: 8487104 Source Call No. 1395909 Type: Film Sheet: 46, The Wood Family in Virginia, by M. B. Wood, page78-80 (written 1892).

Marie Wood; 1820 Scott County Virginia Census: [Name of Head of Household - free white males 0-10, 10-16, 16-18, 16-26, 26-45, over 45, free white females 0-10, 10-16, 16-26, over 45] Wood, Henry - 021101-00201; 820 American Community Survey Scott County Virginia /prepared by the U.S. Census Bureau, 1820 and Wood Henry Jr. m Hannah f 44VA Sarah f 18 VA George m 16 VA Henry m 14 VA Mary f 12 VA Emily f 9 VA Margaret f 7 VA+; 1850 MILLER COUNTY, MISSOURI CENSUS HOUSEHOLDS 1-200; http://www.rootsweb.com/~momiller/miller501.htm Family #22

Henry Wood and Sallie Lawson settled in Moccasin Valley, Scott County, Virginia, about three miles East of Gate City. ; The Wood and Related Families of Southwest Virginia, by James I. Wood, page 80.

Henry Tolbert Wood (1836) & Marie Wood; LDS Family History Center AFN: 24LC-H9

Tolwood Cemetery: Wood, Henry 7 Jan. 1805 - 19 Mar. 1888 h/o Hannah; http://www.rootsweb.com/~momiller/tolwood_cemetery.html

Wood, Henry Vineyard, Hannah 5-1-1831; Scott County Virginia Marriages 1830-1839; ftp://ftp.rootsweb.com/pub/usgenweb/va/scott/vitals/marr2.txt
http://www.rootsweb.com/~vascott/marriage/marr2.html

Marion Wood & Lillian; marriage certificate; researchers' personal files. Marion Wood & Lillian; 1940 American Community Survey Kansas City, Kansas /prepared by the U.S. Census Bureau, 1940.

Chapter Seven

John Birdsong, death certificate; researcher's personal files

John & Della Birdsong marriage certificate; researchers personal files

John & Marie Birdsong marriage certificate; researchers personal files

Interview with John Birdsong, Betty Sue Waldo, Kathy (Birdsong) Smith, Violet Birdsong

Chosin Reservoir, The 1st Marine Division; This Kind of War by T.R. Fehrenbach; http://en.wikipedia.org/wiki/File:Chosin.jpg; http://www.koreanwar.com/MarineCorps.htm

John Birdsong USMC Honorable Discharge; researcher's personal files

Della Birdsong eulogy; Reflections of Della (Rhynerson) Birdsong, eulogy written by Karla Woodward a minster at the Church of the Resurrection

Della Birdsong obituary, Kansas City Star, August 17, 2009

Della Birdsong eulogy; Authored by; Sarah Jade Birdsong

Arent Theunissen Van Hengel b. The Netherland, pb. in or nr. Hengelo in the present province of Gelderland.;Rinearson, Peter M., Arthur P. Rynearson, A Genealogy of the Reyniersen Family, (1997). Pg. 27.

Van Hengel; Olive Tree Genealogy, http://www.olivetreegenealogy.com/nn/17th/dny_22.shtml, retrieved on 12/29/2012.

Jacob (Yacob) Rinearson American Revolutionary War; American Revolutionary War https://familysearch.org/pal:/MM9.1.1/N9KM-Z38

Isaac Hewlick Rinearson - Civil War; United States, Civil War Soldiers Index," index, FamilySearch (https://familysearch.org/pal:/MM9.1.1/F953-KYH : accessed 30 Dec 2012), Isaac Rinearson, 1861-1865. He was a private part of the Union, 85th Regiment, Indian Infantry; "United States, Civil War Soldiers Index," index, FamilySearch (https://familysearch.org/pal:/MM9.1.1/F953-KYH : accessed 30 Dec 2012)

Harry Rhynerson; Social Security Card; researchers personal files. Harry & Vera Rhyneron; Osla Anderson; Cora (Anderson) Stump; 1940 American Community Survey Kansas City, Kansas /prepared by the U.S. Census Bureau, 1940

EDWARD BENNETT sailed from Weymouth, Malcombe-Regis Dorset, England to Weymouth MA with his wife and 4 children in 1636. et.al; Book entitled "The Other Bennetts", authored by Isabel (BENNETT) Ridell and information obtained from the Chemung County Historical Society, of Chemung New York, 415 E. Water Street, Elmira, New York, 14901:

Bennett Family; "Nine Yankee Farmers: A Bennett Line from 1636 to 1916" by Ralph B. Bennett Jr. - San Diego, CA - April 1990 (Self Published).

Will of William Bennett; STATE CAPITOL, HARTFORD, CONN. Historical Records of Stratford, Conn. Page 513, First Volume, 1639-1886

Captain Thaddeus Bennett American Revolutionary War; DEPARTMENT OF THE INTERIOR A. W. Wed. File 17278 Bukeau of Pensions

Battles engaged in Residence of soldier at enlistment, Parish of Stratford et.al; Author:, E. B. Bennett, E. Berlin, Ct. V. Warner, Com'r.

Smith Bennett & Julia E Bailey 1860, Fairhaven, Carroll Co., IL; Van Rensselaer Bailey.Source: Census 1860 [Data: Roll: M653_159, Page: 1001]Resided: 1870, York, Carroll Co., IL Source: Census 1870 [Data: Post Office: Mount Carroll, Roll: M593_191, Page: 286, Image: 574]

Julia Bailey; 1880, York, Carroll Co., IL Source: Census 1880 [Data: Roll: T9_178; Family History Film: 1254178; Page: 641D; Enumeration District: 24; Image: 0485]

Smith Bennett was a farmer; United States Census, 1870," index and images, FamilySearch (https://familysearch.org/pal:/MM9.1.1/M646-QXG : accessed 31 Dec 2012), Smith Bennett in household of Smith Bennett, Illinois, United States; citing p. 1, family 3, NARA microfilm publication M593, FHL microfilm 545690.; Resided: 1860, Fairhaven, Carroll Co., IL Source: Census 1860 [Data: Roll: M653_159, Page: 1001]Resided: 1870, York, Carroll Co., IL Source: Census 1870 [Data: Post Office: Mount Carroll, Roll: M593_191, Page: 286, Image: 574]

Smith Bennett born in 1812, Rhonde Island; 1860, Fairhaven, Carroll Co., IL Source: Census 1860 [Data: Roll: M653_159, Page: 1001]; Van Rensselaer Bailey

Julia E. Bailey; Resided: 1860, Fairhaven, Carroll Co., IL Source: Census 1860 [Data: Roll: M653_159, Page: 1001]; esided: 1870, York, Carroll Co., IL Source: Census 1870 [Data: Post Office: Mount Carroll, Roll: M593_191, Page: 286, Image: 574]; 1889, On own 167 acre farm, with son Granville, in York, Carroll Co., IL Source: Van Rensselaer Bailey

Cora Dell Anderson daughter of Solomon Anderson and Osea Miles, et.al; ; Manley E Bennett; Death Certificate, researchers personal files

Alexander Mills obituary; LaCygne Journal, March 16, 1928

Mary F. Mills obituary; La Cygne Journal, LaCygne , Kansas Nov. 23, 1889

Birdsong Family Genealogyhttp://www.birdsongfamily.com/genealogy/resources.htm

Missouri Death Certificates http://www.sos.mo.gov/archives/resources/deathcertificates/

Daughter American Revolution War (DAR)
http://www.dar.org/library/online_research.cfm

Descendants of Robert Hill http://familytreemaker.genealogy.com/users/h/a/l/Roy-E-Hall/GENE5-0019.html

Message boards: http://www.rootsweb.ancestry.com/

Immigration: William Hanock 1580 – 1621 came on the "Margaret" from Devon shire, England

Randall Holt, Sr 1605 came on the "George" England

SURNAME INDEX

1st Duke of Clarence, 80, 214
1st Duke of Lancaster, 81
1st Earl of Northumberland, 80, 214
Aaliyah Yeldell, 165
Abigal Bennett, 191, 192
Abijah Sterling, 193
Abraham Job, 121
Abraham Jobe, 116, 118, 122, 123, 219, 220
Abraham S. Jobe, 123, 125, 126
Abraham Voorhees Rinearson, 174
Ada E. Rhynerson, 175
Adam Cunningham, 122
Adelaide de Vermandois, 65, 213
Adele de Vexin, 65, 213
Adeline Rinearson, 175
Adria Gurgany, 50
Adriantje Arentsen Van Hengel, 171
Aenor de Chatellerault, 79
Aerent van Hengel, 170
Aernout Reyniersen Van Hengel, 172
Aethelred "Mucil" Ealdormand, 86, 215
Aethelwulf, king of the West Saxons, 86
Agivald of the Bavarians, 76
Agnes, 34, 66, 212
Agnes Nikolls, 34
Agtha von Braunschweigh of Hungary, 88, 215
Albert I, the Pious, 65, 213
Albert Zimmerman, 178
Alexander Mills, 177, 181
Alexis Pena, 165
Alfred "The Great", 1, 86, 215
Alfred the Great, 33

Alice Ann Birdsong, 116, 117
Alice Edington, 189
Alice Judd, 53, 54, 211
Alice Smythe, 32, 54, 55, 67, 211, 212
Alida Reyniersen Van Hengel, 172
Alley D Allee, 106
Alvin Kemp Vaughan, 146
Alycia Pena, 165
Alyssa Toth, 165
Amanda E Rynearson, 174
Amiliyana Birdsong, 165
Amy Bennett, 195
Amy Birdsong, 165
Anderson Birdsong, 98
Andrew Job, Jr, 120
Andrew Job, Sr, 120
Andrew Smythe, 54
Aner Minerva, 194
Angie Birdsong, 165
Ann Brown, 121
Ann Edwards, 45
Ann Gurgany, 50
Ann Stephens, 107, 108, 218
Ann Tomlinson, 95
Anna Hill, 112
Anna M Wood, 146
Anna Safronia, 101
Anne Calthorpe, 67, 212
Anne Devereaux, 82
Anne Drury, 67, 212
Anne Jernegan, 83
Anne Philips, 44
Anne Tomlinson, 94
Annetje Hermans, 171
Annie Birdsong, 98, 101
Anthony Bennett, 191
Anthony Loya, 165
Anthony Spiltimber, 46, 47, 208
Aoife MacMurrough, 66
Arent Teunissen Van Hengel, 170

Arent Theunissen, 170
ARENTSEN, 169
Ariaentje Reyniersen Van Hengel, 172
Arnulf of Flanders, 77
Arnulf of Metz, 76
Arthur Allen, 47
Arthur Birdsong, 116
Arthur Harris, 32, 64, 67, 82, 83, 211, 212, 215
Ashlynn White, 165
Aucke Janse Van Nuyse, 171
Augustine Hancock, 34
Auke Reyniersen, 171, 172, 173, 174
Auke Reyniersen Van Hengel, 171, 172
Baby Birdsong, 101, 116
Bambi Birdsong, 165
Barbara Arentsen Van Hengel, 171
Barent Reyniersen, 173
Bartholomew Jobe, 123
Beatrice de Morvois', 65, 213
Begga to Ansegisel, 64, 76
Benjam Job, 120
Benjamin Allee, 107
Benjamin Birdsong, 91
Benjamin Tomlinson, 93, 94, 95
Bernard, King of Italy, 64, 76
Betsy Bennett, 193
Bill Hansett, 165
Bill Massey, 178
Bill Remington, 181
Brandy Birdsong, 165
Brett Birdsong, 165
Bridgett Yeldell, 165
Brooke Birdsong, 165
Bud Miller, 178
Burell Tomlinson, 94
Burwell Tomlinson, 95
Butts Birdsong, 29

Caleb Job, 121
Capt Stephen Cole, 112
Capt Thomas Harris, 202
Capt. Arbuckle, 113
Capt. Joshua Martin, 113
Capt. Peter Herston, 112
Capt. Thomas Cummings, 113
Capt. Thomas Holt, 38
Captain James Johnson's, 146
Captain Robert Steward, 108, 218
Captain Thomas Harris, 48, 50
Carl Ray Crump, 164
Carloman de Landen, 64, 76
Carter Crafford, 45, 207
Catherine Apperson, 101
Catherine Reyniersen, 173
Catherine Smythe, 54
Catherine Spencer, 82, 214
Cecily Bardolf, 67, 212
Charity Bibee, 114
Charity Birdsong, 98, 99, 100
Charity Bybee, 98, 108, 112
Charlemagne, 64, 76, 214
Charles Birdsong, 22, 29, 216
Charles Hansford, 39, 40
Charles Martel, 64, 76
Charles the Great, 33, 64, 76, 214
Charles VIII of France, 82
Cheryl Birdsong, 3, 7, 151, 165, 197
Cheryl Birdsong-Dyer, 3, 7, 165
Chris Birdsong, 165
Christoffel (Christopher) Reyniersen, 173
Clara Ella Mills, 176, 177, 181, 184
Clara Fern Rhynerson, 177
Clara Rhynerson, 178
Clarinda Chandler, 116, 123, 125, 126, 219, 220
Col. Abraham Penn, 113
Col. Charles Lynch, 113
Col. William Brown's Regiment,

227

146
Colonel of Antwerp, 11
Cora (Anderson) Bennett, 186
Cora (Anderson-Bennett) Stump, 198
Cora Dell Anderson, 195, 200, 224
Cornelius Bennett, 190
Cornelius Reyniersen, 172, 173
Cornelius Reyniersen Van Hengel, 172
Count of Meulan, 65, 213
Cunegundis des Francs, 65, 77, 211, 214
Cunigunde de Gellone, 64, 76
Damaris Hancock, 36, 92
Dan Dickman, 165
Dana Jones, 165
Daniel Bennett, 191
Daniel Boone, 142
Daniel Rand, 113
Daramis Hancock, 1, 28, 29, 32, 36, 206
Daramis Hanock, 33
David Allee, 107, 111, 112, 114, 203, 218, 219
David Bennett, 193, 194
David Birdsong, 98, 102, 129, 131
David Hall, 192, 194
David le Bird, 11
Delaino Loya, 165
Deliverance Bennett, 191
Della (Rhynerson) Birdsong, 159, 186
Della Bennett, 195
Della Birdsong, 161, 162, 163, 164, 165
Della Lorene Birdsong, 5
Della Lorine Rhynerson, 184
Della Rhynerson, 151, 158
DELLA RHYNERSON, 150, 169
Dermot MacMurrough, 66

Diana Lea Birdsong, 164
Dominic Yeldell, 165
Dominick Herrera, 165
Donald Bennett, 186, 196, 203
Donald Burnett, 178
Donald E. Bennett, 195
Dora Adams, 101
Dorothy Waldegrave, 32, 33, 64, 65, 67, 77, 211, 212
Dr. Emile A. Birdsong, 26
Dr. John Potts, 37
Dr. Pott, 37
Duejates Hancock, 35
Dunfermline Abbey, 88
Dylon Birdsong, 165
E. Peterson, 106
Eadgifu, 86, 215
Ealdgyth of Northumbria, 88, 215
Ealfthyrth "the Fair", 87, 215
Earl of March, 80
Ebenezer Hall, 193
Ebenezer Wilson, 192
Edgar "The Peaceful", 87, 215
Edmond Birdsong, 116
Edmund de Mortimer, 80, 214
Edmund I, 86, 87, 215
Edmund II, 88
Edmund Peeters, 40
Edmund S Birdsong, 117
Edward "The Atheling", 88, 215
Edward Bennett, 189
Edward Gray, 111
Edward Gurgany, 50
Edward I, 33, 66, 79, 86, 87, 213, 214, 215
Edward II, 79, 80, 214
Edward III, 80, 211, 214, 215, 217
Edward Longshanks, 79
Edward the Elder, 86
Edwin Birdsong, 116
Edwin Young, 122

Eleanor Beaufort, 82
Eleanor Harbottle, 82, 214
Eleanor of Aqutane, 79, 214
Eleanor of Castile, 79, 214
Eleanor of Provence, 79, 214
Eleanor Rynearson, 174
Eleanor, Countess of Arundel, 81, 214
Eleanor, Lady Poynings, 81, 214
Elena (Helena) Birdsong, 131
Elena Birdsong, 129
Elgifa Gunnarsson, 87, 215
Eli Bennett, 193
Elias Scott, 102
Elijah Bailey, 195
Elijah Bennett, 193
Elisha Henry Wood, 146
Elisha Jobe, 122, 123
Elisha Thomas Jobe, Sr, 124
Eliza Birdsong, 116
Eliza Park, 191
Eliza Patty Bennett, 191
Eliza Redmon, 116
Elizabeth Bennett, 190
Elizabeth Birdsong, 22, 98, 117, 118
Elizabeth Butler, 49
Elizabeth Damory, 66, 212
Elizabeth de Burgh, 80, 214
Elizabeth de Clare, 66, 212
Elizabeth Foliott-Mode, 39
Elizabeth Hansford, 35, 38, 39, 40
Elizabeth Jands, 39
Elizabeth Jane Birdsong, 102
Elizabeth Job, 120
Elizabeth Jobe, 101, 116, 123, 129, 219
ELIZABETH JOBE, 115, 120
Elizabeth Jones, 93
Elizabeth Maxwell, 121
Elizabeth Perdineau, 106, 107

Elizabeth Philips, 32, 35, 36, 44, 207, 208
Elizabeth Phillips, 29, 36, 44, 207, 208
Elizabeth Redmon, 101
Elizabeth Redmond, 116, 117
Elizabeth Seward, 38
Elizabeth Smythe, 54
Elizabeth Stapleton, 67, 212
Elizabeth Tomlinson, 91, 94, 95
ELIZABETH TOMLINSON, 90, 93
Elizabeth Vernon, 120
Elizabeth Wagstaff, 48
Elizabeth Wood, 144
Ellen Jobe, 123
Elmer Beckuau, 178
Eloise (Goldie O) Birdsong, 131
Eloise Birdsong, 129
Elsce Snedeker, 173, 174
Elsey Rinearson, 174
Elvira Jane Vaughan, 146
Emiline Bennett, 195
Emily Elizabeth Wood, 146
Emily Wood, 145
Emma of Alamannia, 64
Empress Matilda, 78, 214
Ennis Mackintosh, 40
Enoch Job, 121, 122
Enoch Jobe, 121, 122, 123, 203
Ermengarde, 65, 213
Ernest Edgar "Ernie" Rhynerson, 177
Ernest Rhynerson, 178
Espriota de Bretagne, 77, 214
Ethel Pearl Rhynerson, 176
Ethelred II, 87, 215
Eudes (Otho), Count de Vermandois, 65, 213
Eugene Birdsong, 129, 131, 135
Eydae Reyniersen, 172
Eysak (Isaac) Reyniersen, 173

229

Eytje Cornelisse Vonck, 172
Ezma Maust, 147
Fenny Reyniersen Van Hengel, 172
Fern (Lula) Birdsong, 131
Fern Lula Birdsong, 129
Floyd Birdsong, 129, 131
Frances Birdsong, 22
Frances Huff, 102
Francies "Fannie" Jobe, 124
Francis Murray, 106
Francis Richardson, 106
Francis Willis, 40
Frank D. Mills, 181
Frank Rhynerson, 178
Frank Theodore Rhynerson Sr, 176
Freda Mabel Rhynerson, 177
Geertie (Charity) Reyniersen, 173
Geertie Reyniersen, 172
Geertje Volleman, 172, 173
Geoffrey Plantagenet, 78, 89, 214
George Bennett, 193
George Case, 194
George Cooper, 25, 34, 37, 67, 82, 94, 100, 108, 121, 146, 181, 194, 205, 206, 211, 212, 215, 217, 218, 222, 224
George Harbottle, 82
George Mills, 181
George Thorpe, 34
George V Wood, 145
George Washington Birdsong, 101
Gerald Birdsong, 131
Geraldine Birdsong, 129, 131, 135, 157
Gerberga of Lorraine, 65, 213
Gerhardn Birdsong, 102
Gerold of Vinzgouw, 64
Gerret Reyniersen, 173
Gerry Birdsong, 129
Gertrudis of the Bavarians, 76
Gertruyd Arentsen Van Hengel, 171
Gilbert de Clare, 66, 213
Gina Birdsong, 164
Giselbert, Duke of Lorraine, 65, 213
Goidie Lucas, 178
Goldie Mae Rhynerson, 177
Granville J. Bennett, 195
Grizell Bennett, 192
Guichard Harbottle, 82
Gunnora of Denmark, 77, 214
H.M Baird, 105, 217, 219
Hannah Freeman, 29
Hannah Job, 121
Hannah McKay, 121
Hannah Vineyard, 145
Harold Carpenter, 178
Harold Henry Rhynerson, 177
Harold Rhinestone, 178
Harry Alexander Rhynerson, 176, 184
Harry Birdsong, 129, 131, 132
Harry Rhynerson, 151, 158, 184, 185, 223
Harry S Truman, 153
Hartwell Phillips, 36, 207
Haylee Birdsong, 165
Heaven Herrera, 165
Hedrick Reyniersen Van Hengel, 172
Helena Arentsen Van Hengel, 171
HENDRICK ARENTSEN, 169
Hendrick Arentsen Van Hengel, 169, 171
Henrietta Wood, 146
Henry Algernon Percy, 82, 214
Henry Bennett, 191
Henry I Beauclerc, 32, 78, 88, 214, 215
Henry II, 79, 214
Henry III, 79, 80, 214
Henry IV, 80, 81
Henry John T. Rhynerson, 175,

176
Henry Percy, 33, 80, 81, 82, 214
Henry Plantagenet, 79
Henry Tolbert Wood, 145, 146, 147, 203, 222
Henry Tomlinson, 94
Henry VIII, 53, 82
Henry Wood, 141, 144, 145, 146, 147, 221, 222
Herbert I de Vermandois, 65, 213, 214
Herbert II, 65, 213
Herbert III, 65, 213
Herbert IV, 65, 213
Herleva, 77, 78, 214
Hildebrante, 65, 213
Hildegarde, 64, 76, 214
Hnabi, Duke of Alamannia, 64
Hrolfr (Rollo the Dane). Rollo, 77
Hugh Magnus, 65, 213
Hugo le Bird, 10
Lydia Hall, 194
Ichabod Lewis, 193
Ida Reyniersen Van Hengel, 172
Imogene Smith, 147
Infant Bennett, 195
Infant Rhynerson, 177
Isaac Bennett, 190
Isaac Hewlick Rinearson, 174, 175, 203, 223
Isaac Odell, 192
Isaac Wood, 140
Isabel Birdsong, 102
Isabel de Beaumont, 66, 213
Isabel de Clare, 66, 213
Isabel de Vermandois, 65, 213
Isabel Marshall, 66, 213
Isabella of France, 79, 214
Isabella, Countless of Anqouleme, 79, 214
Isaphine Birdsong, 116, 117
Jacob (Yacob) Rinearson, 173, 174, 203, 223
Jacob Job, 120
Jacob Rinearson, 175
Jacob S Rinearson, 174
Jaiden Birdsong, 165
Jaile Birdsong, 98, 101
James Allee, 107
James Anderson, 200
James Birdsong, 22, 91, 98, 99, 100, 101, 116, 117, 151, 203, 219
James Franklin (Frank) Cooper, 100
James Henry Rhynerson, 175
James Hill, 112
James Odell, 122
James Osborn, 141, 142
James Osborn Wood, 144
James Sterling Wood, 146
James Tomlinson, 94
James W Birdsong, 101
James, Duke of York, 106
James; Rosa, 182
Jane Alley, 109
Jane Ann Cooper, 100
Jane Handcock, 39
Jane Holt, 35, 38, 207, 208
Jane Smythe, 54
Jane Vanwinkle, 107
Jane Willoughby, 82
Jannetje Aukes Van Nuyse, 170, 171, 172
Jasmine Birdsong, 165
Jayden Daniels, 165
Jayden Hansett, 165
Jean Allee, 107
Jean D Allee, 106, 107
Jean d'Allee, 105, 217
Jeff Birdsong, 164
Jeffrey Birdsong, 151
Jemima Allee, 108
Jenna Dickman, 165

231

Jennetje Aukes Van Nuyse, 171
Jeremiah Stover, 107, 218
Jeremy Daniels, 165
Jerome Birdsong, 151, 165, 198
Jerusha Allee, 112
Jessalyn Birdsong, 165
Jessy Birdsong, 165
Jessy Birdsong, 165
Jim Birdsong, 164
Joachem (James, Joseph?) Reyniersen, 173
Joan (Joanna) Percy, 83, 215
Joan Beaufort, 81
Joan Brounckner, 53
Joan Plantagenet, 66, 213
Joan Smythe, 53
Joan Willoughby Harbottle, 82
Joanna Percy, 32, 33
Job Hale, 113
Johanna Birdsong, 151
Johanna Dickman, 165
Johanna Percy, 65, 211, 215
John Albertson, 106
John Allee, 106, 108, 218
John Allen, 47
John Bailey, 37
John Bardolf, 66, 212
John Bennett, 189, 190, 191, 208
John Birdsong, 7, 9, 22, 26, 27, 29, 30, 32, 101, 118, 129, 130, 151, 186, 205, 221, 223
JOHN BIRDSONG, 32, 128, 150, 169
John Birdsong, I, 9, 22, 26, 27
John D Allee, 106
John Drew, 47, 208
John Edwards, 44, 208
John Hancock, 35, 36, 38, 207
John Hansford, 38, 39, 40, 41, 208, 209
John Harris, 54, 211
John Holt, 38, 209
John J. Rinearson, 174

John Job, 120
John Judd, 53, 211
John Lackland, 79
John Long, 111
John Manford, 106
John Michael Birdsong, 151
John Michael. Birdsong, 203
John of Boston Bennett, 190
John of England, 79, 214
John of Guant, 81
John P Birdsong, 129
John P. Birdsong, 116, 203
John Patrick Birdsong, 5, 131, 135, 151, 152, 153, 157, 158
John Patrick Cooper, 101
John Philips, 44, 211
John Rolands, 40
John Smythe, 54
John Sugars, 47
John T Rhynerson, 175
John Theodore Rhynerson, 176
John Tomlinson, 93, 94, 217
John Tomlinson Sr, 93
John Tomlinson, Sr, 217
John White, 121
John Wood, 140, 141, 221
John Wood, Jr, 140
John Wood, Sr, 140
Jonathan R Wood, 144
Jonathan Wood, 140, 141, 142, 143, 144, 145, 221, 222
Jonathan Wood Sr, 141
Jonathan Wood, Jr, 141
Jonathan Wood, Sr, 140, 141
Jordan Hansett, 165
Joseph Bennett, 190, 191
Joseph Birdsong, 29, 151, 165
Joseph David Birdsong, 165
Joseph Denis, 110
Joseph Dennis, 109
Joseph Holt, 38
Joseph James Birdsong, 165
Joseph Mountfort, 39

Joseph Wilson Bennett, 192
Josephine Bowlin, 101
Joshua Bottom, 121
Joshua Job, 120, 121, 122
Judith de Bretagne, 77, 214
Judith Green, 46
Juleonna Pena, 165
Julia Bennett, 195
Julia E Bailey, 195, 224
Julia Johnston, 181
Julia Marie Hansett, 5
Juliane Rainey, 67, 212
Julie Hansett, 165
Justin Birdsong, 165
Justin Michael Birdsong, 5
Kaitlyn Birdsong, 165
Karla Woodward, 158
Katherine de la Pole, 67, 212
Katherine Swynform, 81
Kemp Birdsong, 98, 101
Kemp Scott, 112
Kennidy Birdsong, 165
Keziah Allee, 107
King Charles I of England, 23
King Edward VI, 53
King Ferdinand III, 79
King James I, 23, 34, 39, 54, 55, 207
King of Denmark, 77
King of Hungary Stephen I, 88
King of Scotland, 33, 78, 88, 215
King of Sigbert III, 64, 76
Kiziah Jane Howard, 101
Klisha Bennett, 190
Lady Elanor Neville, 81, 214
Lady Elizabeth Mortimer, 80, 214
Laura Edna Rhynerson, 176
Laura Miller, 178
Lavina Beeler, 174, 175
Lawton Stoker, 178
Layton Murr, 178

Lena V Wood, 147
Levi Bybee, 101
Lieut. Wm. Hall, 193
Lillian V. Dobson, 130
Lionel of Antwerp, 80, 214
Lioomis G. Bennett, 194
Logan Jobe, 123
Lord de Roger Mortimer, 80
Lord Poynings, 67, 81, 82, 212
Louisa Birdsong, 100
Lt. William Ferguson, 112
Lucile d'Alsace, 76
Lucretia Jobe, 123
Lucy Birdsong, 29, 30, 91
Lucy Hix, 30
Lucy Tomlinson, 94
Luke Cooper, 100
Lula Marie Woods, 101
Lydia Bennett, 190, 193
Lydia Hall, 192
M.W. "Fan" Jobe, 124
Madame Ann Tybout, 105
Magdalen Reyniersen Van Hengel, 172
Magdalena Pieterse, 171
Magdalena Reyniersen, 173
Major Henry Clinton Wood, 145
Malcolm III Cammore, 33
Malcom III Cammore, 88, 215
Manley Bennett, 197
Manley E. Bennett, 195
Margaret "Atheling" Saint of Scotland, 88
Margaret Chichle, 53, 211
Margaret Hill, 99
Margaret McKay, 121
Margaret Wood, 145
Mariah Gulick, 174
Marie (Wood) Birdsong, 131, 133
Marie Lula Wood, 147
Marie Woods, 129, 130
MARIE WOODS, 128, 140

Marion E Wood, 146, 147
Marion Woods, 130
Marissa Herrera, 165
Martha Birdsong, 117
Martha Hancock, 35
Martha Judd, 53
Martha Pucket, 200
Martha Puckett, 200
Mary A. Rhynerson, 181
Mary Amelia Rhynerson, 175
Mary Ann Bennett, 194
Mary Ann Daniels, 175
Mary Arents Van Hengel, 169
Mary Bailey, 37, 38, 39
Mary Beatty, 100
Mary Birdsong, 91, 98, 99, 100
Mary Chappell, 93, 94, 217
Mary Claiborne, 32, 46, 48, 49
Mary Cotton, 91, 94, 217
Mary Dennis, 107, 109
Mary Dipa Sartin Jasper, 101
Mary Edwards, 44, 208
Mary Eliza Jobe, 124
Mary Frances Remington, 177, 181
Mary Gostwich, 35
Mary Graveswas, 175
Mary Hancock, 35
Mary Harris, 32, 36, 46, 48, 208, 210
Mary Jane Wood, 141
Mary Job, 121
Mary Mirfyn, 53
Mary of Lancaster, 80, 214
Mary Philips, 44, 211
Mary Polly Wood, 144
Mary Reyniersen Van Hengel, 172
Mary Seward, 38
Mary Smith Wood, 146
Mary Smythe, 54
Mary Spiltimber, 47, 208
Mary Swan, 32, 210
Mary Swann, 44, 46, 208

Mary Tomlinson, 94, 95
Mary Wood, 145
Marytie Arentsen Van Hengel, 171
Mathew Harris, 48
Mathew Phillips, 47
Mathew Swan, 32, 46, 202
Mathew Swann, 36, 44, 46, 48, 208, 210
Matilda (Edith) Cammore of Scotland, 78, 214
Matilda (Edith) Cammore Of Scotland, 88, 215
Matilda (Edith) Of Scotland, 32, 33
Matilda (Maude) of Flanders, 78, 214
Matilda Adelaid, 89
Matthew Philips, 44
Matthew Swan, 47, 208
Maude de Lacy, 66, 213
Maude Herbert, 81, 214
May Severyn Laurenszen, 170
Meagan Riley, 165
Melissa Birdsong, 165
Merry Birdsong, 98
Michael jr Herrera, 165
Mike Birdsong, 164
Mildred Hines, 112
Miles Birdsong, 29, 30
Minerva Bennett, 193, 194
Montgomery Birdsong, 101
Morgan Morgan, 121
Mr. John McFadden, 134
Mrs Ethel Hoyt, 181
Mrs. Dan Ross, 178
Mrs. George, 147
N.N. de Vermandois, 77
Nancy Allee, 101
Nancy Birdsong, 30, 98
Nancy Davidson, 141, 142, 221
Nancy Jobe, 124
Nancy Wood, 144
Nathan Fairchild, 192

Nathanial Bacon, 46, 208
Nathaniel Jones, 48
Nathaniel Tomlinson, 94
Nellie Dyer, 5, 165
Newton Leonard Birdsong, 101
Nicholas Allee, 107, 108, 109, 110, 111, 202, 218
Nicholas Birdsong, 98, 102
Nicholas De'Allee, 106
Nicholas John Allee, 107
Nicholas Spencer, 35
Niki Birdsong, 165
Noah Scott, 101
Ordgar Ealdormand, 87
Oscar Rhynerson, 203
Oscar William Rhynerson, 177
Osea Miles, 195, 200, 224
Ouke (Auke) Reyniersen Van Hengel, 172
Ouken Reyniersen, 173
Parvie, 65, 213
Patience Job, 121
Paul Guerrero II, 165
Pepin of Heristal, 64, 76
Pepin of Landen, 64, 76
Pepin the Short, 64, 76
Pepin, count of Vermandois, 65
Pepin, King of Italy, 64, 76, 214
Peter Allee, 107
Peter Bayard, 106
Peter Birdsong, 98, 101, 116, 117, 118, 129, 203, 219
PETER BIRDSONG, 115, 120
Peter Mills Rinearson, 174
Peter Wolf, 121
Philippa of Hainault, 80, 214
Philippa Plantagenet, 80, 214
Phoebe H. A. Walker, 175, 176
Pierre de Allie, 106
Polly Allee, 112
Polly Jobe, 123
Polly Patchin, 195

Presley Jacob Stump, 186
Prince Edward, 108
Priscilla Bennett, 189
Queen Elizabeth I, 54
Rachel De Allee, 106
Ralph Bennett, 189
Ralph Neville, 80, 81, 214
Ralph Stafford, 11
Randall Holt, 36, 37, 38, 202, 209, 210, 224
Randall Holt Jr., 37
Raoul III, the Great, 65, 213
Rebecca Birdsong, 29, 30
Rebecca Cooper, 100
Rebecca Tomlinson, 94
Reinald, Count of Bar, 65, 213
Reuben H Jobe, 123
Reubin Jobe, 124
Rev David Allee, 98, 112, 218
Rev. Newman, 189
Rev. W.S. (Bud) Birdsong, 100
Rev. William De Laughder, 178
Reynier Arentsen, 171
REYNIER ARENTSEN, 169
Reynier Arentsen Van Hengel, 169, 170, 172
Reynier Reyniersen, 172, 173
Reyniersen, 173
Rhoda Cox, 111
Richard Bennett, 189, 190
Richard Bowen Jr, 189
Richard Carter, 93
Richard Craford, 27
Richard de Clare, 66, 213
Richard I, 77, 214
Richard II, 29, 77, 81, 214
Richard Poynings, 81, 214
Rinearson, 174, 175
Robert Birdsong, 91
Robert Brounckner, 53
Robert Davys, 54
Robert Evers, 37

235

Robert Harris, 32, 36, 46, 47, 48, 49, 50, 208, 210
Robert I, 65, 77, 213, 214
Robert I, Duke of France, 65, 213
Robert Jones, 40
Robert McCoy, 121
Robert McCoys Ford, 121
Robert McKay, 121
Robert Poynings, 81
Robert Ruffin, 47
Robert Smythe, 54
Robert Tomlinson, 95
Roberta (Rhynerson) Sparks, 186
Roberta Maxine Rhynerson, 184
Roberta Sparks, 164
Rogelio Herrera, 165
Rothaide de Bobbi, 65, 76
Rotrude of Trier, 64, 76
Roy M. Wood, 147
Rynier (Rynard, Reynard) Reyniersen, 173
Saint Aelfgifu, 86, 215
Saint Arnulf of Metz, 64
Saint Begga, 33, 64, 76
Saint Itta, 33, 64
Sally Birdsong, 29
Sally Clary, 30
Samantha Birdsong, 165
Samuel Beeler, 175
Samuel Bennett, 189, 190, 191
Samuel Birdsong, 117
Samuel Job, 121
Sarah (Sally) Ann Birdsong, 100
Sarah Alice (Jane) Birdsong, 101
Sarah Allee, 108
Sarah Bennet, 29
Sarah Bennett, 191, 192
Sarah Birdsong, 116, 117, 165
Sarah C Wood, 145
Sarah Jade Birdsong, 5, 165, 223
Sarah Jane Wood, 146
Sarah M Birdsong, 117
Sarah Melissa Birdsong, 101

Sarah Reyniersen, 173
Sarah Rinearson, 174
Sarah Sally Lawson, 144
Sarah Stephens, 110
Sarah Swann, 45, 46, 47, 207, 208
Sarah Tomlinson, 94
Scott, Buford, 112
Sean Dyer, 165
Sean Riley Dyer, 5
Severyn Laurenszen, 170
Sigehelm Ealdormand, 86
Simon Hancock, 34
Simon Harding, 54
Simon Smythe, 54
Sir Andrew Judd, 53
Sir Brian Stapleton, 67, 212
Sir George Waldegrave, 67, 212
Sir Guischard Harabottle, 82
Sir Henry (Hotspur) Percy, 83
Sir Henry Fanshawe, 54
Sir Henry Smythe, 54
Sir John Egremont of Yorkshire, 82
Sir John Rainey ford, 67, 212
Sir Miles Stapleton, 67, 212
Sir Richard Holland, 83
Sir Richard Smythe, 54
Sir Robert de Beaumont, 65, 213
Sir Robert Drury, 67, 212
Sir Robert Spenser, 82
Sir Roger Damory, 66, 212
Sir Roland Hayward, 54
Sir Thomas Fanshawe, 54
Sir Thomas Mirfyn, 53
Sir Thomas Smyth, 55
Sir William Calthorpe, 67, 212
Sir William Harris, 83, 211
Sir William Herbert, 82
Sir William Marshall, 66, 213
Sir William Waldegrave, 67, 212
Sister Benedict, 135
Sister Claire, 135, 221
Sister Ester, 135

Sister Mary Bonaventure, 134
Sister Theodore, 135
Smith Bennett, 194, 195, 224
Solomon Anderson, 195, 200, 224
Solomon Osborn, 142
Sr. William Wallace, 79
Stephen Bennett, 191
Stephen of Blois, 78
Steven Dickman, 165
Susan Birdsong, 116
Susan Poynter, 34
Susanna Bennett, 190
Susannah Bright, 191
Susannah Vangasco, 107
Susanne Harris, 48
Swan Philips, 44
Tabitha C Wood, 146
Tait Torset, 165
Tempey Hill, 112
Teresa Birdsong, 151, 186, 198
Terri Crump, 164
Teunis Arentsen Van Hengel, 171
Thaddeus Bennett, 191, 192, 193, 194, 203, 223
Thomas Allee, 107, 109, 218
Thomas Bennett, 190
Thomas Bird, 9
Thomas Byrd, 10
Thomas Chappell, 93
Thomas Denis, 110
Thomas Edwards, 39
Thomas Hancock, 34
Thomas Jerden Scott, 101
Thomas Job, 120, 121
Thomas Percy, 82, 83, 214, 216
Thomas Scott, 112, 123, 220
Thomas Smith, 105, 217
Thomas Smythe, 53, 54, 55, 67, 211, 212
Thomas Tomlinson, 91, 93, 94, 217
Thored Ealdorman Gunnarsson, 87, 215
to **Ealhswith of Gaini**, 86
Tryntie Arentsen Van Hengel, 171
Tryntie Reynders, 169, 170
Tryntje Reynderts, 170
Tunis Arentsen Van Hengel, 171
Tyler Birdsong, 165
Tyler Dickman, 165
Unie Orndoff, 182
Uriela White, 190
Ursula Bennett, 190
Ursula Smythe, 54
Valentine Chiche, 53
VAN HENGEL ARENTSEN, 169
Vardie Jackson, 178
Vera (Bennett) Rhynerson, 186, 198
Vera Bennett, 151
Vera Beulah Bennett, 184, 195
Vera Rhynerson, 158
Violet Birdsong, 129, 131, 135, 223
Walla de Corbie, 65, 77
Walter Rose, 178
Webster Dyer, 5, 165
Wido, comte de Senlis, 77, 211
Wildman Bennett, 193
Wilford Birdsong, 98, 102
Willard R Wood, 147
William Allee, 107, 108, 110
William Anderson, 200
William Baffin, 55
William Bardolf, 66, 212
William Bennett, 190, 191, 192, 223
William Berkeley, 46, 210
William Birdsong, 29, 30, 91, 92, 95, 98, 99, 102, 112, 116, 203, 217, 219
WILLIAM BIRDSONG, 90, 93, 97, 105

William Carpenter, 189
William Chambers, 47
William Claiborne, 49, 202
William de Burgh, 80
William Frankline Jobe, 124
William Hancock, 29, 32, 34, 35, 36, 44, 46, 206, 207, 211
William Hanock, Sr, 202
William Harris, 32, 48, 50, 54, 55, 67, 83, 211, 212
William Harris, Jr, 48
William Henry Bennett, 194
William Holt, 38
William Houston, 141, 144
William John Patrick Hansett, 5
William K. Rhynerson, 178
William Kygar Rhynerson, 175, 176, 184
William Milligan Wood, 144
William Penn, 106
William Philips, 32, 36, 44, 208, 211
William Phillips, 46, 47, 208
WILLIAM RHYNERSON, 176, 203
William Scott, 101
William Swan, 46
William Terry, 113
William the Conqueror, 9, 10, 65, 78, 213, 214
William the Longsword, 77, 214
William Tomlinson, 93, 94, 95
William Wesley Wood, 146
William X, Duke of Aquitaine, 79
William, Duke of Normandy, 10
WINAFORD ALLEE, 97, 105
Winaford Birdsong, 98, 99, 100, 217
Winafrod Allee, 98
Winnaford Allee, 112
Wyke Hunnicutt, 93
Yvonne Wood Hamrick, 141

www.ingramcontent.com/pod-product-compliance
Lightning Source LLC
Chambersburg PA
CBHW050106170426
43198CB00014B/2481